THE

SUPREME

COURT

ON TRIAL

THE
SUPREME
COURT
ON TRIAL

How the American Justice System
Sacrifices Innocent Defendants

George C. Thomas III

THE UNIVERSITY OF MICHIGAN PRESS

ANN ARBOR

Copyright © by the University of Michigan 2008
All rights reserved
Published in the United States of America by
The University of Michigan Press
Manufactured in the United States of America
⊗ Printed on acid-free paper

2011   2010   2009   2008   4   3   2   1

A CIP catalog record for this book is available from the British Library.

Library of Congress Cataloging-in-Publication Data

Thomas, George C. (George Conner), 1947–
    The Supreme Court on trial : how the American justice system
    sacrifices innocent defendants / George C. Thomas III.
        p.   cm.
    Includes bibliographical references and index.
    ISBN-13: 978-0-472-11618-8 (cloth : alk. paper)
    ISBN-10: 0-472-11618-5 (cloth : alk. paper)
        1. Judgments, Criminal—United States.   2. Judicial review—
    United States.   3. False imprisonment—United States.   4. Criminal
    justice, Administration of—United States.   5. Due process of law—
    United States.   6. Law and fact—United States.   I. Title.
    KF9685.T48   2008
    345.73'05—dc22   2008011483

TO ALL THOSE WHO HAVE SPARKED MY CURIOSITY,

BEGINNING WITH MY GRANDFATHER, THOMAS IRVINE

CONTENTS

ACKNOWLEDGMENTS

I owe large debts to many people for help during the seven years that this book percolated in my brain and on my computer. I seek here to acknowledge some of these debts. Paul Axel-Lute, a law library faculty member at Rutgers University School of Law in Newark, spent countless hours locating obscure historical material for me. And due to the disorganized way I work, he sometimes had to find it more than once!

Mike Mulligan, one of my best research assistants, played a pivotal role in the early stages. He provided excellent advice, encouragement, and even some language for an article that started me down the road to the book. The book evolved in a different direction from the article, but Mike's help on the article and the initial book proposals helped me shape the idea.

Other excellent research assistants helped very much as the book reached its final stage: Juan Abreu, Kegan Brown, Cassandra Cantwell, Ben Davis, Brian DeBoer, Mike Gadarian, Leigh-Ann Mulray, Dorollo

Nixon, Robert Ulon, Jennifer Virella, and Stefan Wolfe. I also thank those who helped in smaller ways or whose help I have unfortunately forgotten in my years of work on this project.

Many others read parts or all of the manuscript and I thank them for their comments. I benefited particularly from comments by Robert Bartels, Susan Brenner, Joshua Dressler, Peter Henning, John Leubsdorf, Suzanne Goldberg, Nick Humez, Richard Leo, Renee Lettow Lerner, Erik Luna, Daniel Medwed, Paul Marcus, Sam Pillsbury, and Lloyd Weinreb. I thank Gregory Maggs for help with the American military justice system and Kent Roach for information about how Ontario provides counsel to indigent defendants. I thank Daniel Givelber for his provocative article that appeared in 1997 and first created doubts in my mind about how well our adversarial system protects innocent suspects and defendants ("Meaningless Acquittals, Meaningful Convictions," *Rutgers L. Rev.*). When I read his article, I began, in effect, writing this book.

I wish also to acknowledge that some of the ideas presented here have appeared in articles that I published while working on this book. I thank the following journals for permission to reprint: "When Lawyers Fail Innocent Defendants: A Radical Proposal for Change," 2008 *Utah L. Rev.* (forthcoming); "Bigotry, Jury Failures, and the Supreme Court's Odd Response," 55 *Buffalo L. Rev.* 947 (2007); " 'Truth Machines' and Confessions Law in the Year 2046," 5 *Ohio St. J. Crim. L.* 215 (2007); "The Criminal Procedure Road Not Taken: Due Process and the Protection of Innocence," 3 *Ohio St. J. Crim. L.* 169 (2005); "Terrorism, Race, and a New Approach to Consent Searches," 73 *Miss. L. J.* 525 (2003); "When Constitutional Worlds Collide: Resurrecting the Framers' Criminal Procedure," 100 *Mich. L. Rev.* 145 (2001).

Perhaps my greatest debt is to the two readers of the manuscript I submitted to the University of Michigan Press. Susan Bandes and Andy Taslitz said nice things about the project, thus giving me the energy to do what they independently suggested—make substantial revisions in the last chapter. They were then kind enough to reread the last chapter and make additional comments. The book is much better because I took much of their advice.

INTRODUCTION

For thousands of years, Western philosophers have sought an epistemology that reveals the truth. Many late-twentieth-century philosophers essentially gave up on the notion of truth, arguing that everything is subjective and thus an ultimate truth simply does not exist. Whatever the value of that philosophy when speaking of abstract truths, justice systems cannot avoid making an attempt to uncover the truth about the past. Various justice systems approach the truth quite differently. The continental justice systems take, as a given, that it is possible to know the true facts about the crime. In the American system, on the other hand, "truth seems elusive and reality, like the muses, seems always to have another veil."[1]

The notion of "elusive truth" helps explain why American criminal appeals are almost exclusively about procedural errors rather than whether the convicted defendant was guilty of the crime. If truth is elusive, who can say that the jury was wrong? But in continental justice systems, "getting the facts right is normally one of the preconditions to realizing the goal of the legal process."[2]

Mistakes about past events in criminal cases result in convictions of the innocent, well documented now in light of DNA exonerations. I will argue that the prime directive of a criminal justice system is to protect the innocent, at a reasonable cost. The American criminal justice system has both a moral and a legal duty to take reasonable steps not to convict the innocent and to review convictions with an eye toward correcting wrongful convictions. The moral duty comes from the principle that the state can justify imposing sanctions only on proof that the defendant threatens the orderly functioning of society. A false accusation of crime does not provide that proof.

The legal duty to avoid convicting the innocent comes from the right to due process in the U.S. Constitution. The state and federal governments cannot deprive anyone "of life, liberty, or property without due process of law."[3] As Donald Dripps has demonstrated, due process forbids any procedure that creates "an unacceptably high risk of an erroneous decision."[4] Whatever "due process" entails at the margin, its core protection is against the unjustified taking of life, liberty, or property. When government takes life or liberty for a crime that the defendant did not commit, it has violated both its moral and its legal duty.

I should be clear about the limited nature of my project. As to scope, I originally intended a comprehensive review of all the literature, legislative initiatives, and cases on wrongful convictions, but I quickly realized that the volume of material makes a comprehensive review literally impossible in a single-volume work. Thus, the book presents my selective review of a dynamic and continually evolving area of the law. As to substance, I wish to show that the Due Process Clause requires governments to provide reasonable protections against the detention, prosecution, and conviction of innocent persons. Uncovering truth—vindicating the innocent *and* convicting the guilty—is a broader goal but not my goal. Two works have recently sought to advance truth about both guilt and innocence—an ABA monograph, *Achieving Justice: Freeing the Innocent, Convicting the Guilty,* and William Pizzi's book, *Trials Without Truth.*[5]

I will argue that a deeper value than truth is the protection of the innocent. My central thesis is that Sir William Blackstone was correct when he said in 1769 that "the law holds, that it is better that ten guilty persons escape, than that one innocent suffer."[6] A few years later, Benjamin Franklin framed the question as whether "it is better [that] 100 guilty Persons should escape than that one innocent Person should suffer" and concluded that it "is a Maxim that has been long and generally approved; never, that I know of, controverted."[7]

Over half a century ago, Jerome Frank said that the conviction of an innocent person is defensible "only if everything practical has been done to avoid such injustices. But, often, everything practical has not been done."[8] We are still not doing everything feasible "to prevent avoidable mistakes."[9] Erik Luna's evocative metaphor is that there are "'ghosts' in the machinery of criminal justice—the men and women who investigate, litigate, and adjudicate cases—and their erroneous decisions haunt the system."[10]

We know much more than Jerome Frank knew about the failings of the American justice system, thanks largely to Barry Scheck and Peter Neufeld, of Cardozo Law School, who started the Innocence Project at Cardozo in 1992. As of September 13, 2007, 207 prisoners, many convicted of murder and some waiting to be executed, had been exonerated by the Innocence Project. Lack of confidence in the criminal process led Illinois governor George Ryan in 2003 to commute all of the state's 156 death sentences to life in prison.[11]

But with a few exceptions like Ryan, we seem supremely unmoved by the failures we see. The British and Canadians have long been much more concerned about their justice failures. In a book subtitled *The Collapse of Criminal Justice,* David Rose wrote in 1996 that "English criminal justice is in a crisis without precedent, its solutions uncertain and its effects deeply damaging."[12] Three years earlier, a royal commission was "struck by evidence of a disquieting lack of professional competence in many parts of" the English justice system.[13] In Canada, the realization that a single defendant was wrongly convicted of murder led the Manitoba justice minister to commission an inquiry that made an exhaustive study of what went wrong in the case.[14]

Yet Pizzi notes our justice system's "self-confidence, bordering on complacency."[15] The reasons why we don't seem to care about wrongful convictions are many and complex—and probably have much to do with the racial and class makeup of the men and women in our prisons. Governor Ryan asked the right question, "How many more cases of wrongful convictions have to occur before we can all agree that the system is broken?"[16] The reason to write this book is to add to the call for reform of a system that is broken. The problem is not a discrete set of erroneous inputs but a "systemic failure in criminal justice."[17] Andrew Siegel recommends shifting focus of the wrongful conviction scholarship "to broader questions about the structure and administration of the justice system."[18] That is the goal of this book.

The modern Supreme Court has done little to help, and quite a bit to harm, innocent defendants. The core of the problem is that the Court has been satisfied with a procedural focus in its criminal justice doctrine. Pizzi calls American lawyers and judges "procedure addicts."[19] William Stuntz has identified the underlying problem with the focus on process: "more process may actually mean less accuracy, because it encourages defense lawyers and courts to shift energy and attention away from the merits and towards procedure."[20]

The Supreme Court has created a labyrinth of procedural requirements that substitute for substantive justice. Was the suspect given his right to remain silent; was he given counsel if he asked for a lawyer; was he provided a jury; did his lawyer show up and not sleep through the trial? If the answer to all procedural questions is yes, then it does not matter that he was innocent. If the defendant is "procedurally" guilty, his substantive innocence is quite beside the point.

I suspect the reader thinks that I engage in hyperbole here. I wish that were the case. In 1993, the Supreme Court told us that a federal court need not hear a claim of innocence made by a state prisoner whose conviction had been affirmed in the state courts. According to the Court, "Claims of actual innocence based on newly discovered evidence have never been held to state a ground for federal . . . relief absent an independent [procedural] constitutional violation occurring in the underlying state criminal proceeding."[21] Leonel Herrera made no claim that he did not get proper procedure. His claim was that the jury made a mistake *and* that he now possessed newly discovered evidence of his innocence. The Court rejected his claim. In other words, because Herrera got the procedure that was due him, his innocence of the murder was beside the point.[22]

Leonel Herrera was executed on May 12, 1993. His last words: "I am innocent, innocent, innocent. And make no mistake about this. I owe society nothing. . . . I am an innocent man. And something very wrong is taking place tonight."[23]

CHAPTER ONE

INNOCENCE IGNORED

Our mode of trials is often most unfair. It will . . . continue to be, until everything feasible has been done to prevent avoidable mistakes.

—JEROME FRANK

AMERICAN JUSTICE FAILED RAY KRONE

At 8:10 in the morning on December 29, 1991, a female bartender was found, dead, in the men's room of the C.B.S. Lounge in Phoenix. She was nude. The killer left behind no physical evidence save bite marks on her breast and neck. The victim had told a friend that Ray Krone was going to help close the bar that night. Based only on that evidence, police asked Krone to make a bite impression. An expert witness prepared a videotape that purported to show a match by moving Krone's bite impression onto the marks on the victim. According to the Arizona Supreme Court, the videotape "presented evidence in ways that would have been impossible using static exhibits."[1] Although defense counsel had been given the opportunity to examine the dental expert, counsel was not informed of the existence of the videotape until the eve of trial.[2]

The only other evidence against Krone was that he was "evasive with the police about his relationship" with the victim.[3] Of course, without the bite mark identification, being "evasive" about a relationship is practically worthless as evidence. The case thus turned on the bite mark, and the court-appointed defense expert had no experience in video production. Accordingly, counsel moved for a continuance to obtain an expert who could evaluate the videotape. Alternatively, counsel moved to suppress the videotape or to allow testimony about an earlier case in which the same expert's testimony was successfully challenged as not sufficiently scientific. The trial court overruled all defense motions. The prosecution expert used the videotape in his testimony without challenge from a defense expert. The jury convicted Krone of murder and kidnaping. The trial judge sentenced Krone to death.

On appeal, the Arizona Supreme Court held that the trial judge had acted improperly in refusing to allow a continuance. The jury had not yet been selected when the motion was made, the court noted, and the state would have suffered little prejudice.[4] If substantial prejudice would have been caused, the right course of action, according to the supreme court, was to preclude use of the videotape. What the trial judge could not do was what he did—allow use of the tape without giving defense counsel ample opportunity to prepare a defense.

So far, so good. The case was remanded for a new trial, the defense secured an expert, and the jury convicted again. This time, though, the judge sentenced Krone to life in prison, "citing doubts about whether or not Krone was the true killer."[5] This borders on the unbelievable. A trial judge who had "doubts about whether or not Krone was the true killer" *sentenced him to life in prison.* Krone served over ten years in prison before DNA testing conducted on the saliva and blood found on the victim excluded him as the killer. The DNA matched a man who lived close to the bar but who had never been considered a suspect in the killing.

Ray Krone's case is an example of how the current system fails innocent defendants. Police seized on the first plausible suspect and looked no further. The prosecution built a case on a Styrofoam bite impression and mumbo-jumbo scientific evidence. That the case was so weak perhaps explains why the prosecutor did not want the defense to be able to challenge the videotaped "expert" testimony. If true, that violates the first rule of prosecution—to do justice rather than try to win cases. "Doing justice" in Ray Krone's case meant allowing the defense to challenge the prosecution's expert testimony.

The first trial judge failed to give Krone a chance to demonstrate his innocence, and the second one sentenced him to life in prison even though he had doubts about his guilt. These are fundamental failures. To be sure, some parts of the system worked. Krone received what appears to have been effective representation by his counsel, and the Arizona Supreme Court recognized the errors of the first trial judge. Nonetheless, despite these successes, Ray Krone would have spent the rest of his life in prison for a crime he did not commit were it not for DNA testing and the Innocence Project founded by Barry Scheck and Peter Neufeld.

What has gone wrong? In a work published in 1713, Matthew Hale acclaimed the English common-law jury trial as the "best Trial in the World."[6] Several commendable qualities that Hale noted have truth as the goal, and three mention truth specifically. For example, Hale said that having witnesses testify in person—subject to being questioned by the parties, the judge, and the jury—was the "best Method of searching and sifting out the Truth."[7] Today, as chapter 2 will seek to show, any rational system of justice should care more about protecting innocent defendants than any other value. But DNA testing has made plain that our modern adversary system isn't very good at protecting innocent defendants. Or, to be more precise, DNA has made plain that the state adversary criminal systems are not very good at protecting innocent defendants. One of the little-noted features of the DNA revolution is how it is almost completely limited to state convictions.

THE FEDERAL SUCCESS STORY?

All of the 207 exonerations accomplished by the Scheck-Neufeld Cardozo Innocence Project benefited state prisoners. All 340 exonerations uncovered by Samuel Gross and his coauthors were of state prisoners.[8] The Northwestern Center on Wrongful Convictions lists two federal exonerations but provides no details as to either.[9] The Cardozo Innocence Project reports no wrongful convictions in cases tried in federal district courts.[10] What are we to make of the virtual nonexistence of federal wrongful convictions?

Perhaps not too much. Federal criminal law is very different from state criminal law. For example, the Gross study found that 96 percent of the known exonerations were either of murder or a sexual offense, usually rape.[11] Rape is not a federal crime at all and only a few specific kinds of homicide are federal crimes (for example, murdering a federal judge with intent to interfere with his judicial duties[12]). In 2002, the states convicted almost 45,000 defendants for criminal homicide, sexual assault, and rape.[13] In the same year, only 161 federal homicide convictions were entered.[14] Thus, the low number of the offenses most prone to wrongful convictions suggest that federal wrongful convictions should be very rare.

Yet there may be features of the federal system that reduce the likelihood of a wrongful conviction even when we control for the type of offense. The caseloads of the federal public defenders and federal prosecutors are, on average, far lower than their state counterparts. For example, state public defenders typically handle hundreds of cases at a time while the average caseload in at least one federal district is about 30.[15] Even assuming that federal criminal law is more complex and time-consuming than state criminal law, the difference in caseloads is a significant difference in workload. Finally, federal investigating agencies, including the FBI, are probably superior to most state police and thus less likely to settle on innocent suspects.

In sum, much of the federal success in avoiding wrongful convictions is probably attributable to the different types of crimes that concern the federal prosecutors. For that reason, what follows in the book will be addressed exclusively to state prosecution and defense of crime. Still, the federal experience gives us reason to believe that lower caseloads for prosecutors and defenders, as well as better quality investigators, would help reduce the error rate in state courts.

AMERICA'S BEDTIME STORY

In the twentieth century, many criticisms were leveled against the American criminal law process. From the left side of the political spectrum came criticism that criminal justice treated the middle class with kid gloves while targeting the lower classes, particularly those who were racial minorities. Judges had too much discretion in sentencing, for example, and police used their discretion to target and harass the powerless in our society.

From the right side of the political spectrum, we heard that the liberal Supreme Court had tied the hands of the police with rules limiting investigations and suppressing evidence of guilt. The problem was not that too much attention was focused on the powerless. Quite the contrary: The real risks to the fabric of society were those who raped, robbed, and murdered. They should receive the most severe punishments. If it turned out that most were poor and many were racial minorities, so be it.

But in this cacophony of bitter debate, one complaint was rarely heard: that the system was routinely convicting innocent defendants. After all, America has an adversarial system, with procedural protections, unlike the European systems where defendants have to answer questions from judges who seem to assume guilt. We have, in the main, honest police, prosecutors, and judges. Honest police, prosecutors, and judges do not want to convict innocent people. And we provide free lawyers to indigent defendants, lawyers who can achieve an acquittal or a dismissal by deploying the vaunted procedural, adversarial protections—presumption of innocence, right to cross-examine prosecution witnesses, right to call favorable witnesses, right to have the prosecutor turn over favorable evidence, and the right to a jury trial where (in all but two states) if even one juror cannot be convinced of guilt beyond a reasonable doubt, there can be no conviction.

So what's not to like about that story? It is a very soothing story, a bedtime story really. We can lock away 2.5 million people, as of 2006,[16] most of whom are poor and many of whom are racial minorities, and yet we can go to bed at night and sleep soundly—feeling both safe in our beds and justified at taking millions of years of freedom from fellow citizens.

The only problem is that the bedtime story is not true. Over half a century ago, Jerome Frank noted convictions of innocent defendants due to "avoidable court-room errors."[17] Some of these errors result from the very adversary system that many consider a tool for uncovering the truth. As Frank demonstrated, truth is often obscured by our rigid rules of evidence, partisanship of lawyers, and the straitjacket of examination and cross-examination. "[T]he lawyer aims at victory, at winning in the fight, not at aiding the court to discover the facts." Because advocates want *their version of the truth,* the adversary trial system is "the equivalent of throwing pepper in the eyes of a surgeon when he is performing an operation."[18]

Darryl Brown lodges a deeper critique of our criminal process. A system that admits it routinely convicts the innocent might face a challenge to its legitimacy. Thus, American "trial adjudication intentionally conceals some uncertainties in fact-finding to strengthen conflict resolution and the appearance of institutional legitimacy."[19] The principal way our process conceals uncertainties is by assuming that juries are virtually infallible as lie detectors. But, as we will see, juries are all too fallible.

The deepest critique of all is given by John Langbein, who demonstrates that the adversarial system that evolved in England created no institutions whose function it was to seek the truth. Thus, the "well-meaning reforms" in English law that produced our modern adversarial system "had the effect of perpetuating the central blunder of the inherited system: the failure to develop institutions and procedures of criminal investigation and trial that would be responsible for and capable of seeking the truth."[20]

The discovery in the last decade of numerous wrongful convictions demonstrates that Frank, Brown, Langbein, and other critics of our adversarial system were correct. So what are the causes of wrongful convictions? As counterintuitive as it may be to imagine an innocent person confessing, data from the Innocence Project show that 24 percent of wrongful convictions include a false confession.[21] Problems with scientific evidence appear in 39 percent of the Innocence Project wrongful convictions. And the little-known problem of jailhouse snitches and other informants was a cause in 24 percent of wrongful convictions. Perhaps most surprising is that *84 percent* of wrongful convictions include a mistaken eyewitness identification. Gate Germond reports a similar finding for cases taken by the Centurion Ministries.[22]

Andrew Leipold has identified other causes of wrongful convictions—denying bail, delaying trials, trying codefendants together, and forcing defendants to defend in courts far from much of the evidence.[23] But, as Leipold shows, the problems are pervasive and deeply embedded. Given that the criminal process accommodates interests other than seeking truth—"most notably, the conservation of judicial resources"—we have developed a process where each pretrial step "will *explicitly* tolerate a modest amount of error."[24] Darryl Brown agrees, finding that "every major component of criminal adjudication compromises fact-finding to serve competing commitments to government restraint, efficient case disposition, and law enforcement effectiveness."[25]

Our system too often fails. The ultimate problem is a failure to screen weak cases, many of which will involve innocent defendants, out of the system. Moreover, we permit prosecutors free rein to offer very favorable plea bargains to get convictions when the case is weak. Perversely enough, American plea bargaining thus creates huge incentives for innocent people to plead guilty. Our "acceptance of this risk evinces a priority for case resolution over truth-finding."[26]

When prosecutors pursue innocent defendants, they must, by definition, possess false and misleading evidence that can move an innocent defendant to plead guilty. If the case goes to trial, juries will hear this evidence. It is a variation of the GIGO phenomenon first noted when computers were in their infancy: Garbage In, Garbage Out. The "garbage" evidence is part of what the jury hears because of deeper failures—failures of defense counsel, overzealous prosecutors, and judges who are too passive.

I will develop a series of categories of causes of wrongful convictions, cognizant of the ultimately artificial nature of categories. As Siegel has noted, "Like an unhappy family, every wrongful conviction is unique."[27] Richard Leo urges criminologists to develop a criminology of wrongful convictions.[28] In the meantime, I offer categories that are, admittedly, artificial constructs.

INVESTIGATIVE FAILURES

A Department of Justice study of twenty thousand DNA tests of arrested suspects found that one in four of the conclusive tests exonerated the person under arrest.[29] In this sample, the police arrested the wrong person *25 percent of the time.* To be sure, any sample based on DNA testing will overstate the error rate in arrests overall. In many cases, the identity of the actor is known to the police, and there is no reason to conduct a DNA test. On the other hand, DNA tests are used, presumably, only in cases of serious crimes where police have incentive to do a better job of investigation.

In the end, it is impossible, I think, to estimate the wrongful arrest rate. But a 25 percent failure rate in a sample of serious crime cases should give us reason to inquire into how police investigations fail. Though stories of corrupt or evil police surface—and Sam Pillsbury has one of the best accounts[30]—it is unlikely that bad motives cause many of the failures. If police as a group do not care whether they arrest the guilty or the innocent, the system is in chaos and nothing anyone can recommend can help. Thus, I assume that almost all police, like almost all prosecutors and judges, want to convict guilty people and avoid convicting innocent people. So what goes wrong?

EYEWITNESS FAILURES

We have long known that eyewitness identification produces a high degree of error. "The identification of strangers is proverbially untrustworthy," wrote Felix Frankfurter in 1927.[31] Under the best of circumstances, humans are just not very good at remembering faces and picking the right one from a lineup or photo array. To make matters worse, police routinely conduct identifications in ways that enhance their unreliability.

Consider the Clark McMillan case in Memphis, Tennessee, in 1979.[32] A black man accosted a white couple in a park, forced them to strip, and raped the girl. She was sixteen years old and a virgin. The girl and her boyfriend gave descriptions of the assailant. Neither mentioned a limp. The police arrested McMillan, a black man who had a profound limp and wore a leg brace. At the first photo array, which included a picture of McMillan, the girl said the assailant was not among the photos, and the boyfriend picked a "filler" (a photo added to fill out the array). The police held a lineup despite these failures. At the lineup, the girl picked McMillan, and the boy again selected a filler.

At trial, the victim testified that her attacker had a limp. She and her boyfriend identified McMillan from a lineup conducted in the courtroom. That the male victim had never identified him in any procedure prior to trial makes one wonder how he came to identify him in court. Perhaps he was coached, by the other victim if not by the police or prosecutors. Clark McMillan served twenty-two years in a Tennessee prison before he was conclusively exonerated by DNA testing. And the Tennessee prosecutors? They admitted a mistake on *this rape charge* but suggested that McMillan was nonetheless a dangerous rapist who must be kept off the street. One prosecutor said that he might "resurrect two other rape charges for which McMillan was indicted but never brought to trial" because of the wrongful conviction.[33]

The unreliability of eyewitness identifications is heightened when the eyewitness is a child. Researchers Cohen and Harnick found that nine-year-old children were almost four times as likely as college students to be led to an incorrect selection by suggestive questions.[34] In 1987, an intruder raped an eight-year-old child. Jimmy Ray Bromgard was a suspect in the case but was not under arrest. His act of agreeing to appear in a lineup was thus the act of a probably innocent man. While the child victim picked Bromgard, she said she was not sure, perhaps only 60 or 65 percent sure. "When asked at trial to rate her confidence in the identification without percentages, she replied, 'I am not too sure.'"[35] What system would permit the jury to hear a child identify a man as her attacker when her certainty was so low? The answer: The one we have today in the United States.

It is not only defendants whose lives are damaged by identification errors. After Jennifer Thompson identified Ronald Cotton as her rapist, he served eleven years in prison. Then Thompson was visited by a detective and the district attorney—"good and decent people who were trying to do their jobs—as I had done mine, as anyone would try to do the right thing. They told me: 'Ronald Cotton didn't rape you. It was Bobby Poole.'" DNA had exonerated Cotton, the "man I had identified so emphatically on so many occasions," but he "was absolutely innocent. . . . I live with constant anguish that my profound mistake cost him so dearly."[36]

We now know that mistaken identifications contribute to far more wrongful convictions than any other cause. It is time for a radical solution. Chapter 9 will deliver that radical solution.

THE "FLAT EARTH" THEORY OF POLICING AND THE FAILURE TO PURSUE OTHER SUSPECTS

Police investigators are, after all, human like the rest of us. When they put together a theory of the crime, and identify the likely perpetrator, they often close their minds to other theories and to other suspects. And if they discover new data, they are tempted to force it into their preexisting theory. When Galileo's observations confirmed the Copernican theory that the earth rotated around the sun, the church "police" ignored the new data and forced Galileo, under threat of torture, to renounce his belief in the Copernican theory of the solar system.

Radelet and his coauthors call this phenomenon "making the defendant fit the crime."[37] Deborah Davis and Richard Leo refer to it as a "presumption of guilt."[38] The Manitoba Department of Justice, in a report chronicling the wrongful conviction of Thomas Sophonow (to which I shall return), called it "tunnel vision":

> Tunnel Vision is insidious. It can affect an officer or, indeed, anyone involved in the administration of justice with sometimes tragic results. It results in the officer becoming so focussed upon an individual or incident that no other person or incident registers in the officer's thoughts. Thus, tunnel vision can result in the elimination of other suspects who should be investigated. Equally, events which could lead to other suspects are eliminated from the officer's thinking. Anyone, police officer, counsel or judge can become infected by this virus.[39]

The case of Michael Crowe is a good example of police holding on for dear life to their flat-earth theory.[40] Only hours after discovering Michael's twelve-year-old sister, Stephanie, murdered in her bedroom, the police seized on fourteen-year-old Michael as the murderer. The inept police investigation led them to conclude that it was impossible for anyone to have broken into the house. Once that flawed assumption was in place, it led quickly to Michael because of remarks he had made about being angry with his sister. Remarkably, the police rejected Raymon Tuite as a suspect even though they knew he was a drifter with "a prior criminal record and a history of mental problems" and that he had been seen "knocking on doors and peering in windows in the Crowe neighborhood on the night of the killing."[41]

Michael repeatedly denied killing his sister during day after day of interrogation while in police custody. He offered to take a lie detector test. It was, at worst, inconclusive, but the police lied and told him he had failed. Despite his denials, a weak motive at best, and no evidence that he was lying, the police stuck to their theory. They chose to believe Tuite when he admitted being in the Crowe neighborhood but denied entering any homes. The myopic police investigation that focused too quickly on Michael began a seven-month ordeal in which Michael and two of his friends were incarcerated awaiting trial for murder. The boys, all fourteen years old, were to be tried as adults. I will return to the Crowe case in the next subsection, dealing with false confessions. The boys were ultimately saved from wrongful convictions by a test that found Stephanie's DNA on the clothes of—you guessed it—Raymond Tuite.

THE "FLAT EARTH" THEORY OF POLICING AND FALSE CONFESSIONS

Until the advent of sophisticated DNA testing, many lawyers, judges, and academics believed that false confessions from mentally competent suspects were extremely rare. We now know otherwise. About a quarter of all wrongful convictions in the Innocence Project data include false statements of innocent suspects. As Mark Costanzo and Richard Leo write, "We might hope that judges and jurors could easily tell the difference between true and false confessions. Unfortunately false confessions often *look and sound true*."[42]

Perhaps the best-known case is that of the young men, then fourteen to sixteen years old, who confessed to the brutal rape and beating of the so-called Central Park Jogger. Four of these confessions were videotaped. Yet we now know that someone else committed this brutal crime and that the young men were completely innocent.[43] Why would an innocent person confess to committing a crime?

The mechanisms that produce false confessions are not fully understood. A critical component, as Leo has observed, is the increasing use of police trickery as the interrogation tool of choice.[44] Facing what appears to be a certain conviction, even an innocent suspect— perhaps *particularly an innocent suspect*—can falsely confess in exchange for lenient treatment. For example, when police questioned Jackson Burch about a murder, he maintained his innocence for hours.[45] Police then fabricated incriminating evidence against him to "lever a confession," including a phony lie detector test that he, naturally, "failed." The detective told Burch that it was up to him whether he got charged with capital murder or second-degree murder. If he confessed, and explained the circumstances, he might be charged with second-degree murder and serve as few as seven years. Burch confessed to being present at the scene but said he could not remember the assault that killed the girl.

After Burch incriminated himself, the state charged him with capital murder, of course, not second-degree murder. He was convicted and sentenced to die, but the state supreme court overturned the death sentence. As Alex Wood described the situation faced by Burch, the police told him, "We've got you, and you could face the death penalty. But if you confess, you may be able to persuade us to send you to prison for as little as seven years." Wood asks, "Why should that kind of pressure work only on a guilty person?"[46] It is a very good question.

Return to the Crowe case. Fourteen-year-old Michael was repeatedly interrogated while in police custody. The interrogators told him over and over that there was no doubt as to his guilt and all that remained was to "get down to why it was done."[47] The interrogators lied to him repeatedly about various tests they did that indicated he was engaging in deception. They told him over and over that if he cooperated with the police and confessed, he would receive help and not jail time. They said if he didn't confess, he would go to an adult prison and perhaps be raped. As Leo described the police strategy, "Through the use of multiple lies, relentless pressure, threats and promises, the interrogators succeeded in breaking down Michael Crowe's confidence in his memory: 'I don't remember. That's the truth. I can't remember what happened. The very fact anything happened—the only reason I know is you've been telling me I did this. That's the only way.'"[48]

Crowe eventually "confessed," though he did not reveal any details of the crime. How could he? He was innocent. His pathetic confessions all resembled the following: "I know I did it, but I don't know how."[49] Based on the manufactured, unbelievable "confessions," the prosecutors charged him with murdering his sister. He was incarcerated in juvenile hall for seven months, awaiting trial. But for DNA, he would be in a California prison today.

The picture here is clear even if the psychological mechanism is still shrouded in mystery. Ofshe and Leo describe a two-step process by which police move a suspect "from denial to admission: The first stage culminates in a state of hopelessness and despair produced by the realization that denying involvement in the crime is futile." The second step involves offering the hopeless suspect inducements "to motivate the suspect to perceive that it is in his self-interest to comply with the interrogator's wishes and confess."[50]

The Michael Crowe case is a perfect example of what Ofshe and Leo describe. Crowe was fourteen years old, in shock over the murder of his sister, removed from his home and family, and subjected to relentless interrogation from adults who were certain of his guilt. When the interrogators repeatedly lied to him about the evidence against him and then promised to help him rather than jail him, Michael could no longer sort the truth from what the adults believed was the truth. Two friends of Michael's were arrested and also ultimately gave incriminating, and false, accounts of their involvement in Michael's murder of his sister.

It is a mystery why Michael was viewed as a better suspect than the drifter seen looking in windows in the very neighborhood and on the very night Stephanie was murdered. Perhaps the police thought that the crime would be more sensational, and thus draw more attention to their work, if the killer was the victim's brother. Perhaps the answer is found in the dark psyches of the police. Or perhaps the answer is as simple as that their first theory had Michael as the killer.

I agree with Richard Ofshe that, in most cases, police do not want to produce a false confession. Of course, there are exceptions. Susan Bandes has written movingly about the willingness of police to use brutality to get confessions.[51] But I think those are outliers. In the typical case, as Ofshe notes, police "manage to keep themselves believing" that the suspect is guilty. And "the passion, the pursuit, the desire to finish the case that takes over interrogators when they interrogate blinds them to what they are doing in some cases, and they blunder into making a horrible mistake that they did not want to make and they will never admit that they made once it's over."[52]

We have so far seen stories of how the investigation and arrest process can misfire. Now I consider how the prosecution and adjudication of criminal cases is flawed.

PROSECUTION AND ADJUDICATION FAILURES

The vaunted adjudicative process that gave Matthew Hale so much pride is not very good at screening out innocent defendants today. The parts that are adversarial—the courtroom drama—are not very good at uncovering truth. And the parts that are not adversarial are under control of the prosecutor. What we have today, Gerry Lynch demonstrates, is an "administrative system" of criminal justice where the prosecutor's office is more important than the courtroom.[53] The value of the procedural protections in the eighteenth century was to keep the king and his cronies from fabricating cases against their political opponents. But errors today are routine and difficult to detect. Defense counsel failures make routine errors even harder to detect and correct. I begin with these failures.

DEFENSE COUNSEL FAILURES:
A "TRUE CONSTITUTIONAL CRISIS"

The Constitution Project and the National Legal Aid and Defender Association will soon issue a major report on the provision of defense counsel to indigent defendants in the United States. Two of the reporters have just published an article concluding that the present provision of counsel is a constitutional crisis. Mary Sue Backus and Paul Marcus comment: "The pervasiveness of this failure is particularly shocking in light of the decades of repeated attempts to call attention to and repair the deep flaws in the indigent defense systems across the nation."[54]

And while the guilty as well as the innocent deserve competent counsel, the profound failure to create a functional system falls more heavily on the innocent. "If defense counsel are juggling hundreds of cases, clients' claims of innocence will not likely receive the attention they deserve."[55] While one should not confuse fiction with reality, Perry Mason provides an aspirational model of what defense counsel could accomplish in the service of the innocent. His clients were, of course, always innocent, and he always believed their protestations of innocence. One problem faced by defense lawyers in the real world is that they, like the judicial system itself, lack an epistemology to separate the guilty from the innocent. If the defendant looks guilty to the prosecutor, she probably looks guilty to the defense lawyer as well.

In addition to his steadfast belief in his client's innocence, Perry Mason had other advantages over those who labor in the real world of indigent defense. He had Paul Drake, a private investigator who conducted his own fact investigation and developed alternative theories of the case. This was an effective antidote to "flat earth" policing. Second, Drake and Mason appeared to have only one case at a time and thus vast quantities of time and energy to devote to proving the client's innocence. Compare this to data collected by the American Bar Association showing that lawyers for indigent defendants in four Alabama counties failed even to request investigators or experts in 99.4 percent of the cases.[56]

While the Perry Mason model is unattainable, the reality is often so far removed as to be unrecognizable as criminal defense. Kent Roach notes that the "battle theory does not work well when one of the gladiators is inexperienced, incompetent, woefully under resourced, drunk or asleep."[57] Return to Jimmy Ray Bromgard, who spent fifteen and a half years in a Montana prison for a crime he did not commit. Despite an extremely thin prosecution case, Bromgard's lawyer "did no investigation, hired no expert to debunk the state's forensic expert, filed no motions to suppress the identification of a young girl who was, according to her testimony, at best only sixty-five percent certain, gave no opening statement, did not prepare a closing statement, and failed to file an appeal after Bromgard's conviction."[58] To say that Bromgard's lawyer provided the "assistance of counsel" guaranteed by the Sixth Amendment is to make a mockery of the words.

What might explain the lawyer's indifference to his innocent client? Consider a picture of indigent clients meeting their lawyer for the first time in New York City:

> In disgusting pens holding as many as forty prisoners, I would interview clients. I was the first person many prisoners saw after they had spent up to four days waiting to appear before the court.
> The holding pens were filled with huddling defendants, most of whom were standing because there was only one bench. Virtually the entire population of the pens was nonwhite and poor, without the resources or stable families to allow them bail. Most were in shock or panic, yelling questions and begging for help. "What am I charged with?" "When will I ever get out?" "Can you call my mother?" "What if I didn't do it; will they still keep me?" "Will you call my boss because if I don't show up I'll lose my job?"
> I came to see that most of them were not really represented at all. Not only would they not make bail, *but most would ultimately plead guilty to something, anything, just to move out of the system.* I realized that with a lawyer who had a few days to spend with the client instead of a few minutes, a proper fight could be waged, both to get the defendant out on bail and ultimately, to get a favorable disposition.[59]

The Supreme Court in *Gideon v. Wainwright* said that providing counsel to a "poor man charged with crime" made him "equal before the law."[60] But as Corinna Barrett Lain puts it, *Gideon* is just a "piece of storybook Americana."[61] The huddled masses in holding pens will be surprised to learn that they are "equal before the law." Indigent defendants are lucky to have a warm body and even a few minutes to discuss their case with that warm body. Some public defenders handle seven hundred cases a year—almost three dispositions per working day.[62] A caseload of this magnitude means that even the most able and dedicated defense lawyer has insufficient time to investigate a client's innocence, insufficient time to file motions to discover the state's case, insufficient time to develop alternative theories of the case or do the barest investigation.

Backus and Marcus conclude that by "every measure in every report analyzing the U.S. criminal justice system, the defense function for poor people is drastically underfinanced."[63] The *New York Times* reported in 2003 that five states pay nothing toward indigent defense, relying on counties to provide funds.[64] In one county in Mississippi, appointed lawyers are paid next to nothing and sometimes coerce clients into pleading guilty. Most states pay public defenders less than prosecutors, and both groups make far less than private lawyers. Many lawyers who represent indigent defendants seem uninterested, drugged, burned out, incompetent, crushed by the workload, or all of the above.

As Susan Bandes puts it, for some defense lawyers the "time arrives when the lawyer simply can no longer continue to do the work effectively."[65] Michael Mello describes his book about death cases as "rife with exhausted sadness." Part of his sadness is "that our criminal justice system and the law itself, so noble in theory, are so shabby and seedy in practice."[66]

The very person who should be laboring to prove her client innocent may be throwing up her hands and pressuring him to plead guilty. Indeed, though criminal procedure has "many of the trappings associated with confrontation and contest," in reality, it is not "adversarial in theory nor adversarial in fact."[67] Instead, "a major objective of all participants is to achieve a settlement without recourse to contested trial."[68] A pivotal role played by defense lawyers is to "transmit *to* the client the system's imperatives" that include "co-operation with the police or the administrative convenience of a guilty plea."[69]

To be sure, a study from the early 1970s found no difference between outcomes obtained by appointed counsel and retained counsel.[70] But this study suggests that the problem is deeper than indigent defense. Because rich people are statistically irrelevant among criminal defendants, the clients who retained lawyers in the study were of modest means. Clients of modest means cannot generally afford to pay for a lengthy trial and would likely face greater temptation to take a plea bargain deal than defendants represented by public defenders. Thus, rather than give us confidence in the quality of appointed counsel, the study makes me wonder how flawed is the provision of criminal defense to all but the wealthy.

Does it matter if the client says he is innocent? Probably not, or at least not very much. In addition to the epistemological problem shared by all others in the criminal justice process, defense lawyers are burdened with an attitude problem. Over time, most defense lawyers become cynical if not jaded. Professor Alan Dershowitz has "discerned a series of 'rules' that seem—in practice—to govern" the criminal system: "Rule I: Almost all criminal defendants are, in fact, guilty. Rule II: All criminal defense lawyers, prosecutors and judges understand and believe Rule I."[71] We are beginning to understand that Rule I is an exaggeration, but it is unclear how effectively this message has percolated through the criminal justice system.

Defense lawyers thus face relentless caseload pressure with a cynical mask firmly in place and a myopic focus on getting a plea deal. Is it any wonder that defense lawyers are not inclined to believe the client who protests his innocence? Is it any wonder that defense lawyers who have hundreds of cases are exasperated when a few clients reject a very favorable plea bargain on the ground that they are innocent? And given their very own lawyer's impatience with their plight, is it any wonder that innocent defendants are tempted to take plea offers if the "deal" is good enough?

I do not mean to say that most defense lawyers are incompetent. Nor do I mean to say that most defense lawyers become jaded or burned out. As Andrew Taslitz pointed out to me, big-city public defender offices have relatively large numbers of "ideologically passionate left-wing libertarians who view prosecution as a dirty, evil business, aiding state oppression of powerless groups."[72] But with millions of criminal cases each year, if only a small percentage of the low-paid defense bar provide poor representation, hundreds of thousands of defendants are poorly served by their lawyer. Poor representation increases significantly the risk that an innocent defendant will plead guilty or be found guilty after a trial in which her lawyer will not provide the adversarial testing that the Sixth Amendment is meant to require.

PROSECUTOR FAILURES: IGNORING INNOCENCE

Kent Roach observes that "[w]rongful convictions inevitably implicate multiple stages of the criminal process. Mistakes made during the initial investigation by the police or witnesses are repeated in subsequent proceedings."[73] Precisely. When the system fails, the police give the prosecutor a case file that contains evidence, and the prosecutor sees only that evidence. She does not see, unless she grills the police, the tentative or flawed investigative procedure. Belloni and Hodgson report the same phenomenon in England: Prosecutors remain "dependent upon the information provided by officers" and do not probe that evidence for weakness.[74] In sum, once a case file is created that makes an innocent defendant look guilty to the prosecutor, the appearance of guilt tends to intensify at every stage of the process.

Moreover, even if the prosecutor asks probing questions, she is unlikely to uncover the flat-earth failure to follow other leads or develop other theories. The prosecutor has no epistemology by which she can access the truth about guilt. It is difficult to prove a negative, and roads not taken rarely announce themselves to the prosecutor when she reviews the file.

As Susan Bandes has demonstrated, "tunnel vision" is not limited to police officers. Prosecutors also have a "tendency to develop a fierce loyalty to a particular version of events: the guilt of a particular suspect or group of suspects."[75] This helps explain what otherwise is inexplicable: Prosecutors sometimes continue to insist on the guilt of suspects who have been conclusively exonerated by DNA testing.[76] The prosecutor's "[l]oyalty to a particular version of events may develop at a very early stage, and may prove mightily resistant to reconsideration."[77]

As stories of wrongful death-row convictions mounted in Illinois in the late 1990s, the Illinois Supreme Court explicitly recognized the problem of tunnel vision and amended the ethical rules governing the conduct of prosecutors. The first paragraph now states, "The duty of a public prosecutor or other government lawyer is to seek justice, not merely to convict."[78] The committee report notes that the duty to seek justice has been an explicit part of Illinois law at least since 1924. That the state supreme court saw fit in 1999 "to remind prosecutors that the touchstone of ethical conduct is the duty to act fairly, honestly, and honorably"[79] reveals the depth of the court's concern with prosecutorial tunnel vision.

Beyond the problem of tunnel vision, most state prosecutors are burdened with too many cases. The incentive to dig into the police work looking for flaws or for other suspects is muted by the constant need to get cases plea bargained or ready for trial. In addition, McConville and coauthors note that the close working relationship between police and prosecutors creates a "desire to achieve a result which legitimates police action in the case."[80]

The biggest problem may be the job we ask prosecutors to do. The goals of serving justice and being an advocate are in tension, if not downright contradictory, as Susan Bandes, Daniel Medwed, Fred Zacharias, and others have noted.[81] The career incentives for prosecutors are also in tension with protecting innocence. Prosecutors typically have ambitions that transcend their current position—to advance in the ranks of prosecutors, to become a judge, to run for political office. The current system rewards conviction rates and either ignores or penalizes dismissals and acquittals. In short, we have failed "to develop an incentive structure for prosecutors that rewards the pursuit of justice rather than the pursuit of competitive advantage."[82]

The adversary system and the American method for selecting prosecutors aggravate the problem with incentives and the tension of being an advocate while seeking justice. In France, prosecutors receive additional education and training and go directly into prosecuting when their internships end. They never practice law as an advocate. The French believe that practice "at the bar could produce a cast of mind which would be a defect" in seeking truth. "The lawyer, whose duty is to win the case for his client, is often led not to favor the emergence of the truth."[83] In the United States, prosecutors are chosen, often for political reasons, after years or decades of practicing law and honing their skills as a dogged advocate. Michael Tonry would remedy some of these problems by having the states adopt a career civil servant model for prosecutors, in essence moving us toward the French system.[84]

Laboring under these tensions and burdens, prosecutors can influence the process in a variety of ways and at many points. If she does so fairly, striking (in the Supreme Court's words) "hard blows," the adversarial process is served, and the prosecutor is not to be blamed for inherent flaws in our adversarial approach. But the prosecutor can aggravate these flaws by striking what the Court calls "foul blows." This is forbidden. It is as much the prosecutor's "duty to refrain from improper methods calculated to produce a wrongful conviction as it is to use every legitimate means to bring about a just one."[85]

The difference between "hard blows" and "foul blows" is often a difficult call, but prosecutors sometimes go far over the foul line. The prosecutor in the rape case against the Duke lacrosse players, Mike Nifong, offers a good example. The state attorney general investigated the case after Nifong dismissed the rape charges, but not the charges of kidnaping and sexual assault. The attorney general concluded that the defendants were innocent of all charges.[86] An ethics panel found Nifong guilty of misleading defense lawyers and a judge about a lab report that showed DNA evidence from four unidentified men on the alleged victim.[87]

What is unusual about the Nifong case is not the presence of foul blows. It is the response of the legal community. "There is no discipline short of disbarment that would be appropriate in this case," said F. Lane Williamson, a Charlotte lawyer who led the ethics panel.[88] I will return to the issue of sanctions for foul blows later in the chapter.

An example of foul blows noticed by the Supreme Court appears in the Lloyd Eldon Miller case. It appears that police and prosecutors made "the defendant fit the crime"—the authorities "needed a suspect and quickly convinced themselves of Miller's guilt."[89] The case also involved flawed science that defense counsel failed to challenge. Because this case took place in 1955, we do not know whether Miller was an innocent defendant convicted in part because of foul blows of the prosecutor. But his case remains a good example of police and prosecutorial tunnel vision.

Two days after Thanksgiving, Janice May was raped and brutally murdered in Canton, Illinois. Settled in 1825, halfway between St. Louis and Chicago on the Chicago, Burlington, and Quincy railroad, Canton was a small, sleepy Midwestern town. The horrible crime in the small Midwestern town gave rise to a "manhunt" that the local newspaper called "the most intensive" in the county's history.[90]

The family dog led two boys to their sister, who was moaning and bleeding from multiple wounds about the head. The day was bright and very cold—the high of ten degrees was reached at noon—but she had set out to meet her brothers at a playground. She apparently decided to take a short-cut through the rail yard, where she was apprehended. She died in a local hospital three hours after her brothers found her. Her mother was a nurse, her brothers were twelve and fourteen years old, and the dog that found her was named Cuddles.[91] Her father worked for the International Harvester Company[92]—a business so important to Canton that four years later an "International Harvester Appreciation Week" was held in the town.[93]

Early the next morning, suspicion settled on twenty-nine-year-old Lloyd Miller because he did not return his cab to the taxi company the night of the murder and could not be found at his home. The police questioned a waitress who had ridden in Miller's cab shortly after the murder. The interrogators over several sessions kept "endlessly" asking her whether Miller said he did it. She later testified, "By this time I was very confused and crying, and I said, 'I guess he did.' . . . And from that moment on, I told lies."[94]

Miller agreed to take a lie detector test. Though the results were inconclusive, the police polygraph operator told Miller that the machine said he was lying. He insisted on his innocence during an eight-hour interrogation. He insisted on his innocence even when the police told him, falsely, that a pubic hair was found on the victim that matched his. He insisted on his innocence even when police showed him the waitress's statement in her presence. He said to her, "Tell these people I didn't say no such thing to you."[95]

According to Miller, he finally signed a written statement that he did not read because the interrogating officer said that it was the only way he could avoid the electric chair.[96] At trial, the lie detector results were not introduced. The pubic hair "match" was not introduced. These phony pieces of evidence were used to get a confession. When the phony or inconclusive evidence did not do the trick, the police moved to the next stage. They threatened the electric chair.

However persuasive Miller's confession might have been, the prosecutors had a technical problem. Anglo-American law requires corroboration of a confession, and the waitress had repudiated her original accusation in a written statement in possession of the defense. The defense was permitted to read to the jury the portion of her statement denying that Miller confessed.[97] At trial, she changed her story again, and testified that Miller told her that he committed the crime.[98] While her testimony provided corroboration if the jury chose to believe what she said on the stand rather than what she told the defense, it was hazardous to rely on the testimony of someone who changes her story repeatedly.

That brings us to the bloody undershorts, found not far from the murder scene. In his statement to the police, Miller said that he had abandoned the shorts because they were bloody.[99] The existence of the shorts and the presence of blood on the shorts would serve as physical corroboration of the confession and would probably send Lloyd Miller to the electric chair.

Later investigation, in preparation for Miller's habeas corpus hearing, revealed that the shorts were almost certainly not his. Moreover, it is unclear whether there was any blood on the shorts. Sophisticated tests performed eight years later found no blood.[100] As the police and prosecutor knew at the time, at least some of the stain was brown paint. But the way the prosecutor questioned the expert on the witness stand, and the way he answered the questions, made it seem as though *all* of the stain was blood.[101]

The prosecutor referred to the bloody shorts in his closing argument. The testimony that the shorts were stained with blood corroborated Miller's confession and ensured a conviction. Was the use of shorts stained with brown paint a hard blow or a foul blow? The Supreme Court of the United States, unanimously, took the view that it was foul, concluding that the "prosecution deliberately misrepresented the truth."[102]

The Court's conclusion was rejected by the Grievance Committee of the Illinois Bar Association. In a defiant report completely at odds with the ethics investigation of Mike Nifong in the Duke case, the committee accused the Court of "misapprehend[ing] the facts of the case."[103] The committee concluded that the prosecutor violated no ethical duties when he failed to inform the defense, the court, or the jury of the existence of paint stains on the shorts.

The report would make the Pharisees proud. The committee correctly noted that the presence of paint on the shorts was not inconsistent with the presence of blood and thus the testimony was not a lie. But the critical question for my purpose is whether the prosecutors served justice by hiding from the defense that the stains were mostly paint.[104] Consider the effect on the jury when the prosecutor presented shorts that appeared to have been soaked in the blood of an innocent child. The committee's conclusion that justice was served by hiding the paint stain is simply incredible.

Now compare the response to the foul blows in the Miller case with those in the Duke lacrosse players case. Perhaps times have changed in the last fifty years. I hope that is the explanation. But knowing the way our justice system routinely underserves and even oppresses the marginal suspect and defendant, I am doubtful. I think the Illinois ethics commission vindicated the Miller prosecutors because Miller was an itinerant drifter with no powerful family or friends. The Duke lacrosse players were white, upper-middle-class college students.

Leaving aside notions of fair play and propriety, prosecutors who abuse their power threaten the innocent, as the Duke case makes clear. Perversely, prosecutorial abuses are likely to be found more often in cases of innocent defendants than guilty ones because cases against innocent defendants will be, on balance, weaker than cases against a guilty defendant. The attitude of the Illinois Grievance Committee helps create the climate in which some prosecutors feel justified in overreaching. Willard J. Lassers concluded that the "Miller case has a fearful message" for America. He then asked very hard questions about the conduct of the authorities. Miller's

> confession was inconsistent with, and indeed contradicted, known facts. Even convinced as they were of Miller's guilt, one would have expected the authorities to be troubled by this, but they made little or no effort to resolve the inconsistencies or contradictions. When they learned, for example, that the hair on the vaginal swab did not match Lloyd's, they should (one thinks) have had profound doubts about the confession and bent every effort to study the matter. Yet they did not. On the contrary, at the trial, they misrepresented key evidence and suppressed evidence favorable to the accused. Why did they behave in this fashion?
>
> It is my view that the answers to these questions lie in the nature of the criminal process. . . .[105]

The state's conduct in the Miller case can only be understood as the by-product of an adversarial process that emphasizes winning the case rather than achieving justice. It is one kind of problem if a party in a civil suit fails to investigate or present its case fairly. We can safely leave those cases to the adversary system, confident that in a universe of cases civil justice will be done. We cannot afford to take such a laissez-faire approach to criminal cases. We need to find a way to encourage prosecutors to seek justice as their principal goal. In chapter 9, I will propose a radical change that I believe will have that effect.

FAILURE OF JUDICIAL SCREENS

Screening innocent suspects and defendants out of the justice system depends initially on police and prosecutors. But flat-earth policing and tunnel vision prosecuting suggest the need for a meaningful judicial screen. In most states, and in the federal system, a preliminary hearing before a judge takes place a week or two after arrest. The defendant has a right to have his lawyer present evidence, and to cross-examine prosecution witnesses. Unfortunately, the prosecutor need only show probable cause to believe the defendant is guilty—a very low standard that is almost always met. The prosecutor would not proceed with the preliminary hearing if she did not have probable cause. When the defendant is innocent, the case file necessarily contains evidence that falsely implies guilt. But it will still *look* like probable cause. Indeed, the standard is so easily met that few savvy defense lawyers present evidence at the hearing, contenting themselves with probing the state's case through cross-examination of prosecution witnesses.

Some states do not require a preliminary hearing, permitting a prosecutor's sworn information to bring the case before a grand jury. Forty-eight states make use of grand juries in some fashion,[106] and the Fifth Amendment requires grand juries in federal felony prosecutions. This nationwide embrace of grand juries suggests that they are an important protection. They are not. Grand juries are very unlikely to screen for innocence. The grand jury hears only the state's side of the case. The defendant and defense lawyer are not present. Nor is there a judge in the room. The prosecutor presents the evidence and answers any questions that the grand jurors might ask. A grand jury controlled by a prosecutor who believes the defendant is guilty is not an effective screen for innocence. As a chief judge of New York's highest court is reported to have said, any prosecutor worth his salt can get a grand jury to "indict a ham sandwich."[107]

But what about the trial—Hale's "best Trial in the World"? What about the presumption of innocence and the requirement that guilt must be proved beyond a reasonable doubt? What about the requirement, in almost all jurisdictions, that no conviction can be entered unless all members of the jury vote guilty? Surely all (or almost all) innocent defendants will insist on a trial and will benefit from powerful procedural protections. Surely a guilty verdict from a jury against an innocent defendant is a truly rare occurrence.

This is what most observers of the American criminal justice system believed until DNA testing proved us wrong. Upon reflection, we were naive to believe that procedural protections will catch almost all the mistakes made by police and prosecutors. Our justice system is like our world—viewed from the inside, it looks different than when viewed from the outside. When we see a piece of granite, for example, it looks solid. Little did we know until the discovery of atoms and subatomic particles that even a piece of granite is mostly empty space. It remains difficult to comprehend at an intuitive level that a solid object is 99.99 percent empty space.[108]

It is the same with the justice system. The procedural protections look solid when viewed from outside but contain far more empty space than we thought. The fundamental point here is that, when the system fails, the case of an innocent defendant *will look like any other case throughout the entire criminal process.* The "garbage in, garbage out" problem leaves juries pretty much in the dark.

JURIES AND THE GIGO PROBLEM

The Framers would be surprised to learn that the jury system they so valued is sometimes part of the reason innocent defendants are convicted. To the Anti-Federalist Framers, the proposed central government was oppressive and dangerous. The jury was to stand between the citizen and the tyrannical central government. The right to counsel, to free speech and religion, to be free of unreasonable searches and seizures were all potential nullities if the government could bring its case before corrupt or biased judges. Thus, the principal focus of the debate over the Constitution was directed at assuring trial before an impartial jury drawn from the defendant's community.

But by the nineteenth century, juries were viewed by some as a joke. Mark Twain said in 1873: "We have a criminal jury system which is superior to any in the world; and its efficiency is only marred by the difficulty of finding twelve men every day who don't know anything and can't read."[109] Criticism mounted in the twentieth century. Historian Carl Becker said in 1945 that trial by jury was "antiquated" and "inherently absurd."[110] Present-day critics abound. The common refrain is that jurors are amateurs too easily fooled by lawyers, unable to get the facts right or apply the law fairly.

Juries also have their contemporary, and eloquent, defenders. Jeffrey Abramson uses political theory to demonstrate that, while the jury is not without flaws, it is the best way for a deliberative democracy to decide criminal culpability. On Abramson's view, the various jury criticisms are not just wrong, but incoherent. When the jury fails, it is because we as Americans have failed.

> The direct and raw character of jury democracy makes it our most honest mirror, reflecting both the good and the bad that ordinary people are capable of when called upon to do justice. The reflection sometimes attracts us, and sometimes repels us. But we are the jury, and the image we see is our own.[111]

Or as Scott Sunby puts it, in the death penalty context, "At bottom, a jury's effort to decide between life and death is a distinctly human endeavor infused with emotion and moral judgment."[112]

On the question of how well juries find facts, Jonakait's thoughtful book persuades that jury verdicts are determined by the evidence presented.[113] Hans and Vidmar reached a similar conclusion, based on a study of British judges taken after jury verdicts in their courts.[114] The classic and rigorous Kalven and Zeisel study found that the judges found the jury verdict without merit in 9 percent of the cases.[115] Pizzi describes the judge-jury difference in the Kalven and Zeisel data as "substantial,"[116] but given the drumbeat of criticism of juries, 9 percent does not sound all that high.

The jury's role in creating criminal culpability out of facts crucially depends, of course, on an accurate presentation of the facts. If the jury is presented facts that falsely imply guilt, the jury is not to be blamed for a false conviction. Four categories of false evidence can be usefully constructed—erroneous eyewitness identifications, false confessions, perjury, and failed science.

I discussed false confessions and eyewitness misidentifications in the subsection about police failures. Here I discuss perjury and failed science. We know little about police perjury. As Morgan Cloud observed, "No one can know with certainty the extent of the problem, but no one familiar with the criminal justice system would deny its existence."[117] Pizzi argues that the Warren Court's penchant for creating rules that exclude reliable evidence made police perjury more likely and the justice system more cynical.[118]

Whatever the scope of the problem, it is extremely difficult to remedy. Lawyers who suspect that a witness is giving false testimony will attack it during cross-examination, a type of questioning where lawyers are permitted to attempt to confuse or discredit the witness, to show inconsistencies in the testimony, and even to suggest motives for its falsity. But a veteran police officer who decides to risk discipline, and his pension, to tell a smooth and coherent, but false, story at trial is a difficult target for cross-examination. In the current American criminal justice system, where the trial is viewed more as a contest than a careful search for the truth, not much can be done. My reformed criminal justice process, described in chapter 9, will indirectly create a greater disincentive for police to lie on the stand.

Informants and accomplices are another source of perjury. One commentator argues that the amount of "fabrication" that results from deals with the government "is potentially staggering."[119] Stephen Trott, a former federal prosecutor who now sits on the Ninth Circuit Court of Appeal, said that informants' "willingness to do anything includes not only truthfully spilling the beans on friends and relatives, but also lying, committing perjury, manufacturing evidence, soliciting others to corroborate their lies with more lies, and double-crossing anyone with whom they come into contact, including—and especially—the prosecutor."[120]

The problem is not so much that those charged with or convicted of crimes are willing to lie to get a benefit, but that prosecutors are so willing to believe the lies. Begin with Saul Kassin's proof that humans are just not very good at detecting lies.[121] A study by Paul Ekman and Maureen O'Sullivan demonstrated that police detectives and FBI and CIA agents could detect lies only 56 percent of the time, which is only marginally better than flipping a coin.[122] Ellen Yaroshefsky conducted interviews with assistant United States attorneys and concluded that several, overlapping factors contribute to the willingness to believe informants—a lack of corroboration of the informant's story; lack of investigation; naive belief that the prosecutor could trust the informant and could tell who was telling the truth; lack of experience as a prosecutor; and the prosecutor's belief in the guilt of the defendant.[123]

While jailhouse informants do not carry the credibility of police officers, and can be savagely attacked on cross-examination, juries too often believe informants who are lying. The Canadian justice system was shocked by the revelation of two wrongful convictions based, in large part, on false informant testimony. In one, Thomas Sophonow was tried three times for the brutal murder of a sixteen-year-old girl. The jury could not reach a verdict in the first trial. The second trial ended in conviction, but the Canadian Court of Appeal directed a new trial.[124] When he was convicted a second time, the Canadian appellate court acquitted him.[125] Here is how the prosecution used informants at Sophonow's three trials:

> In addition to the three jailhouse informants called in the case, police had offers from nine other jailhouse informants, including Terry Arnold, who is currently the prime suspect in the killing, to testify against Sophonow. In the end, one of the three called [to testify], Thomas Cheng, had twenty-six counts of fraud withdrawn. While proclaiming the best of motives for his testimony, a police report from a polygraph operator, which was not disclosed to the defence, confirmed Cheng's primary motive was to secure his liberty and have his charges dropped. After testifying at the first and second trials, he was released and never seen again. The Crown read in his evidence at the third trial.[126]

The commission that later investigated the failures of justice in the Sophonow case described another informant witness as "a prime example of the convincing mendacity of jailhouse informants. He seems to have heard more confessions than many dedicated priests."[127]

After his acquittal Sophonow continued to insist that he was innocent. The Winnipeg Police Service reinvestigated the murder, ultimately announcing that Thomas Sophonow "was not responsible for the murder and that another suspect had been identified. On that same day, the Manitoba Government issued a news release which stated that the Attorney General had made an apology to Thomas Sophonow as he 'had endured three trials and two appeals, and spent 45 months in jail for an offence he did not commit.'"[128]

It is not just "flat earth" or "tunnel vision" policing that can lead prosecutors to put forth jailhouse informants. What if an ambitious, zealous young attorney general became convinced that the Teamsters' union leader was involved with organized crime? If Robert Kennedy believed in his heart that Jimmy Hoffa was damaging the fabric of the union movement, would he not use whatever tools at his disposal to get Hoffa? And if federal prosecutors heard rumors that Hoffa was trying to bribe jurors in his trial for, ironically enough, accepting bribes as head of the Teamsters, wouldn't the prosecutors welcome a jailhouse informant and make a very generous offer to encourage him to join Hoffa's entourage and become a spy? That, or something close, is how Robert Kennedy finally got Jimmy Hoffa.

The jailhouse informant was Edward Partin. He was languishing in a Louisiana jail, facing indictments for state and federal crimes of embezzlement, kidnapping, and manslaughter, when he apparently conceived a plan to save his own skin. He told his cellmate, "I know a way to get out of here. They want Hoffa more than they want me."[129] It is impossible to argue with Partin's logic, however much we may condemn his ethics or lack of honesty. He contacted federal authorities and offered to seek to become part of the Hoffa inner circle as the bribery case was about to begin. Chief Justice Warren, in dissent, explained why Partin cooperated with the federal prosecutors:

> A motive for his doing this is immediately apparent—namely, his strong desire to work his way out of jail and out of his various legal entanglements with the State and Federal Governments. . . . [H]e has not been prosecuted on any of the serious federal charges for which he was at that time jailed, and the state charges have apparently vanished into thin air.[130]

That the federal authorities found a way to shield Partin from state as well as federal charges tells us how badly they wanted him inside the Hoffa circle. And why would a man charged with embezzling, kidnapping, and manslaughter (and about to be charged with perjury) not be willing to lie to save himself? I am not suggesting that Partin did lie, or that Hoffa was innocent, only that if the government wants a conviction badly enough, the price for jailhouse informants can reach the point where lies about innocent people become a very real possibility. As Chief Justice Warren put it,

> This type of informer and the uses to which he was put in this case evidence a serious potential for undermining the integrity of the truth-finding process in the federal courts. Given the incentives and background of Partin, no conviction should be allowed to stand when based heavily on his testimony. And that is exactly the quicksand upon which these convictions rest, because without Partin, who was the principal government witness, there would probably have been no convictions here.[131]

But Chief Justice Warren dissented alone, and the Court has done nothing in the intervening forty years to solve the problem of jailhouse informants or to warn jurors that the testimony might be false. As lying jailhouse informants were a factor in 16 percent of the wrongful convictions, it is a problem that needs addressing.

Another problem for juries is failed science. Some writers refer to this as "junk" science, but that allows us to feel too smug about the problem. If the problem were only the fraudulent or completely indefensible expert testimony, the fix would be easier. But it extends even to evidence that we have long accepted on faith as good science. One writer called failed science the "most insidious and least noted" of the problems facing the legal system today.[132]

For example, it now appears that fingerprint matches are not the gold standard that we have been assured. Even if it is true that no two fingerprints are the same—and how can that proposition be proven?—when the FBI computerized identification system cannot produce a definitive answer, "human analysts make the determination, and their conclusions often differ."[133] The reader might recall the high-profile FBI mistake that led to the arrest of Brandon Mayfield, a Portland lawyer, who was incorrectly linked to one of the Madrid terrorist bombings in March 2004. Although three FBI examiners and an external expert agreed that the prints were Mayfield's, Spanish authorities eventually matched the prints to an Algerian, and the FBI agreed with the Spanish experts.[134]

Moreover, even evidence that is "bulletproof," such as DNA, can be produced or stored in ways that undermine its accuracy. If fingerprints and DNA evidence can sometimes produce false results, the label *junk science* does not completely contain the category of failures. I prefer the term *failed science,* which is broad enough to cover reliable tests that misfire as well as the fraudulent and incompetent science.

Because most juries want to believe expert testimony and because juries lack the training to distinguish good science from bad science, juries are at the mercy of expert witnesses. If the defense lawyer is incompetent or the state does not give the defense a chance to counter the expert testimony, failed science can lead to a conviction and a death sentence. We saw in Ray Krone's case a prosecutor who so badly wanted a conviction that he did not give the defense a fair chance to rebut the failed science that was being served the jury. The prosecutor was aided and abetted by a judge who refused to give the defense time to rebut the new type of testing that was revealed to the defense, literally, on the eve of the trial.

Failed science can cross-contaminate other errors, such as overzealous prosecutors and incompetent defense lawyering, to create a truly foul mixture. Return to Jimmy Ray Bromgard's case. The state called a forensic expert who had examined hairs found on the sheets where the young victim was raped. (The semen found on the victim's underwear did not yield results from then-available testing.) The expert "testified that there was less than a one in ten thousand (1/10,000) chance that the hairs did not belong to Bromgard." But this testimony was fraudulent because "there has never been a standard by which to statistically match hairs through microscopic inspection. The criminalist took the impressive numbers out of thin air."[135] Bromgard's incompetent defense lawyer did not challenge the expert's methodology or seek funds for a defense expert. Recall the Alabama data showing that defense counsel failed to request investigators or experts in 99.4 percent of cases.[136]

Belloni and Hodgson report failed science in the British "Birmingham Six" case, where six men served seventeen years each for a pub bombing before their convictions were overturned.[137] The prosecution's forensic expert reported the results of a "Greiss test" on the hands of the defendants for which he claimed a 99 percent certainty that two of them had handled nitroglycerine. But on the same night, a scientist in the same laboratory dismissed positive results from a Greiss test in two cases because the suspects had handled adhesive tape.[138] A test that can be fooled by adhesive tape cannot be very reliable. More troubling, the scientist who testified about the Greiss test failed to testify about (and the prosecution failed to disclose to the defense) the negative results from other sensitive tests for nitroglycerine residue on the defendants' hands.

In 1993, prosecutor William C. Forbes asked the West Virginia Supreme Court to investigate "the willful false testimony of Fred S. Zain, a former serologist with the Division of Public Safety" who had testified for the state in many cases.[139] That a prosecutor would allege willful false testimony by a scientist the state had frequently used shows the seriousness of the problem.

Two independent investigations followed, one by the American Society of Crime Laboratory Directors. Both found numerous acts of fraud that included "misreporting the frequency of genetic matches," "reporting inconclusive results as conclusive," "repeatedly altering laboratory records," and "reporting scientifically impossible or improbable results."[140] Though no one knows how many innocent defendants were convicted because of Zain's subversion of the justice system, a state police investigation "identified as many as 182 cases that might have been affected by Zain's work."[141]

Was Fred Zain an evil man? Was he an avenging devil, aka Charles Bronson's vigilante character? The truth is apparently more about mendacity and incompetence than evil. Zain claimed to be a chemist when he was, in fact, a mediocre student who had failed organic chemistry. Incredibly, "no one looked at his transcripts until the house of cards he had built came tumbling down."[142]

The Zain saga is a good example of cross-contaminating errors. A flawed bureaucracy hired Zain without examining his credentials. Overzealous prosecutors used him without checking his qualifications. Lax judges did not demand much from the prosecutors who qualified him as an expert. Most disturbingly to those who embrace the adversarial system, *not a single defense lawyer from the hundreds of cases even bothered to challenge his credentials.* It is easy, too easy, to dismiss Zain as a spectacular failure that we can avoid by careful screening of experts. But that is a mistake because experts do not have to be utter failures to interject false science into criminal cases.

In sum, we have a problem with police perjury, jailhouse informants, false confessions, eyewitness misidentifications, and failed science. I agree with the conclusion Jonakait reaches in his study of the American jury system. It is the too frequent failure of the adversary system itself that produces wrongful convictions.[143]

ESTIMATING THE FREQUENCY OF CONVICTIONS OF INNOCENT DEFENDANTS

So far, we have innocent defendants arrested, charged, and convicted of crimes they did not commit. These cases cause immeasurable harm to the innocent people, to their families, and to the public trust in government. But they cause another harm that should not be ignored. In every case in which an innocent person is convicted, the real criminal remains free to prey on victims yet again. Thus, the interests of all "sides" in the debate over crime control are in confluence on this issue. Whether you believe we are "soft" on crime or that our criminal laws cover too much conduct with insanely severe sanctions, you do not want an innocent defendant sitting in jail while the real criminal goes unpunished.

We have known for centuries that an occasional failure in the system convicts an innocent person. We now know they are far too common. But how common? Is there any way to estimate the frequency of convictions of innocent people? Radelet and his coauthors documented four hundred cases of wrongful convictions of crimes punishable by death, which they suggest merely scratches the surface of wrongful convictions.[144]

A statistical model developed by Gelfand and Solomon estimates a 2.21 percent probability that a jury of twelve will convict an innocent person.[145] Baldwin and McConville studied actual English cases and concluded that 5 percent of the convictions were of doubtful validity.[146] I will use 2 percent as a conservative estimate. Of course, not very many defendants go to trial, so perhaps the problem of innocents being convicted is serious, unforgivable really, but not widespread. Only thirty thousand felony convictions result from a trial each year.[147] Two percent of that universe gives us six hundred innocent defendants convicted of felony.

What about plea-bargained convictions? The 1993 Royal Commission on Criminal Justice "acknowledged that 'it would be naive to suppose that innocent persons never plead guilty because of the prospect of the sentence discount.'"[148] I agree. Perversely, as noted earlier, the weaker the case, the more favorable the plea deal is likely to be. Even an innocent defendant who has never committed a crime must be tempted to take a deal in which a felony is reduced to a misdemeanor and the sentence will be the time served before bail was arranged or, if the defendant was out on bail, a suspended sentence.

McConville and Baldwin concluded that 2 percent of the guilty pleas in their study were of doubtful validity.[149] If we halve that estimate, to be conservative, and apply it to the roughly one million felony convictions each year,[150] it gives us ten thousand guilty plea felony convictions of innocent defendants. Moreover, there are roughly eight million nonfelony convictions each year.[151] Prosecutors with weak misdemeanor cases will probably offer steeper discounts and thus induce a greater percentage of innocent defendants to plead guilty to lesser penalties. But if we stick with a rough estimate of 1 percent, we get eighty thousand wrongful misdemeanor convictions. We are thus close to one hundred thousand wrongful convictions each year.

Andrew Leipold's estimate of wrongful convictions is more conservative than mine.[152] But even if my estimate is too high by a factor of ten, it is intolerable that ten thousand innocents are convicted each year. It is impossible to prove the rate of erroneous convictions with any precision. But the number is ultimately beside the point. I seek to defend, in the next chapter, the proposition that due process requires a set of procedures that protect innocent defendants, at a reasonable cost. However many innocent defendants are saved by these procedures, if due process requires the procedures, then states must make them available.

In chapter 9, I will propose dramatic changes in the pretrial screening of cases, plea bargaining, the way the counsel is used to prosecute and defend, and the appeal of criminal cases. These will be revolutionary, not incremental, changes. I believe these procedures will save many innocent defendants from conviction at the same time they satisfy due process.

History will, I believe, see the early years of the twenty-first century as an inflection point in the protection of innocent defendants. DNA is the best, but not the only, example of how science is now offering us a partial epistemology of innocence. In a book generally critical of the way the Supreme Court has handled scientific evidence in the past, David Faigman nonetheless concludes that "there is reason to be hopeful. Science and technology today are so pervasive that the Court cannot continue its slapdash ways."[153]

With science and technology as our trusted lieutenants, it is time to declare war on the convicting of innocent defendants, which brings me to "narcoanalysis."

ERNIE TRIPLETT AND "NARCOANALYSIS"

Jimmy Bremmer was raped and murdered in Sioux City, Iowa, on August 31, 1954, but his body was not found for almost a month. The case was eerily similar to the Lloyd Miller case that would occur a year later in the adjoining state of Illinois. Both victims were eight years old; both were raped; and both were brutally murdered. The suspect in the Sioux City case was, like Lloyd Miller, a drifter.

Ernie Triplett was an itinerant laborer who worked different jobs—including carnival worker—for a few weeks and moved on.[154] He was AWOL from the army in 1922 when someone told him that the army could not take action against him if he were married. So he married a prostitute with whom he was living. He tried to convince her to stop prostituting herself and, sometime during the Great Depression, left her because she would not stop. He eventually married again, without bothering to get a divorce. His second wife threw him out of the house in 1952. By the time of his contact with police in 1954, he had tertiary syphilis.[155]

In August 1954, Triplett went to work for the Flood Music Company in Sioux City selling music lessons.[156] We do not know what drew the police to question Triplett, but it is possible that he had been in the Bremmer neighborhood while soliciting buyers for music lessons. The police interviewed Triplett two days after Jimmy disappeared, and he admitted seeing a boy matching Jimmy's description on August 31. He told several versions of his encounter with Jimmy, always denying that he touched or harmed him. In the weeks that followed, "he continued to give the police evasive and inconsistent answers to their questions."[157] When he was interviewed twenty years later, Triplett said he purposely told different stories because he wanted to stay in jail.[158] Indeed, he bragged about outsmarting the police to get free food, cigarettes, and coffee. It is also possible that his tertiary syphilis was causing memory loss. And it is possible that he killed Jimmy Bremmer and was clumsily trying to cover up the truth.

At some point in September, the police persuaded Triplett to admit himself to the State Mental Health Institute in Cherokee, Iowa, for a psychiatric evaluation and treatment. After finding Jimmy's body, the police conferred with the clinical director until midnight about Triplett's possible involvement in Jimmy's murder.[159] A couple of weeks later, and presumably in response to a communication from the hospital, two Sioux City police drove to the hospital to interview Triplett. In the morning, he told the same basic story he had told a hundred times: After getting out of Triplett's car, Jimmy had "gone into his house, returned briefly, and then disappeared around the side of the house."[160]

But a completely different story emerged in the afternoon session, with one of the psychiatrists taking the lead in the questioning. Triplett now admitted that he had made a sexual advance, that Jimmy had run from him, and that he knocked him down. What changed? While it is possible that Triplett's conscience finally moved him to tell the truth when he had been telling a different story for a month, a more likely explanation is found in the doctor's notes. They had, for some time, been subjecting Triplett to "narcoanalysis"—questioning him while he was under the influence of powerful drugs. The doctors gave him barbiturates that caused drowsiness and euphoria, as well as LSD, a powerful and unpredictable hallucinogen. Triplett would later tell his lawyers of "fabulous pictures" he saw while at the mental hospital.[161] He was sometimes given a combination of barbiturates and a stimulant that could produce delirium.

Prior to and during the October 6 afternoon interrogation, the doctors gave Triplett large dosages of Seconal (a barbiturate) and Desoxyn (a stimulant commonly known as "speed"). The intravenous dosages of Desoxyn were so large, an expert witness would later testify, that they could have been lethal, "but apparently were not, as he is alive."[162] Even swimming in this sea of powerful drugs, Triplett denied killing Jimmy. Indeed, his choice of words at one point shows the control of the doctors and their narcoanalysis: "Nobody told me I killed the Bremmer boy."[163] The head of the mental hospital, seventeen years later, concluded after his study of the records that "the likelihood was that Triplett said whatever his interrogators wanted him to say."[164]

Triplett's lawyer was a former schoolteacher who had never attended law school but who had "read for the law." He made no effort to inspect the doctors' notes even though Triplett told him he had been drugged at the hospital. The confession was admitted into evidence. The jury convicted of second degree murder—evidently his confused confession persuaded the jury that there was no premeditation. The judge sentenced to the maximum permitted, life in prison. Just before he entered the Iowa State Penitentiary, he turned to the sheriff and said, "This thing didn't turn out the way I thought it would."[165]

At some point during his seventeen years in prison, Triplett began writing letters insisting on his innocence. Unfortunately, his letters were bizarre, nonsensical, and mostly sent to people who were not in a position to help him, such as the president, the secretary general of the United Nations, and the "Poster Master General." One of his letters, however, reached the legal clinic at the University of Iowa College of Law. It said that his legal problem was "Fraud Contract—Pinkerton Dects Real Murder Case." Helpful information, he said, could be found in the "Anglo Saxion American Law Contract Poaster General's Office at Sioux City, Iowa." In an almost comprehensible part, the letter read, "Judge Vanp Pelt of Lincoln Neb. Absent the confession would not support the conviction."[166]

Two years out of Stanford Law School, Robert Bartels joined the Iowa law faculty in July 1971, "to take over and develop a fledgling 'clinical legal education'" program begun by Professor Philip Mause.[167] By now, Triplett had been in prison seventeen years. How the Iowa legal clinic proceeded in court and how the lawyers and law students unearthed the notes about the "narcoanalysis" is a good read but beside the point for my project. I am, however, interested in the strategic decision the Triplett defense team made after discovering the narcoanalysis.

A hearing had been scheduled on the question of the voluntariness of Triplett's confession. The defense could wait and spring the information on the state at the hearing. Another possibility was to show the evidence to the prosecutor beforehand, in the hopes that he would join, or at least not resist, the motion to vacate the conviction. The danger in the second course was that, once warned, the state lawyer might find counterevidence.

Complicating the decision was that the state's lawyer was William Sturges, who had been one of the prosecutors at Tripplet's trial. Might Sturges feel that he needed to vindicate the verdict by seeking opposing expert witnesses? Ultimately, Bartels decided to show Sturges what the defense had found. It was the right thing to do. And the evidence of involuntariness was so strong, it would be hard to rebut.

But still Bartels fretted about Sturges's reaction. He needn't have. After examining the defense evidence, and doing some investigation of his own, Sturges "conceded that the October 6, 1954 confession was involuntary and that the conviction should be reversed."[168] He would join the motion to vacate and, because without the confession there was not enough evidence to convict on retrial, he would dismiss the indictment. At the close of the hearing, Sturges rose and said, "On this the State moves for a dismissal." His voice cracked and tears welled up in his eyes.[169]

Ernie Triplett was a free man. He later won a modest amount of money from Iowa as partial compensation for the seventeen years of freedom he had lost. He lived out the rest of his life in Iowa City, getting around on his bicycle. Robert Bartels managed the modest sum of money and did what he could to help Triplett.

I end what is mostly a tragic chapter with the Triplett story because we have heroes here. Professors Robert Bartels and Philip Mause recognized a valid claim beneath the haze of Triplett's confusion. Bartels and the Iowa law students spent countless hours investigating the case. Without the notes about "narcoanalysis" that they uncovered, it is unlikely that Triplett would have won his freedom. Bartels decided to trust that prosecutor William Sturges would do the right thing when he saw the evidence. And Sturges did.

CHAPTER TWO

THE FUNDAMENTAL VALUE

OF DUE PROCESS

> There is no worse error in American criminal justice than the wrongful prosecution, conviction, and incarceration of an innocent person.
>
> —RICHARD A. LEO

> [T]he conviction and punishment of someone who is wholly innocent is the most plain and unequivocal denial of justice.
>
> —LLOYD WEINREB

The knowledge that modern justice systems are prosecuting and convicting innocent persons led John Jackson to conclude that "the criminal trial is undergoing perhaps one of the greatest challenges that it has faced since trials by ordeal came to be challenged and replaced in the thirteenth century."[1] I agree. The task of this chapter is to provide a proof that the paramount value in any criminal process is to protect innocence at a reasonable cost. Protecting innocence is, I will seek to show, a critical part of the due process of law guaranteed by the Constitution.[2]

One goal of a criminal process is to determine truth, often expressed in terms of reliable or accurate outcomes. Protecting the innocent is a subset of the reliability goal. Donald Dripps has offered a comprehensive account of procedural due process that seeks both to advance reliability and to protect innocence. On Dripps's account, due process would reject procedures that impede gathering of evidence of guilt as well as those that pose an "unnecessary risk of false conviction."[3]

I have no objection to the part of Dripps's account that would remove barriers to convicting the guilty. I do not go that far, though, in part because I believe that protecting the innocent is a more fundamental goal than reliability. Recall Blackstone's famous dictum that "it is better that ten guilty persons escape, than that one innocent suffer."[4] If undifferentiated reliability were the fundamental value of the criminal process, trading ten wrongful acquittals for one wrongful conviction would be perverse. To be sure, reliability is important to the protection of innocence because accurate information about what happened will demonstrate innocence. But erroneous acquittals of factually guilty defendants do not weigh in the due process balance of protecting innocent defendants.

Another reason I focus on the less ambitious goal of protecting the innocent is that wholesale legislative changes in American criminal procedure are monumentally difficult to achieve. Indeed, no such changes have been made at the federal level since the Judiciary Act of 1789. One goal I set for myself is to seek to move law as far as necessary to protect innocence but no farther.

The difficulty of getting changes in law unconnected to the protection of innocence can be seen when we examine the second set of values, or normative demands, identified by Antony Duff. These have to do with respecting the autonomy, dignity, and privacy of those affected by the process. Dripps would change the law to provide less privacy and autonomy in the search of more convictions of the guilty. Duff would change the law to provide more privacy and autonomy of those suspected of crime, many of whom will be guilty. It is difficult enough to persuade legislatures to adopt salutary provisions designed to protect innocent defendants without also getting involved in the long-standing debate about where to draw the lines that protect other values.

Herbert Packer's work is instructive here. After discussing reliability as a goal, he argued that due process has "tended to evolve . . .

into values quite different and more far-reaching [than reliability]. These values can be expressed in, although not adequately described by, the concept of the primacy of the individual and the complementary concept of limitation on official power."[5]

This is a remarkable analytical move. Due process, for Packer, begins with the goal of reliability but moves quickly to values that are "more far-reaching." The "primacy of the individual" and the "limitation on official power" manifest themselves most clearly in the values of privacy and autonomy. Privacy at its core is the right to exclude the uninvited eye or ear from some enclave in our life. Autonomy at its core is the right to make decisions without interference from the government.

Packer did not invent the idea that constitutional criminal protections are importantly about privacy and autonomy. He got it from the Warren Court, which found the protection of privacy and autonomy implicit in several rights. So, for example, the Court held that when police violate privacy by conducting an unreasonable search, the evidence is usually inadmissible in court.[6] And the Court famously held in *Miranda v. Arizona* that suspects must be warned of their right to silence and to counsel before being interrogated to give the suspect the "free choice" to decide whether to cooperate with the police.[7]

What was unsettling about Packer's argument was that, in one stroke, he relegated the protection of innocence to the periphery of constitutional values and trumpeted the evolution of due process into a protector of the individual against official power. Odd though the Packer view sounds to my ears now, it informed an entire generation of scholars, teachers, lawyers, and judges. Echoes of it resonate today. Belloni and Hodgson define "miscarriage of justice" to include failures to treat suspects and defendants fairly. Thus, it would be a miscarriage for police to target unpopular groups, such as black males, immigrants, the Irish, pickets, demonstrators, squatters, gays, and feminists.[8] Targeting unpopular groups is an abuse of power, I quite agree, but it is not a miscarriage of justice that compares to the conviction of an innocent person.

Packer's concern with privacy continues to manifest itself. In *Hudson v. Michigan*,[9] the issue was whether a police officer's failure to knock before executing a valid search warrant required suppression of the evidence found pursuant to the warrant. Four members of the Court would have held that the evidence should be suppressed. The dissent bristled at the privacy intrusion caused by the failure to knock.

> Many years ago, Justice Frankfurter wrote for the Court that the "knock at the door, . . . as a prelude to a search, without authority of law . . . [is] inconsistent with the conception of human rights enshrined in [our] history" and Constitution. How much the more offensive when the search takes place without any knock at all.
>   Over a century ago this Court wrote that "it is not the breaking of his doors" that is the "essence of the offence," but the "invasions on the part of the government . . . of the sanctity of a man's home and the privacies of life."[10]

Hudson is an example of Packer's continuing influence—albeit in the dissent—and of the Court's current rejection of Packer. To the extent that the law of search and seizure protects innocent people, its protection lies in the requirement that the police have probable cause before they act. Requiring probable cause protects against random searches that are more likely to include the innocent. For five members of the *Hudson* Court, the key fact was that the magistrate issued a warrant, based on probable cause, authorizing the search for evidence of crime. *Hudson* thus chose to value the protection of innocence over the homeowner's privacy that was infringed by the failure of the police to knock. The dissent would have put privacy on a par with the value of reducing searches of the innocent.

We can test the notion that protecting the "primacy of the individual" is a due process value on a par with protecting innocence by using police interrogation as a laboratory. Three overlapping due process norms evolved in the American law of interrogation: Police should be fair, the suspect's autonomy should be respected, and false confessions must be avoided. One method for obtaining confessions that violates all three norms is torture. Torture is obviously unfair, the suspect's autonomy is rejected as irrelevant, and the resulting confession will often be false.

But once we move away from torture, the fairness and autonomy norms become surprisingly difficult to implement. Assume we have a universe of confessions and an epistemology that allows us to determine which confessions are false. Begin with the subuniverse of true confessions of guilt. Here we know the suspect is guilty, and the value of protecting innocence is thus fully served. Some of these cases of true confessions will generate a consensus that the police methods were unfair or trenched too harshly on the suspect's autonomy—for example, if the police questioned the suspect for thirty-six hours with only one break for food.[11] Some cases will sharply divide us on fairness and autonomy issues. Consider the case where an inmate confessed the rape and murder of his stepdaughter to a police informer to get protection from "some tough treatment and whatnot."[12] As the five-to-four split on the Supreme Court reveals, able lawyers can argue both sides of the fairness and autonomy issues in this case.

Studies show that the stubbornly difficult cases of fairness/autonomy are a very small subset of actual interrogations conducted in the field. In most cases, observers would agree that the police methods were acceptable. Richard Leo observed 182 interrogations and found coercion in only 4 of them, a 2 percent rate.[13] In my study of 212 interrogations from reported decisions on Westlaw, I found 5 cases of coercion, roughly the same rate as Leo found.[14] These studies suggest a very small area of controversy in the subuniverse of true confessions from guilty suspects. Courts should, therefore, admit almost all of these confessions.

Now move to the subuniverse of confessions that are false. Is there anything here that would generate controversy about whether to admit the confession? The answer of course is no. Whatever the virtues of suppressing the confession of a guilty suspect—promote respect for the process; punish offending officers; deter future coercion—no argument can be deployed to justify admitting a false confession from an innocent suspect. Moreover, this judgment holds *even if the suspect was treated fairly and even if his privacy and autonomy were fully respected.* It follows that the single due process value that trumps all other values in police evidence-gathering is to avoid eliciting incriminating statements from innocent persons.

A real-life example of the crucial importance of innocence in the law of confessions is *Connelly v. Colorado.*[15] Connelly, a paranoid schizophrenic, approached a Denver police officer and confessed to a murder while the startled officer tried to provide *Miranda* warnings. Connelly was suffering command hallucinations causing him to believe that God had given him a choice of killing himself or confessing. If we assume that the confession is false, it is inadmissible for any purpose even though the police conduct was as respectful of individual privacy and autonomy as we could imagine. To use a false confession would make the outcome illegitimate, however much Connelly's autonomy was respected and however fairly he was treated. On the other hand, if we view the confession as true, as did the Supreme Court, then courts might admit it even though Connelly lacked the robust rational capacity to choose to confess and his autonomy was thus impaired.

Of course, we lack the epistemology that would permit us always to be certain that any confession is false. Thus, due process demands a set of procedures that create an acceptably low risk that the confession is false. The greater the risk of false confessions from any given set of procedures, the less likely it is that due process is satisfied. An example of a practice doomed to fail this due process test is the "third degree" police interrogation method that developed around the turn of the twentieth century. In Freemasonry, the third degree is the test to become a master Mason. American police used the "highest test" of interrogation to get confessions when the suspect refused to answer questions or continued to deny involvement. The third degree utilized various forms of physical coercion to break "tough guy" suspects and induce a confession.[16]

The Wickersham Commission reported in 1931 that "third degree" police interrogation methods were "widespread."[17] In 1949, Jerome Frank wrote, "To our shame be it said that the English, who do not tolerate the 'third degree,' call it the 'American method.'"[18] The lawlessness uncovered by the Wickersham Commission threatened values other than innocence, to be sure. Fairness and autonomy were also mugged by the misconduct documented in the report. But what prompted the outcry against the third degree was the fabrication of evidence and the use of coercion to produce confessions that might be false. Due process requires, more than any other parameter, that the criminal process not threaten innocent people.

I offer two additional examples of the fundamental nature of protecting innocence. The first keeps the focus on the law of confessions. In case A, the police use the third degree, beating the suspect with a telephone book until, wracked with pain, he confesses. In case B, the police lie to the suspect about finding his fingerprints at the crime scene. Both cases involve unfair police methods that do not respect the suspect's autonomy. But the critical difference between these methods is that the third degree seriously threatens innocence and the trick does not.[19] The Court recognizes this fundamental difference. It has many times condemned the third degree.[20] It has never held that a trick, by itself, renders a confession inadmissible.

A second example concerns the Court's right to counsel doctrine. Providing counsel to indigent defendants protects innocence. To force innocent defendants to defend themselves while a trained prosecutor seeks to make them look guilty is to burden innocence far too heavily. The Court recognized the truth of that proposition in 1963 in *Gideon v. Wainwright*.[21] Quoting the Court's first intervention in a state criminal justice system, *Powell v. Alabama* (the Scottsboro case), the Court noted that without counsel, a defendant cannot adequately prepare his defense "even though he have a perfect one." Without the "guiding hand of counsel, he faces the danger of conviction because he does not know how to establish his innocence."[22]

The right to counsel, of course, also protects the values of autonomy and fairness. If we knew ex ante that the defendant was guilty, he would still have the right to counsel. But once we satisfy the innocence value by providing effective assistance of counsel, fairness and autonomy have little work to do. Indigent defendants do not have a federal constitutional right to counsel of their choice,[23] a rule that might be unfair and certainly denies indigent defendants the robust autonomy enjoyed by defendants who can afford counsel.

Systems that provide indigent defendants no choice in counsel can fairly be criticized, but unlike the conviction of an innocent, the refusal to allow choice is not illegitimate. James Tomkovitz, for example, notes the valid governmental interests served by the no-choice rule. It avoids "unacceptable administrative burdens and costs in criminal justice systems already taxed to their limits."[24]

Fairness and autonomy simply recede once we pay sufficient attention to the innocence parameter. Indeed, why would we want to give a guilty suspect a level playing field or robust autonomy? I suppose one could say, as Chief Justice Earl Warren said on behalf of overturning Jimmy Hoffa's conviction, that police trickery is simply not "in keeping with the standards of justice" to which we should aspire.[25] But that imposes a moral code on police. We would need to know *why* trickery is not "in keeping with the standards of justice."

Moreover, in Hoffa's case, Chief Justice Warren's principal concern was whether the evidence that the government had obtained by shoddy means *was in fact true*. As long as we hold to our assumption that the evidence is true—that the suspect really did what the police tricked him into admitting—we should not hold the police to the same standards that we hold lawyers or accountants. This means that we must ensure against unacceptable risks of false confessions, but once that is done, the morality of police conduct is of lesser importance.

In sum, it is time to tell the truth about Packer's due process theory and the Supreme Court opinions on which it is based. Every book, every court opinion, is necessarily a product of its time, and it is perhaps unfair to criticize what was written forty years ago for its romantic notion that protecting innocence is somehow less important than protecting privacy and autonomy. But we should be clear that Packer's notion is inextricably linked to the 1960s and should be examined afresh today. As Kent Roach concludes, Packer's arguments "may still strike a chord, but slowly and surely, they are becoming as out of date as other hits of the 1960's."[26] And as Sherry Colb has demonstrated, the idea that guilty people deserve privacy while committing their crimes is an odd one indeed.[27]

I believe that I have established that protecting innocent suspects and defendants is more fundamental than the values of fairness, privacy, and autonomy. Now I must meet a different kind of objection, this from the pragmatist. Lacking an epistemology that permits us to know who is innocent, we can never completely protect innocence. Thus, the pragmatist asserts, the best that a system of justice can do is to provide the right procedures.

The Sixth Amendment fits the bill here, providing the right to counsel, to subpoena witnesses, to confront the state's witnesses, and to have a public and speedy trial. Moreover, due process requires procedures explicitly designed to tilt the balance in favor of innocent defendants. The state must prove the defendant guilty beyond a reasonable doubt; defendants are presumed innocent and need not present any evidence; in almost all jurisdictions, a jury must vote unanimously for conviction; and prosecutors are supposed to disclose exculpatory evidence to the defense.

Once these procedures are in place, the pragmatist can trust the outcomes. He need not engage in a searching inquiry about whether the jury conviction was justified by the evidence. He can be content with an appeals process that creates a very strong presumption in favor of sustaining the conviction.

The pragmatist can make a deeper claim. If you asked a physicist why gravity exists, he would say, "That is the way the universe is constructed." An adversarial system is the way Anglo-American law was constructed. For at least a millennium, Saxon and then English law viewed trials as a contest between parties. The purpose of law was to offer a forum for the parties to settle their differences. Mirjan Damaska calls this a laissez-faire approach to justice; John Rawls refers to it as "pure procedural justice."[28] The pure procedural approach, in its most robust form, would find the concern with right outcomes incoherent. A fair procedure was put in place. The contest was held. One side won. That is the meaning of an accurate outcome viewed within the robust laissez-faire/pure procedural framework.

One vivid manifestation of "justice as a contest" can be seen in the reliance in England on private citizens to prosecute most crimes until well into the nineteenth century. The state provided the judge, the jury, the courtroom, and a set of procedural rules. The rest was left up to the parties. Another piece of evidence that Anglo-American law simply accepted the outcome of the contest as justice is the lack of appeals until the nineteenth century. If there is no reason to question the outcome of the contest, what would be the point of an appeal?

Of course, modern American law is not laissez-faire in the eighteenth-century sense, but the pragmatist's point is that we have the system we have, for good reasons, and it works well enough. I think the pragmatist fails to persuade. He makes two fundamental errors. First, to say that we lack an epistemology to protect innocence *perfectly*, which everyone concedes, is not to say that we cannot do a *better* job of protecting innocent suspects and defendants. As Antony

Duff concludes, we cannot have a "process that guarantees acquittals for all the innocent; but [we can have] a process that provides fair and equal protection against mistaken convictions."[29]

Moreover, to claim that the Bill of Rights procedures are sufficient to protect innocence today is to fail to understand the forces that led to the Bill of Rights. The Framers were not concerned with ordinary cases of "garbage in, garbage out." They were, instead, afraid of abuse of the federal prosecutorial and judicial power to harass those who opposed the government.[30] The Bill of Rights protections, particularly the guarantee of a jury trial, was probably a good buffer against conviction by an aggressive federal prosecutor pursuing an enemy of the government.

Today, the threat to innocence is systemic and benign, caused by system failures of the types that include the factors we saw in chapter 1. If innocence is insufficiently protected, and if sound ideas exist that can improve the protection, why should we insist that the Framers did enough 225 years ago? The Criminal Justice Section of the American Bar Association recently published a monograph with dozens of ideas about how better to protect innocence.[31] While I will be critical of some of those ideas later in the book, the report makes clear that we need not surrender the high ground to the pragmatist for lack of ideas about how to protect innocence.

Thus, the remaining issue is not whether the system should care about the accuracy of a conviction but, rather, *the extent to which we should care.* The issue is how much various protections of the innocent cost and how much benefit they bring. If cost were no object, we might decide to have ten panels of appellate judges review the transcript of every case and declare an acquittal if only one panel found the State's evidence insufficient. As this is obviously impractical, we must decide how much innocence protection we can afford.

The protection of innocence must be achieved at a reasonable cost, both in terms of dollars and in terms of freeing the guilty. As Erik Lilliquist has recently pointed out, false negatives are not cost-free.[32] If freeing one thousand guilty murderers was the cost of preventing one wrongful conviction of murder, even I would find that a bad deal. I feel the same way if the ratio were one hundred to one. But Blackstone gets it about right in my view: ten to one is an acceptable balance. And as for the financial cost, Jerome Frank identifies the appropriate variables: We must do "everything *feasible* . . . to prevent *avoidable* mistakes."[33] I will return to the cost of protecting innocence in chapter 9.

Duff and coauthors argue that criminal procedure theory is radically undertheorized and that no one has offered a normative theory of the criminal trial.[34] I agree. What I offered in this chapter is not a complete normative theory, but it is a start. The critical question is innocence. Donald Dripps has demonstrated that "preventing the punishment of the innocent has priority over punishing the guilty."[35]

In sum, I disagree fundamentally with writers like Heike Jung who assert that truth is not itself a fundamental value because truth is "modulated by legal principles which include particular human rights standards and above all else fairness."[36] I do not demean other values and, indeed, would be happy to have other values added to the meaning of "due process of law." But let's first do all we can to protect the innocent.

The history of justice systems in the Western world, beginning with the ancient Greeks, provides important insights into ways of sorting the guilty from the innocent. The next chapter begins our historical journey.

CHAPTER THREE

IN THE BEGINNING:
GOD, JURIES, AND GOD AGAIN

I'll appoint human judges of this murder, a tribunal bound by
oath—I'll set it up to last forever. . . . Once I've picked the finest men
in Athens, I'll return. They'll rule fairly in this case, bound by a
sworn oath to act with justice.

—ATHENA, GODDESS OF WISDOM

Ancient Western cultures viewed the sorting of the innocent from the guilty as critically important in maintaining an orderly society. The self-help blood feud of the ancient Greeks and Romans had proved destabilizing by the fifth century BC, as we can see in Aeschylus's *Oresteia* trilogy. The notion that juries should judge guilt first appears in Athens in this period, and it flourishes during the Roman republic, only to lose traction as the empire sought more efficient means of determining guilt. When Rome falls, the principal truth-determining procedures in the Western world are the ordeals—elaborate rituals in which men ultimately call upon God to reveal who is telling the truth about guilt and innocence when that truth is hidden from humans.

As told by the great dramatist Aeschylus, the Athenians by 460 BC had begun to use juries to decide guilt and innocence in homicide cases. In the *Oresteia* trilogy, the curse on the House of Atreus leads Orestes to kill his mother to avenge his father's death at her hands. As commanded by the law of the old gods, the Furies now seek Orestes' death to avenge his mother's murder. Apollo, a newer god with a different law of justification, had ordered Orestes to kill his mother. But now, facing the Furies, the god Apollo seems incapable of protecting Orestes.

Orestes flees to the Temple of Athena, where he clings to her statue, seeking her judgment. The Furies arrive before Athena can say a word and, calling up the image of the ground soaked with mother's blood, promise to suck his blood. "Drinking your living bones sustains me—I feed upon your pain."[1] Then a terrifying prediction: "Apollo's power will not save you—nor will Athena's. You're slated to die abandoned and alone, without a sense of heartfelt joy, a bloodless criminal sucked dry by demons, just a shade—no more."[2]

This, then, is the conundrum faced by Athena, the goddess of wisdom. The curse on the House of Atreus had caused many human actions, including incest. It had also caused several murders, each new murder having to be avenged by yet another death. In effect, the blood feud of the ancient gods allowed the past to control the present and thus the future. The only way to deny the past its power over the future in these cases was to allow an actor in the present to judge guilt.

Athena refused to decide whether Orestes was justified in killing his mother, contending that it was too difficult even for a goddess. Instead, she created a "tribunal bound by oath . . . to last forever," consisting of the "finest men in Athens."[3] The jury was to be charged to "rule fairly" and to be "bound by a sworn oath to act with justice."[4]

Thus, in the telling of Aeschylus, was born the jury as an institution to discern the truth and deliver justice. The change in the view of justice manifested by the story of Orestes is striking. Before this time, justice was mechanical and determined by ancient rules laid down by the gods. But all of that was replaced in Athens with the idea of a court of "finest" men to pass judgment on the justification of a killing. The truth no longer resided exclusively in the gods that Athenians still worshiped. Now, Athenian citizens could determine justice.

This fictional account fits with the traditional history that has uncovered the use of judicial governmental bodies in Athens as far back as the seventh century BC. Historian John Fine concludes that during this period "government was more and more trying to change the administration of justice from the dangerous system of family self-help to a regular governmental function."[5] We know that the Athenian council, called the Areopagus, had exclusive jurisdiction in homicide cases.[6]

Indeed, Fine notes that Aeschylus wrote the final play in the *Oresteia* trilogy four years after legislation deprived the Areopagus of some of its powers, an act that "inflamed" passions in Athens.[7] Fine concludes that Aeschylus was delivering the message that homicide cases belonged to the Areopagus as the true voice of the people.[8] Thus, as early as the sixth century BC, the people (at least the nobles) were deciding guilt or innocence in some cases. When self-help became too destabilizing, guilt or innocence could not be left to the gods or to family members. It had to be decided otherwise. In the Athenian state of the sixth century BC, that function would naturally fall to the people.

ROME

According to historian O. F. Robinson, "Early Roman criminal law is both obscure and hotly debated."[9] Guilt during the earliest period in the Roman republic was determined by republican magistrates, who succeeded kings as rulers of Rome around 510 BC.[10] The principal function of magistrates was to be military commanders, but they also had executive and judicial powers.[11]

The Twelve Tables probably date from 450 BC, about the time Aeschylus wrote the *Oresteia* trilogy.[12] The surviving fragments make clear that the Twelve Tables were "a comprehensive codification of the law in force at the time."[13] Like Greek law of the period, criminal law "was in very large measure based on the idea of the right of an injured party to private vengeance."[14] As in Greek law, the prosecution of a murderer was left to the victim's relatives. Unlike early Greek and early Roman law, the relatives were entitled to blood vengeance only after the killer's guilt "had been judicially established."[15] For the authors of the Twelve Tables,

> [T]he natural and only result of a crime was the victim's right of vengeance, and they were merely concerned to restrict [the victim's right] of physical vengeance to the more serious crimes, to keep this right under judicial control, to isolate the wrongdoer who had been found guilty, and thus to protect the commonwealth from the effects of devastating family vendettas.[16]

By the time of the Twelve Tables, it was "the custom, possibly the duty, of the magistrate to refer this or that point in dispute to the decision of one or more jurymen."[17] The reference to "jurymen" should not be confused with modern juries. A juryman from this period was merely "a temporary creation" of the magistrate's will, "a private man on whom the magistrate, by virtue of his [office], chooses to lay the task of finding an answer to some question, whether of law or of fact, which the magistrate thinks fit to put to him."[18]

The evolution in Roman law from jurors who assisted the magistrate at his pleasure to jurors who decided guilt and innocence is hidden from view. It might have been a natural evolution, over three centuries, as Romans became more comfortable with self-governance. It might "have been inspired by Greek jury courts, which were familiar to the Roman upper class" by the second century BC.[19] Or it could have been the brilliant innovation of a single man, Calpurnius Piso. A tribune, Piso is given credit by Cicero for creating, in 149 BC, the first standing jury courts.[20] The proceedings before these juries were civil in nature, and "the only penalty was simple restitution."[21]

Little is known about how Roman juries functioned prior to the reign of Sulla in 81 BC. Sulla routinized the use of jurors and created a new system of courts that would eventually draw "from the three orders of senatorials, equestrians, and *tribuni aerarii*."[22] Robinson suggests that equestrians were roughly equivalent to English knights, and *tribuni aeraii* were "closely akin" in status to, though below, the equestrians. The *lex Aurelia* in 70 BC may have fixed the size of the jury at seventy-five, "25 from each order."[23]

The Roman trial procedure was much like modern American procedure. The prosecutor began with a "long speech detailing the charges."[24] The advocate or advocates for the accused then spoke. "The weapons in the legal duel are the speeches of the advocates and the evidence of the witnesses. It appears that speeches were mixed in with the evidence of witnesses."[25]

Witnesses who appeared in court were examined by the advocate, who offered them as evidence. A witness was subject to cross-examination "to show his want of credibility" by the advocate on the other side of the case.[26] Cross-examining one witness, "Cicero 'cut him up to the applause of gods and men' with extraordinary, but probably calculated fury."[27] In Cicero's words, "That impudent swaggering fellow Vatinius was overwhelmed with confusion and thoroughly discredited."[28]

The Roman jury was given much greater latitude to hear different kinds of evidence than Anglo-American juries. There was no law of evidence, thus permitting both sides to introduce evidence that was hearsay or even irrelevant, as well as opinions about character.[29] The Roman magistrate played a ministerial role, opening court and tending to practical matters about conducting the trial. There was no summing up of the evidence by the magistrate or any instructions about the law. Voting was by secret ballot, except for a twelve-year period under the laws of Sulla when it was up to the defendant to choose.[30] The "different classes voted separately, so that it was possible to say the senators had condemned, the equestrians absolved."[31] The judgment was decided by a majority of the entire jury. Thus, it was possible for one or two classes to vote narrowly one way and yet have a majority for a contrary verdict. A tie vote produced an acquittal.[32]

By 70 BC, Roman justice depended on the voice of the community. That would change with the rise of the empire. The later Roman Empire "was a savage period; the arbitrary exercise of power was, in a sense, increasing."[33] The dependence on the voice of the community in sorting the guilty from the innocent began to fade. The emperor, or his delegate, could insist on sitting as judge in trials, exercising jurisdiction that had previously belonged to the standing jury courts.[34] The Senate ceased to function as a regular court.[35]

By the time of Nero, the jurisdiction of the emperor's courts was coextensive with the jury courts.[36] "From this time, the jury courts dwindled, though traces of their existence remain till the end of the second century after Christ," when the final reference to jurors appears in a work of Papinian.[37] Thirty years later, Papinian's student, Paulus, would say that the Roman jury trial in criminal cases "has fallen out of use."[38]

The disappearance of the jury courts does not seem to have been a conscious usurpation of power by the emperors. Indeed, Strachan-Davidson speculates that Augustus "doubtless intended the jury courts to last on as part of his own machinery of government" despite the alternate courts he created.[39] What led to the demise of the jury courts in the empire seems to have been what has led to their virtual disappearance in England today: Nonjury determinations of truth about guilt and innocence are simply more efficient than jury determinations. Criminal proceedings in the emperor's courts were "more effective, more flexible" and were conducted with "greater speed and elasticity than in the jury-courts."[40] As the empire expanded and then collapsed, it was probably inevitable that the emperors would turn to more efficient means of ascertaining truth.

"The law courts in the fourth and fifth centuries [AD] share in the general demoralization of the age" and participated in the "machinery of cruelty and rapacity" of the later empire.[41] Judges were "merely the nominees of the emperor and his courtiers, and form but a section of the all-pervading bureaucracy" at work in the empire.[42] Corruption was also a problem. When Cicero prosecuted the governor of Sicily for extortion, the jury was "heavily bribed."[43] Cicero said that criminal defendants relied "not so much on [their] eloquence as on [their] influence to obtain a verdict."[44] The search for truth about guilt and innocence had surrendered to power and rapacity.

Taking stock at the end of the third century AD, we see that juries had been the principal mechanism for finding the truth about guilt or innocence in the two leading Western civilizations—ancient Greece and Rome—for roughly eight hundred years. When the jury light flickered out in the middle of the Roman Empire, it would stay mostly dark, with only a glimmer here and there, for almost a millennium.

Tribunals were used in Europe to settle disputes for many centuries. The Frankish inquest is the likely origin of the English jury. The history here is murky but clear enough for our purposes. As early as the ninth century, the Frankish kings used the inquest to help them govern. The king "orders that a group of men, the best and most trustworthy men of a district, be sworn to declare what lands, what rights, he has or ought to have in their district."[45] Kings also used the inquest to uncover corruption among their subordinates as well as "grave crimes" that threatened the peace.[46] These functions roughly parallel the modern grand jury. The Frankish kings also used the inquest in place of the battle and the ordeal when the king was a party to the litigation. The common man had to rely on what Pollock and Maitland call the "formalism of the old folk-law" found in the ordeal. The king could use what amounted to his own jury.[47]

But after the ninth century, "the deep darkness settles down. When it lifts we see in the new states that have formed themselves no central power capable of wielding the old prerogatives" such as the inquest.[48] Scattered uses of the inquest persist in France and Germany until it is "finally overwhelmed by the spread of the romano-canonical procedure"[49] that led to the modern European inquisitorial form of justice. We will see the modern French version in chapter 8. Indeed, the irony here is that the inquest as a method of ascertaining truth would have "perished and long ago have become a matter for the antiquary" but for the Norman conquest of England.[50] I will return to the link between the Frankish inquest and the early English jury in the next chapter.

The task in the rest of this chapter is to sketch how truth was uncovered in Europe and England when the inquest was not used. Truth, of course, is often both obvious and acknowledged. A baron in ninth-century England who had presided over a castle for decades was not going to have his ownership rights challenged. But when truth was hidden from view during this period, it was commonly sought by inviting God's direct judgment. While the Greeks relied on the judgment of their gods indirectly, through the requirement that deaths be avenged to satisfy the blood guilt, the Germanic cultures asked God to intervene directly. This should be no surprise. In the view of these pre-Enlightenment cultures, God was everywhere, knew everything, continually judged the behavior of man, and revealed himself in miracles. Who better to reveal the truth about criminal guilt?

To be sure, we must be careful to separate the cases where criminal guilt was apparent from the cases where it was hidden. Only in the latter category did the Saxons and Franks need an appeal to God. If the offender was found in the possession of stolen goods, his fate was sealed. He would be found guilty by "a court hurriedly summoned for the purpose," and "without being allowed to say one word in self-defence, he will be promptly hanged, beheaded or precipitated from a cliff, and the owner of the stolen goods will perhaps act as an amateur executioner."[51]

As we approach the time when the English jury would reclaim the task of sorting, the hand of man can be seen gradually exercising more influence over the outcome. The English jury did not spring from a void but was, rather, an evolution hastened along by the Lateran Council of 1215. I will return to this transformation in the next chapter. But if we limit the period to the tenth, eleventh, and most of the twelfth centuries, guilt was either self-evident to man or revealed by God.

The Frankish kingdom, which ruled a large part of Europe by 534, used the water ordeal as one method of settling disputes. The accused was required to plunge his hand into a boiling cauldron and retrieve a stone or other object at the bottom. If his wound remained "clean," he was innocent, but if the wound became "dirty," his fault or guilt was demonstrated.[52] The Saxons who inhabited England also used the ordeal by fire and by water. As Sir William Blackstone described these ordeals:

Fire-ordeal was performed either by taking up in the hand, unhurt, a piece of red-hot iron, of one, two, or three pounds weight; or else by walking, barefoot, and blindfold, over nine redhot plowshares, laid lengthwise at unequal distances; and if the party escaped being hurt, he was adjudged innocent; but if it happened otherwise, as without collusion it usually did, he was then condemned as guilty. However, by this latter method queen Emma, the mother of Edward the confessor, is mentioned to have cleared her character, when suspected of familiarity with Alwyn bishop of Winchester.

Water-ordeal was performed, either by plunging the bare arm up to the elbow in boiling water, and escaping unhurt thereby: or by casting the person suspected into a river or pond of cold water: and, if he floated therein without any action of swimming, it was deemed an evidence of his guilt; but, if he sunk, he was acquitted.[53]

Trial by battle was a uniquely European ordeal that the Normans brought with them to England. It was "another species of presumptuous appeals to providence, under an expectation that heaven would unquestionably give the victory to the innocent or injured party."[54] Again in Blackstone's words:

The [accused], when [charged with] felony, pleads *not guilty,* and throws down his glove, and declares he will defend the same by his body: the [accuser] takes up the glove, and replies that he is ready to make good the [trial], body for body. . . . The battel is then to be fought with the same weapons, *viz.* batons, the same solemnity, and the same oath against amulets and sorcery, that are used in the civil combat: and if the [accused] be so far vanquished, that he cannot or will not fight any longer, he shall be adjudged to be hanged immediately; and then, as well as if he be killed in battel, providence is deemed to have determined in favour of the truth, and his blood shall be attainted [his lands forfeited to the king]. But if he kills the [accuser], or can maintain the fight from sunrising till the stars appear in the evening, he shall be acquitted.[55]

Blackstone published his four-volume *Commentaries on the Laws of England* in the period 1765 to 1769. By most accounts, the *Commentaries* are "the most important legal treatise ever written in the English language."[56] One of Blackstone's contributions was to evaluate the law while describing it. By Blackstone's day, of course, England and Europe were experiencing the Enlightenment. Thus, it is not surprising that Blackstone dismissed the ordeals and trial by battle in a haughty manner: "One cannot but be astonished at the folly and impiety of pronouncing a man guilty, unless he was cleared by a miracle; and of expecting that all the powers of nature should be suspended, by an immediate interposition of providence to save the innocent, whenever it was presumptuously required."[57]

This is one Blackstone criticism that misses the mark. In his day, juries decided guilt or innocence by weighing the evidence and choosing which witnesses to believe. If Blackstone had allowed himself to see the world as it existed for the pre-Enlightenment cultures, he would have realized that the ordeals and trials by battle were *superior* to juries in sorting the innocent from the guilty when the truth was hidden from human eyes. Juries could only guess at innocence. God knew.

The following case from around 1175, reprinted in its entirety, shows a deep belief that God would reveal the truth-teller.

> Two men who had been condemned to judicial combat came together, one being much bigger and stronger than the other. The stronger man catches the weaker one, lifts him high up above his head ready to throw him hard on the ground; the smaller man hanging thus in the air lifts up his spirit to heaven and says a short prayer: "Help, holy Thomas [Becket] martyr." The danger was great and sudden, and the time for prayer short. There are witnesses who were present: the stronger man, as if oppressed by the weight of the holy name, suddenly collapsed under the one he held and was vanquished.[58]

In addition to the water ordeal, the Franks used a method to determine guilt or innocence that, on the surface at least, more closely approximated modern-day trials. In the trial by oath, sometimes called "compurgation," both the accuser and the accused gave an oath and then presented oath takers or oath helpers to support their oath. The oath helpers swore "their willingness to support the oath of the principal, whether accuser or defendant."[59]

In a trial by oath, the "defendant swore on the Bible—or, better still, on holy relics (saints' bones)—that he didn't do it. Then he brought in oath helpers in numbers and prominence designated by the justices to swear that his oath was 'clean,' that he couldn't possibly have committed, say, murder or armed robbery."[60] Norman F. Cantor characterizes trial by oath as "organized lying,"[61] but this may be too cynical, at least for the period that preceded the Norman

Conquest. As Trisha Olson puts it: "Historians must pluck out their skeptical eye when viewing the sources [relating to oath taking]."[62]

In the Middle Ages, belief in an omniscient and omnipotent God was total. Oath helpers who lied could expect to be "revealed by the Deity."[63] So, for example, in an 1186 case in a manor court of a lord, the "men of the whole vill" were ordered "to speak the truth on this [issue], testifying for the truth on peril of their souls and their goods."[64] It is difficult to accept Cantor's notion that simple men, who believed in God's judgment after their death, would routinely lie to save others from earthly judgment.

Whether or not one views oath helping as organized lying, litigants had plenty of reason to fear trial by oath. It was exceedingly formal, with draconian consequences for the litigant whose oath helpers did not follow the procedure exactly. "A punctilious regard for formalities is required of the swearers. If a wrong word is used, the oath 'bursts' and the adversary wins. In the twelfth century such elaborate forms of asseveration [swearing] had been devised that, rather than attempt them, men would take their chance at the hot iron."[65]

Indeed, in the 665 cases in Van Caenegem's collection of English lawsuits, spanning the years 1066–1216, I found only one case in which the litigants made oaths on relics, and oath helpers swore to the truthfulness of the litigants.[66] And even in that case, the litigants compromised on a judgment before the oath taking was finished. To be sure, there were cases where twelve or twenty-four lawful men would be required to make an oath before the king or another judge, but the oaths in these cases were about some fact in the universe that was at issue, usually who owned particular property.[67] In one case, the hundred "wanted to swear upon relics," but it was to persuade the sheriff who was judging the inquest that the property belonged to the church of Andover.[68] The defendant in a criminal case would sometimes be required to take an oath, but, in these cases, the judge would decide whether to permit an oath of purgation that would result in acquittal.[69] So it appears that the judge was determining guilt; there was no mention of oath helpers.

It is important to understand that trial by battle, by ordeal, and by oath were not in any sense an attempt to discern the facts of the case. Rather, they were forms of proof. Today, a party to a legal action makes proof by witnesses and documents. In the eleventh and twelfth centuries, litigants offered the results of the battle, the ordeal, and the oath as proof. But the proof was not whether or not the accused committed the crime with which he was charged. The results of the ordeal revealed, instead, which party was innocent before God.

Thus, the ordeals were reserved for cases when normal methods of inquiry would not discern the facts. Because of my focus on the various forms of the ordeal, it might appear to the reader that they were the order of the day, used to settle most disputes. Nothing could be farther from the truth, at least in England in the years following the Norman Conquest. The most frequently litigated issue in that period was ownership of property, and the most common method of resolving disputes, as we will see in more detail in the next chapter, was to have an inquest consult its collective memory and declare who was the rightful owner. Ordeals were outliers when the relevant universe is all cases rather than just cases seeking to determine guilt or innocence of acts that we today consider crimes.

But in the cases when the facts were obscured from humans, innocence was a holistic state rather than a crude question of whether X did act Y. As Olson points out, X could very well have done Y and yet be innocent because X had atoned.[70] An example, from the early thirteenth century, is of a man who had lived, out of wedlock, with a woman for a long time. Fearing that he would be confronted with this sin,

> He went to his priest, confessed, and was advised "if you have a firm purpose never to sin again with her, then you may carry the white-hot iron without further care and deny your sin; for I hope the virtue of confession will free you." He was adjudged innocent. Rather than signifying approval of perjury, the priest's advice to guilty probands [those being tested] reflected a faith in the Deity's willingness to cloak from men's eyes evidence of crimes that a proband, unabashedly and without rationalization, had regretted at private confession.[71]

The result of the ordeal thus did not need to be explained to humans. Perhaps God judged innocence on a standard "incomprehensible" to men.[72] Of course, as long as humans believed that God was rendering the judgment, it mattered little whether the result made sense. Nor did it matter whether those who harmed society escaped justice if it was God's will. The medieval acceptance of God's verdict in the ordeal was, in Olson's terms, "bowing to the unknowable."[73]

This view of justice, innocence, and truth about facts that were unknowable to humans was firmly embedded in European and Saxon culture in 1066 when William the Conqueror crossed the English Channel and defeated King Harold on the field of battle. The ordeal was still flourishing in 1166 when William's great-grandson was king of England. A few decades later, however, the ordeal would be dead letter in England and in Europe. How did this cultural revolution happen so quickly? That is the story for the next chapter.

CHAPTER FOUR

TRUTH FROM JURIES: WILLIAM THE CONQUEROR, HENRY II, AND THE CATHOLIC CHURCH

King Henry ordained . . . for preserving peace and maintaining justice that inquiry be made . . . [by jurors] upon oath that they will tell the truth, whether . . . there is any man cited or charged as . . . being a robber or murderer or thief . . . since the lord king was king.

—ASSIZE CLARENDON, CH. I (1166)

The story about how juries replaced the medieval modes of proof in criminal cases has three major players: William the Conqueror, Henry II, and the Catholic Church. I begin with William the Conqueror.

WILLIAM THE CONQUEROR

Despite his name, William came not to destroy but to preserve.[1] In 1085 William embarked on the most ambitious inquest of that, or perhaps any, era. He ordered his commissioners to list all property in England, personal property as well as real estate, and to determine ownership. This was compiled into what became known as the Domesday Book. Knowing the extent of property gave William an idea of the productive capacity of the English economy. Determining ownership allowed him to tax the property. A near-contemporary account noted that after the compilation "there was no single hide [of land] nor a yard of land, nor indeed one ox nor one cow nor one pig which was there left out: and all these records were brought to [William] afterwards."[2]

According to a contemporary publication called the Ely Inquest, "All this was to be recorded in triplicate; as it was in the time of King Edward, as it was when King William granted it and as it is now."[3] What made this different from a tax collection process is that the king dispatched commissioners to verify or correct the information obtained by the initial collection of data. The commissions traveled throughout England, to every town and hamlet, to ask questions of the villagers designed to produce facts that could be used to check the records.

These answers were duly recorded, usually in a legal proceeding before the county court, and ownership of property was legally determined. Sometimes the claim would entail an element of proof, rather than a mere assertion of fact. In one case, an abbot claimed a manor because he "had it in the time of King Edward and the men of the hundred [subdivision of a shire] confirm this."[4] Sometimes, the ownership was disputed. In those cases, the disputes were decided by the men of the county. So, for example, "Baldwin holds [the land] for the king, but the abbot claims it for St. Peter by the testimony of the men of the whole county."[5]

It was thus natural that when property disputes arose after the Domesday Book was complete, they would normally be settled by local men. Early in his reign, King Henry I ordered the sheriff to "call together the hundred of Andover and to inquire from it what belonged to that church, and it was done."[6] In 1120, a dispute over jurisdiction was settled by the sworn oaths of eighteen men of the hundred.[7] In 1136, King Stephen ordered that it be "recognized by the oath of twelve lawful men of the county" which woods King Henry I had "afforested in his lifetime."[8]

The notion of "recognition" of the ownership of property quickly became the standard verbal formulation of what English juries did. Their task, like that of the Domesday commissioners, was to recognize who had lawful title to the property. Early English juries thus did not "find" facts in the way modern juries do. They simply operated as the repository of community knowledge about title to property. This early function of juries helps explain why juries were not initially used in criminal cases. While there was a community knowledge about title to property, no similar knowledge existed about whether X was innocent or guilty of a crime, unless of course X was caught red-handed or confessed. But in that case, X would be summarily convicted without the need for formal proof.

To be sure, other forms of proof were used in property cases during this period. Property cases were decided by reference to charters, by the king taking testimony of monks, and by writ of the king simply declaring who owned property or what someone should do with property.[9] Sometimes, a property case would be decided by having the land surveyed, or "perambulated," as it was called.[10]

Sometimes these methods were combined. In 1098, William II, son of William the Conqueror, ordered the sheriff to restore to the monks of St. Augustine the rights to Newington as "in the time of my father" and then allowing objection to be pleaded in court.[11] The effect of this was to permit a jury to overrule the king's judgment if a litigant challenged his verdict. Combining two forms of proof also explains a case where King Stephen ordered two shires to meet before him to decide whether two of his knights had sought "the betrayal and the death of the king."[12] The lord abbot asserted that the knights were in service of the church of St. Edmond and that the church's "privileges and charters" gave the ecclesiastical court the sole right to decide their guilt. In sorting out this jurisdictional issue, the king's justice had the charters recited in court and also relied on the testimony of a "very old man" who remembered "many things that happened in the time of King Henry and before."

Even cases involving crimes were usually resolved by means other than the ordeal. In a rural environment where strangers rarely appeared, criminals were often caught red-handed by the victim or by the hue and cry. Moreover, then as now, criminals would tell others about their crimes.[13] Some defendants confessed in court.[14] Sometimes, the king served as the judge. One case involved a man who had cleverly forged the royal seal. "When this became known to the king, he ordered the man to be hanged" but commuted the sentence to confinement because the man's brother was weeping.[15] So, for all these reasons, even in criminal cases the ordeal was the outlier, the method reserved for cases beyond the capacity of humans to judge.

But in the absence of proof of criminal wrongdoing or intervention of the king, English courts—typically the county court and the hundred court—made use of the ordeals that we saw in the last chapter. Henry II and the Catholic Church would combine forces, quite unintentionally, to end the use of the ordeal. The story begins with his grandfather, Henry I.

HENRY I

Henry I, son of William the Conqueror, was king for thirty-five years and continued to consolidate control of England in the Norman barons and lords. Moreover, after much travail, he was successful in "firmly uniting the kingdom of England and the duchy of Normandy."[16] While not as significant as his father or his grandson in affecting the English legal system, Henry I made important contributions to the regularization of legal proceedings. Like his father, Henry I "had a passion for order, or at least a dislike for disorder as an insult to their kingship."[17]

In his charter of 1100, issued upon ascending to the throne, he bound himself to the law by putting limits on what he could do, most importantly (for the time) to keep the church whole and not to use the death of an archbishop, bishop, or abbot as an opportunity to take from the church.[18] He also condemned "unjust exactions" and promised that he would "take away all the bad customs by which the kingdom of England was unjustly oppressed."

In 1108, he created jurisdictions for different kinds of land disputes. For example, those involving his barons, who held property by grace of the king, would be tried in the king's court, while disputes between vassals of two lords would be tried in the county court.[19] The decree mandated that land disputes be settled through trial by battle. But even here, we see emerging a role for human judgment. The 1108 order permits the parties to give up the combat "through their own fault." An alternative translation ends with "if it be not there settled."[20] Compromise of a legal dispute is clearly recognized here. By the middle of the reign of Henry II, most of the recorded suits are nothing more than memorializing a "final concord" or settlement.[21]

Henry had no legitimate sons and planned for his daughter, Matilda, to succeed him. Though he publicly announced her as his successor and "required his barons to swear fealty to her," most of the barons ultimately preferred Henry's nephew, Stephen, who seized the throne upon Henry's death in 1135.[22] But some barons honored their oath to Henry, leading to a protracted struggle between castles loyal to Stephen and those loyal to Matilda. As this sporadic war continued for year after grinding year, Henry of Anjou, Matilda's son and the duke of Normandy, was growing stronger and gathering an army in Normandy.

HENRY OF ANJOU

Seventeen years after Henry's death, in December 1152, Stephen moved to destroy Matilda's final supporters. He knew that Henry of Anjou had an army in Normandy, but he believed the weather too rough for a crossing of the English Channel. Stephen and his supporters "had mistaken their man; Henry of Anjou never allowed himself to become a victim of circumstances—he molded situations to his will."[23] Two weeks after Christmas, in early January 1153, Henry crossed the channel in a terrible winter storm with an invasion force of around three thousand men, including 140 knights.

They undoubtedly made the trip in an armada of sailing ships called the cog. A wide flat-bottomed transport ship, probably made of oak and held together with iron rivets,[24] the cog was gradually replacing Viking vessels by the twelfth century. Cogs had sails by 1153, but the winter gale made it unlikely that Henry's armada depended on the sail. More likely, it was powered by rowing and steered by an oar that operated like a rudder. A good guess is that it would take fifty to one hundred cogs to transport three thousand men.[25]

So we can see perhaps seventy-five ships, loaded with men, weapons, and armor, rowing furiously in galelike winds while traversing the English Channel. The armor of the day was a shirt of mail consisting of interlocking iron rings.[26] Knights were equipped with helmet, shield, lance, and sword. Soldiers likely had only the mail shirt (if that) and a sword. It was dark, it was bitter cold, the waves came one after another, and the ships took seawater as well as rain. Ships were surely lost, but much of Henry's army made it safely to shore. Such was the mettle of the man who would reinvent the English criminal justice system to make it an effective tool for damping down the crime wave left over from Stephen's failed reign.

Unable to defeat Henry's army, Stephen saved his kingship by compromise—he acknowledged Henry as his heir and successor. Less than a year later, when the great-grandson of William the Conqueror was twenty-one years old, he was king of England. W. L. Warren writes:

> It is remarkable that he inherited none of the well-known characteristics of his parents. He had neither his mother's haughty demeanor, nor his father's dashing charm. All the signs are that he was indifferent to rank and impatient of pomp, careless of appearance, and disdaining of the trappings of monarchy. He did not even have the booming authority of his grandfather's awful presence [King Henry I]. He was stocky, freckled, restless and unkempt. Yet the force of his personality was unmistakable. Great men, be they barons or bishops, quailed before his sudden surges of anger, and ran for harbor like fishing smacks before a storm.[27]

Upon taking the throne, Henry II proclaimed that he wanted to restore the kingdom of England "to ancestral times," by which he meant its privileges and customs as they existed at the end of the reign of his grandfather, Henry I.[28] So, for example, three years into his reign, he issued a royal writ to a sheriff "that the church of Chesterfield shall hold and have all things as . . . fully as it best and most freely held them in the time of King Henry my grandfather and as it was recognized by lawful men of the hallmoot [court of the lord of a manor] and the wapentake [subdivision of a shire]."[29]

In addition to restoring the "ancestral" privileges and customs, Henry II sought to establish the primacy of the crown over the church at the same time that he sought to establish a system for the detection and prosecution of crime. These ventures were not as unrelated, as they would be in today's world. They were linked, oddly enough, by the ordeal.

Henry II was not the first king to doubt the accuracy of the outcomes of the ordeal. William II—son of William the Conqueror and great-uncle of Henry II—openly mocked the ordeal of hot iron when fifty men accused of taking the king's deer in 1098 presented themselves with unburned hands three days after undergoing the ordeal. According to an account written about twenty years later, the king exclaimed in disgust, "What is this? God a just judge? Perish the man who after this believes so."[30]

But the ordeal exerted power over the mind of most men, as can be seen in the very account that gives us William's indignation. Written by Eadmer, a theologian and historian, the account assumes that the fifty men were innocent, a fact that God "by mercifully preserving the hands of all of them from burning made clear to all." To Eadmer, God's "just judgment declared how unjust was the malice of the men who so wickedly sought to ruin them." So to Eadmer the king was wrong and the ordeal a true manifestation of God's judgment. He makes no effort to reconcile his assumption that God intervened with William's skepticism about God's judgment.

Indeed, to understand the position in which Henry II found himself, we must understand the relationship between the church and the ordeals. Though the ordeal was of pagan origin, clerics had become involved in its administration. Clerics could bestow a blessing on the one undergoing the ordeal. Of critical importance, clerics were the judges of whether the accused came through the ordeal of hot iron "clean" and whether he "passed" or "failed" the ordeal of cold water. Bartlett notes that roughly two-thirds of those who underwent the water ordeal were acquitted.[31] Records at a twelfth-century Hungarian monastery revealed about an even chance that the ordeal of hot iron would reveal the one carrying the iron to be telling the truth.[32]

Moreover, early in this period, clerics sometimes functioned as the local reeve or sheriff,[33] putting them firmly in control of the administration of justice. Depending on the degree of cynicism one brings to the issue, the acquittal of defendants who appeared to fail the ordeal could have resulted from bribes, a penitent's private confession making him innocent in the eyes of God, or God's mystical judgment. Paul Hyams tells of a tenth-century ordeal of hot iron in which the reeve banked the fire higher than usual, gave the accused a heavier hot iron than usual, and, to his amazement, three days later observed that the severely injured hand was clean.[34] "The rest of the onlookers were even more surprised, for *they* could clearly discern the signs of guilt, the pus and decay on the hand." Bartlett notes that the explanations offered to explain outcomes inconsistent with what men could see with their eyes were often the "tortuous arguments of a man trying to reconcile a deep belief in God's immanent justice with a most intractable sequence of events."[35]

By the twelfth century both the church and Henry II had grown impatient with the role of clerics in administering justice. The chaos created in Stephen's reign continued in the early years of Henry's reign, leading to "an unprecedented crime wave."[36] Twenty years of castle warfare had strengthened the barons at the expense of the countryside. They built castles, thumbed their nose at the king, and tortured and killed many for their gold and silver. They "levied payments upon the villages," and when all the money was gone, they "plundered and burned all the villages."[37] Contemporary monks said that "[i]f if two or three men came riding into a village, all the villagers would flee, for they thought they were robbers."[38] In the second year of his reign, Stephen was prosecuting "plunderers who had grievously ravaged" the countryside.[39] More broadly, one man told Stephen's bishops and barons in 1150 that "justice has fled and laws have fallen silent and the liberties of churches, like other good things, have been lost in many places."[40]

Under the existing legal order, little could be done to stop these brash criminals. The prosecution of crime depended, in large part, on the victim or the victim's family accusing the perpetrator. In a stable, agrarian society, the perpetrator would usually be known and could be required to defend himself against an accusation of crime. But marauding bands of thugs were another matter. Moreover, to the extent the violence was implicitly or explicitly authorized by the barons of the castles, the chance of obtaining justice was low even when the offenders were known because English law permitted lords to protect from arrest those who served them.

Finally, "One lesser but awkward aspect of the problem was the prevalence of crime committed by members of the clergy."[41] The church insisted, with Rome's support, that it had exclusive jurisdiction over the trial and punishment of clerics. Henry II found himself hemmed in on two fronts. Lords would protect those who served them, and the bishops would protect clerics who committed crime.

THE CHURCH AND THE ORDEAL

The church of the era independently doubted the ordeal, believing that it "allow[ed] many a hardy heretic to go at large."[42] Cantor concludes that Pope Innocent III was an "austere, learned, aristocratic Roman lawyer" who simply "thought it high time that this German barbarity of the ordeals was abandoned."[43] Olson notes that in "the period from 1050–1215 arguments were advanced that the ordeals lacked authority, were internally inconsistent, and that the Deity's judgment was inaccessible."[44]

Peter the Chanter of Notre Dame in the late twelfth century "led a scorched earth attack against the ordeals, going so far as to argue his case before the cardinals."[45] His objection was not, as modern readers might think, some pre-Enlightenment glimmering that man was able to make better judgments about guilt or innocence than could be achieved by depending on God to heal burned flesh or cause the innocent to sink below the surface of water. Chanter's objection was, rather, a condemnation of mankind. He wrote that, "in an age where sin is so prevalent, miracles are not to be found." Thus, a wrongdoer could not "perfect himself with his god through purgation."[46]

On this view, the ordeal was flawed to the core. Because God's judgment, in the view of the skeptics, did not manifest itself in miracles on behalf of the innocent, all outcomes were either random or corrupt. In that light, the church could not continue to sanction the ordeal. And, as we will see, less than two decades after Peter the Chanter died, the church brought an abrupt halt to this method of sorting the guilty from the innocent.

HENRY II, THE CLERICS, AND CRIME CONTROL IN TWELFTH-CENTURY ENGLAND

If Henry II and Rome had, by 1164, reached the same conclusion about the need to reform the administration of criminal justice, they were nonetheless on a collision course as to how to go about reform. In the Constitutions of Clarendon, Henry sought to establish the primacy of the crown over the church by "confronting the bishops with a document setting out in unequivocal terms 'the customs and privileges of the realm' in respect of the exercise of royal authority over ecclesiastical affairs, and demanded that they take an oath to observe them."[47] The bishops saw some of the provisions of Henry's document as inconsistent with canon law and, naturally, "resisted taking an oath which would compromise their adherence to the dictates of canon law."

In 1164, Thomas Becket was the archbishop of Canterbury. A friend of Henry's, and Henry's chancellor for a time, he was now resisting the Constitutions of Clarendon. But Henry had not gotten where he was by accepting no for an answer. He attempted to "browbeat the bishops into submission."[48] Then came a most remarkable occurrence. Beckett changed his position and urged the bishops to obey the king. Moments later, he changed his mind again "and imposed a penance on himself."[49] Henry was furious and set out to remove from power his old friend, who fled England and ultimately persuaded the pope that Henry intended "to destroy the authority of the Church in England."[50]

After his hotheaded response to Becket, Henry II had to engage in "astute diplomacy" to "avoid an open breach with the Papacy."[51] The problem would worsen. Four of Henry's knights would kill Becket in 1170. Three years later, facing a rebellion that included his son and his wife, Eleanor, Henry would seek to regain the support of the papacy. In July 1174, at "Becket's tomb in Canterbury cathedral he prayed and wept and was then beaten as a penance."[52]

In the meantime, Henry tried another, more indirect, route to minimize the influence of the clerics. If he could not put the clerics under his direct control, he could at least get them out of the business of deciding which criminals to free. At the same palace in Clarendon that had seen the contentious meetings with the bishops, Henry convened his barons in 1166 and issued what is known as the Assize of Clarendon, a modification of the customary law about the administration of criminal justice.

In chapter 1, Henry proclaimed the goal of "preserving peace and maintaining justice." To that end, the Assize consolidated power in the royal courts, gave sheriffs far more power, and deprived the lords of the ability to protect those in their service. The sheriff was ordered to seek out those suspected of murder, robbery, and theft wherever they might be found and "none shall forbid the sheriffs to enter into their land."[53] This was clearly a blow against the castle tyranny that plagued Stephen's reign.

The Assize also ordered the local inquests to make inquiry "whether in their hundred [subdivision of a shire] or in their vill there is any man cited or charged as himself being a robber or murderer or thief."[54] No longer would justice have to await private prosecution. The crimes of murder, robbery, and theft immediately became crimes against the king, to be prosecuted by order of the king. Moreover, the scope of the inquests was extended back to the time when "the lord king became king,"[55] giving these inquests authority to correct injustices that had lingered for over a decade.

Each inquest consisted of "twelve more lawful men of the hundred," and "four more lawful men of each vill." Though the Assize does not make this clear, in practice the four "lawful men" of the village by custom were knights, and their judgment came to carry more weight than that of the twelve men of the hundred.[56] The effect of all of this procedure was to let trustworthy men decide who was probably guilty of murder, robbery, or theft and then force the accused to defend what amounted to a presumption of guilt. It was only after this human judgment that those who were accused had a chance to clear themselves by inviting God's judgment.

The use of the inquest as the accusing body assisted in solving crimes in another, more subtle, way. In cases of private accusations, the reeve could choose either the accused or the accuser to carry the hot iron or be thrown into the water. The accusers' potential to be made to endure the ordeal surely suppressed the number of accusations. But after 1166, serious crimes would be prosecuted whenever the inquest judged someone to be guilty, and it was the accused who had to undergo the water ordeal to prove his denial of the crime.

Following customary law of the time, the ordeal could be avoided altogether if the culprit was caught red-handed—if he was found "with the spoil of his robbery or theft in his possession" and was found to "bear an ill name and have a notoriously bad reputation."[57] In those cases, "[L]et him not have law," meaning the accused would not be given the opportunity to cleanse himself by the ordeal of water. That man was summarily punished. Summary punishment, without law, also followed a confession made "in the presence of lawful men or the hundreds."[58]

If he was permitted to "have law," the only ordeal that could avoid the judgment of an inquest was that of water. Oath helping could not be used to rebut the charge of the inquest. Nor could the ordeal of hot iron (which would have pleased Henry's great uncle, William II) or the offer of judicial combat.

Henry II fully realized the revolutionary nature of what he had done. In his writ that sent royal justices in eyre to enforce the Assize, he soothingly reassured his subjects, "I do this temporarily because of the aforesaid necessity" to do justice "to thieves and murderers and robbers."[59] That he modified and strengthened it ten years later in the Assize of Northampton shows that he found the changes in criminal procedure useful in controlling crime.

For my project, the significance of the Assize of Clarendon is that it moved English justice toward a system in which Englishmen judged criminal guilt for themselves. Indeed, after 1166 the English communities could even avoid God's judgment at the ordeal entirely in cases where the inquest found probable guilt. In chapter 14, the Assize provides that "those who make their law and are quit thereby, if they have a very bad reputation and are publicly and scandalously decried on the testimony of many lawful men, shall forswear the king's lands." Technically this did not "overrule" God's judgment because the accused was still "quit." But he could no longer live in the community. In effect, the cleric's judgment to release into the community a dangerous man was now subject to veto by the community.

Having been stalemated in his attempt to bend the English bishops to his will, Henry managed by a brilliant move of indirection to blunt their power over the administration of justice. Henry gave authority to the community to regulate itself, to cleanse itself of wrongdoers through the inquest, and to overrule the clerics when they refused to convict probable wrongdoers. We see here an unmistakable trend toward the judgment of the community and away from God's mystical and incomprehensible judgment.

The reader should keep the Assize of Clarendon in perspective. As revolutionary as it was, little change is noticed in the existing records a few years after the Assize. Juries of recognition continued to be used to settle land disputes, trial by battle occurred with some frequency, and trial by hot iron can be found in a few cases. Moreover, Glanvill, who may have been one of King Henry's justicars, does not mention the Assize of Clarendon in his pioneering treatise published some twenty years after the Assize. His description of English criminal procedure is largely consistent with the Assize but differs in ways suggesting that either Glanvill did not know of the Assize or did not think it was still binding.[60]

Part of its lack of effect was intended. In chapter 5, Henry makes clear that the procedure created in the Assize would not displace proceedings other than those ordered by the local inquests.[61] Thus, disputes about land (always the most common form of action in these early records), private prosecutions, and prosecutions by the church were unaffected. Beyond that, the greatest effect of the Assize would have been seen in the eyre rolls and few survive from this period. To be sure, we do find in the years immediately following the Assize, records of increased building of county jails, "the digging and blessing of ordeal pits, and lists of men from most shires who 'perished in the judgment of water.'"[62]

Why did this activity decline? Other problems pressed on Henry II in the 1170s and 1180s, not the least of which was the rebellion led by his wife and young son. There was also the far-reaching Inquest of Sheriffs in 1170 and the difficulty of finding men "of character, position, and training" to supervise the shire courts.[63] Moreover, it is fair to assume that Henry's changes in procedure had diminished lawlessness. If roving bands of criminals had largely disappeared, there would have been less need for the innovations of the Assize.

The significance of the Assizes of Clarendon and Northampton for my purposes is not whether they effected a permanent change in how all criminal cases were handled in the English courts but, rather, that they pointed the way to men making a judgment about guilt when it was not apparent.

It is likely that the role of the inquest jury in England would have gradually expanded to finding guilt in criminal cases if left alone. But along came the Lateran Council of 1215 and blew apart the stable order. The church condemned the participation of clerics in "a rite of blessing or consecration on a purgation by ordeal of boiling or cold water or of the red-hot iron."[64] The ordeal of water and hot iron disappeared from English law with amazing rapidity. Pollock and Maitland discovered that the ordeal was "[f]lourishing in the last records of John's reign," which ended in 1216, but "we can not find it in any later rolls."[65] It seems to have ceased earlier than 1219, but in that year the end was official: Henry III, then twelve years old, issued an order forbidding royal courts from using the ordeal.[66]

By the clear language of the Lateran Council, clerics could no longer participate in the ordeals of water and hot iron. Thus, courts in England were, in 1216, caught between the Lateran Council and the Assize of Clarendon. Henry's law required that those accused by an inquest could defend the accusation only by going "to the judgment of water."[67] But God's law removed that option. What to do with those accused by the inquest of murder, robbery, and theft? How would truth be discerned now that God was out of the business?

In Europe, the ascertainment of guilt and innocence moved into the hands of judges who conducted "a searching examination both of the accused himself and of witnesses."[68] In England, by contrast, the ascertainment of guilt and innocence moved into the hands of juries. Part of the reason for this is the Norman Conquest. In Europe, no similar event had put the ownership of property into question. In England, the juries of recognition were critical to settling property disputes, and judges had thus become accustomed to the role of juries in settling disputes. Also important was the revolution affected by the Assize of Clarendon. The community was permitted to outlaw the accused even if he was "quit" at the ordeal. How was it really any different letting a jury—as proxy for the community—discharge that function without the intervention of the ordeal?

Glanvill's treatise was published only twenty-two years after the Assize of Clarendon. It noted that in private prosecutions, which were not governed by the Assize of Clarendon, there was a distinction between those accused based on ill fame and those accused by a specific accuser. The former could absolve himself without an ordeal if the "probable facts and possible conjectures both for and against the accused" are favorable.[69] Where a specific accuser appeared and the "accused denies everything in court in the proper manner, then the plea shall be settled by battle."[70]

Roger Groot documents several cases from the period around the turn of the thirteenth century showing that the stronger the evidence of guilt, the more likely was the inquest to require an ordeal rather than the easier proof of compurgation.[71] That compurgation, rather than the water ordeal, was sometimes used to rebut the finding of the inquest suggests that the Assize of Clarendon had lapsed. But the important point for my project is that both Glanvill and Groot find evidence that men were injecting themselves into the decision-making process. Indeed, Groot has discovered that, in some cases, a distinction was made between the finding of the twelve jurors and that of the vill.[72] The latter consisted of four knights, and their view carried more weight than the twelve jurors. All of this evidence suggests an evolution from God's unknowable judgment to that of the community.

To be sure, in the immediate aftermath of the Lateran Council of 1215, English criminal justice experienced a period of confusion. Historian William Holdsworth describes this interregnum as follows:

> [Henry III's] writ addressed to the judges in 1219 tells them that nothing had as yet been determined [as to how to deal with those accused of crime]. It directs that those accused of great crimes and suspected should be imprisoned—but not so as to endanger life or limb; that those whose crimes were less heinous should abjure the realm; and that those accused of small offenses should be released if they would find securities to keep the peace. But, it concludes, much must be left to the discretion of the justices.[73]

The justices, very quickly, in criminal cases came to prefer trial by jury, known as "putting oneself on the country," to whatever was left of the ancient modes of proof. *The Mirror of Justices*, written in the thirteenth century, criticized as an "abuse" that defendants "were driven by the judges to put themselves on their country, when they had offered to defend themselves by their bodies [trial by combat]."[74]

Why would judges prefer the jury to the ancient forms of proof? Judges were political animals, appointed by and serving at the discretion of the king. What the king wanted, judges wanted. And what the king wanted was to rid the communities of the murderers, thieves, and robbers. As Henry II had realized, a local inquest was perfectly capable of identifying dangers to the community.

In the beginning, unsurprisingly, criminal juries were modeled after juries in property cases. Criminal jurors were selected a fortnight before the trial and were expected to learn all they could about the case.[75] Early criminal juries essentially functioned as a review of the inquest. Records of early trials state "the commission of the judges, the presentment of the grand jury, the indictment, the plea, the fact that the accused places himself on his country, the summons of the jury, the verdict, and the judgment."[76] *There is no mention of evidence!* The criminal trial jury would simply confirm or deny the verdict of the inquest based on its own knowledge of the relevant facts and the character of the defendant. Indeed, Musson has discovered that in the first half of the fourteenth century, there was a "substantial overlap between the presenting and trial juries," thus making it easier for the trial jury to review the presenting jury's verdict.[77]

To Holdsworth, the early "jury is regarded as a formal test to which the parties have submitted. The judgment follows, as under the old system, the result of that test."[78] Their verdicts "inherited the inscrutability of the judgments of God." Pollock and Maitland concluded that early jury verdicts in criminal cases were simply another proof from God.[79] "If a man came clean from the ordeal or successfully made his law, the due proof would have been given; no one could have questioned the dictum of Omniscience." So, too, the early jury verdicts were unimpeachable: "The justices seem to feel that if they analyzed the verdict they would miss the very thing for which they are looking, the voice of the country." In effect, the acceptance of the jury verdict represented a triumph of what Pollock and Maitland call the "arbitral and communal principles"—the notion that twelve men could manifest the view of the community.

To be sure, these views may overstate the analogy between the older forms of proof and the thirteenth-century jury verdicts. We know, for example, that juries from this period could be "attainted" —convicted of perjury—as far back as William the Conqueror.[80] That the conviction was for perjury is further proof that juries of the time functioned as witnesses and not as finders of fact. Moreover, Musson has discovered that, by the early fourteenth century, litigants could challenge jurors on the ground of bias.[81] Both of these developments suggest a view of juries as a distinctly human endeavor, subject both to intentional and inadvertent error.

Skepticism about jury verdicts would increase in the fifteenth and sixteenth centuries. Perhaps it was the fear of crime, just as in the days of William II and Henry II. Perhaps later monarchs were more afraid of treason conspiracies and thus needed to make certain that their enemies were convicted.

Whatever the reasons, the Star Chamber rode to the rescue in 1487 during the reign of Henry VII. For some readers, the idea of the Star Chamber performing a benevolent function is startling because it is best known as a ruthless, politically inspired inquisition. But its charge and early function were at least superficially benevolent. It was created to oversee the operations of the lower courts. Part of this function included routinizing the long-established practice of "attainting" juries that had returned erroneous or corrupt verdicts.

The difference between the Star Chamber and the early attempts to determine whether verdicts were corrupt is illuminating. From William the Conqueror's reign to the Star Chamber, a jury verdict could be examined, but only by a second jury. The innovation of the Star Chamber, one that would ultimately lead to its own corruption, was that judges reviewed the jury verdict. While the power to punish jurors who returned corrupt verdicts could have been used only to punish those who had been influenced to return false verdicts, "in the sixteenth century, the Star Chamber was apt to treat any verdict of acquittal which it considered to be against the weight of the evidence as corrupt."[82] Holdsworth noted that almost every judicial term in the sixteenth century saw a fine imposed on "some grand inquest or jury . . . for acquitting felons or murderers."[83]

The rise of the divine right of kings played a critical role here. Truth in the relevant sense was no longer God's truth or the community's truth expressed through a jury but was, instead, located in the mind of the king and his judges and prosecutors. Indeed, in the sixteenth and seventeenth centuries, felons, and particularly felons charged with treason, were presumed guilty, and all the criminal law needed do was to pronounce that judgment. Recalcitrant jurors who favored acquittal were thus an impediment to the royal justice. And a threat to the monarch. We can safely call this the "presumption of guilt" period in English criminal law.

TRUTH IN THE PERIOD OF PRESUMPTION OF GUILT

By the seventeenth century, the Reformation began to spread to the political arena, posing a threat to the concept of monarchy. If governments were all answerable to an unchanging and fundamental natural law, as Grotius and other philosophers argued, a monarch was at best unnecessary and at worst a terrible hindrance. One response to this challenge, probably the only one, is the theory of the divine right of kings. English monarchs embraced this response to Grotius.

Thus, seventeenth-century treason trials were self-consciously arranged so that the Crown was favored.[84] The "tilt" was profound. While juries technically decided the case, the trials "took place before a special commission of court-appointed judges with government attorneys leading the prosecution."[85] Treason defendants were not permitted to see a copy of the indictment and, until late in the seventeenth century, were denied both counsel and pen and paper during the trial.[86] Treason defendants could not swear witnesses to give testimony at trial or cross-examine the crown's witnesses.[87] "[W]hether guilty or not, the accused were expected to confess their crime, pray for forgiveness, and exalt the goodness of the sovereign."[88]

Whig opponents of treason trials alleged that crown prosecutors self-consciously used perjured testimony to make their cases, even to the extent of "hiring or blackmailing criminals or the poor to make false statements."[89] Writing of treason prosecutions, legal reformer John Hawles said in 1689, "It is downright tying a man's hands behind his back, and baiting him to death."[90] One might think that the tilt toward the crown was a ruthless perversion of the truth, designed to keep a corrupt or ineffective monarch in power. But so smug a view is anachronistic. The monarch was lord sovereign. The monarch had enemies, to be sure, but why would their view of the truth be more accurate than the monarch's? The divine right of the monarch privileged the public good over the individual. If the existence and health of the collective is more important than the individual, it makes perfect sense to presume guilt in treason cases. Convicting innocent defendants is, in this scheme, less threatening to the social order than freeing from the gallows those who would kill the divine king.[91]

The prevailing view was that truth was better uncovered if defendants spoke alone in court so that they "could not easily hide either their knowledge or ignorance of the facts."[92] Sir Edward Coke in his *Institutes* argued that truth was, on balance, preserved by denying all felony defendants the right to counsel and generally the right to present an effective defense. To those who would say that muzzling a treason defendant is an injustice, Coke responded that the role of the judge was to represent the defendant if matters tilted too strongly toward the prosecution and thus imperiled truth.[93] Coke defended the denial of counsel in felony cases on the ground that serious felony indictments should not be brought, or maintained, unless "the evidence to convict" is "so manifest, as it could not be contradicted."

While Coke's notion seems almost laughable today, we must seek to see the world through the eyes of those who believed in the royal prerogative and in the collective over the individual. We should reject Coke's view of truth because it is not our view of truth, but there is nothing incoherent about saying that defendants lie, that lawyers hide the truth, and that those indicted for treason pose, on average, a greater risk to the collective than those who are not indicted. Thus, even though treason trials prior to 1700 look like kangaroo courts to us, they were, like the ordeal, merely a search for the truth by methods that we view as unlikely to provide a truth that we would recognize.

In 1603 Sir Walter Raleigh was indicted for conspiring to commit treason against King James I.[94] The indictment revealed a complicated plot to depose James, imprison him in the Tower of London, and replace him with his cousin, Arabella Stuart. The prosecutor was Coke, some forty years before he would publish his *Institutes*. The only evidence of treason against Raleigh was a statement of his alleged accomplice, Cobham, given before the Privy Council and also in a letter.

Raleigh's defense was that Cobham's statements were untrue, that after confessing his own guilt, Cobham had lied about Raleigh's guilt to obtain favor from the king. Raleigh asked the judges to call Cobham as a witness because the "common Trial of England is by Jury and Witnesses."[95] A judge replied, "I marvel, sir Walter, that you being of such experience and wit, should stand on this point; for so many horse stealers may escape, if they may not be condemned without witnesses." Raleigh replied, "I know not how you conceive the Law." The Lord Chief Justice said, "Nay, we do not conceive the Law, but we know the Law."

Raleigh's next move was to the law of God. The "wisdom of the Law of God is absolute and perfect . . . . Remember, it is absolutely the Commandment of God: If a false witness rise up, you shall cause him to be brought before the Judges."[96] Raleigh argued that Cobham's accusation was false; it was but "a means to excuse himself." Even a plea of innocence grounded in the law of God was unavailing to the Lord Chief Justice: "There must not such a gap be opened for the destruction of the king as would be if we should grant this. You plead hard for yourself, but the laws plead as hard for the king."[97]

Raleigh tried again, asking the court to let Cobham "be brought, being alive, and in the house" to testify.[98] If he repeated his accusations in court, Raleigh offered "to confess the whole Indictment, and renounce the king's mercy." The court dismissed the argument on the ground that Cobham was a party to the treason and thus not permitted to testify under oath.[99]

The concern with the safety of the monarch over the welfare of the defendant is palpable in these exchanges. The jury was not to be trusted to produce the truth without tilting the case against the defendant accused of treason. Cobham was not produced. Raleigh's earlier protestation that he was being tried "by the Spanish Inquisition"[100] was borne out. In his closing argument, he said to Coke, the prosecutor, "You have not proved any one thing against me by direct Proofs, but all by circumstances."[101] Coke responded: "Thou art an odious fellow, thy name is hateful to all the realm of England for thy pride."

But Coke's ultimate argument was more to the point: "The king's safety and your clearing [acquittal] cannot agree."[102] Unable to confront his accuser, condemned by the court as a danger to the king, Raleigh was convicted after the jury deliberated a mere fifteen minutes.[103] Judgment of death was passed, though it was not carried out for fifteen years.

Raleigh spent the next thirteen years in the Tower of London, where he began writing his *History of the World* that would total one million words when published.[104] In 1616, he was released and sent to the New World to search for gold on behalf of James I and, while there, he broke his promise not to attack or harass Spanish possessions or ships.[105] When he returned to England, the King of Spain insisted that James execute Raleigh, and he was beheaded in 1618.[106]

That Raleigh was not executed immediately after his conviction is evidence that a treason conviction was but the opening gambit in a chess game with the monarch. The presumption of guilt in treason trials was so strong that few were acquitted. But given a large universe of convicted treason defendants, the monarch could pick and choose which ones to execute. That James did not execute Raleigh for the treason "proved" in 1603 probably means he doubted Raleigh's guilt. But when politics required Raleigh's death, it was convenient to have the treason conviction in hand.

Times would soon change. Whig political theory emerged, rejecting the divine right of the king to govern and the protection of the collective over the individual. John Locke developed a theory of the natural right of the individual to resist when government sought to injure or destroy him. This right of self-preservation sets the stage for a reversal from a presumption of guilt to a presumption of innocence. Fueled by the Whig principle of self- preservation, reformers began to question the elevation of the collective over the individual.

The Glorious Revolution of 1688 swept James II from power and brought William and Mary to the English throne. It also vastly increased the power of the Whigs, who were instrumental in the change of monarchs. "The Glorious Revolution . . . concentrated power in the hands of an oligarchy of Whig nobles."[107] It also led, directly, to the English Bill of Rights of 1689 that manifested the sea change in the relationship between the crown and its subjects. In

1691, for example, Sir Richard Grahme drew explicitly on the self-preservation principle to argue for greater procedural rights in his treason trial: "I am bound *in duty to myself,* in such a case, to insist upon all advantages I can have by law."[108]

But one more victory had to be achieved for the jury to return to its role as the English medium through which truth about guilt is manifested.

TRUTH AND JURIES: WILLIAM PENN'S CASE

We saw earlier the power of the Star Chamber to punish jurors who gave corrupt verdicts. Trial judges too would sometimes threaten jurors in an attempt to have them return a conviction. Judicial meddling in jury acquittals reached a critical moment in 1670.

The story begins August 14, 1670, when William Penn and William Mead were arrested for conducting a Quaker meeting in public. They were indicted for "unlawfully and tumultuously" assembling and congregating themselves together "to the Disturbance of the Peace of the said Lord the King."[109] What follows is William Penn's account of the trial.[110] No official transcript exists.

Tried at the Old Bailey before commissioners who included the mayor of London, the defendants challenged the legitimacy of the indictment and the power of the court to convict them. Matters quickly grew heated. At one point, the mayor told Mead, "You deserve to have your Tongue cut out."[111]

When Penn and Mead insisted on making their defense to the jury, the court ordered them removed to the hole. Otherwise, they would "talk all Night . . . that I think doth not become the Honour of the Court, and I think [the jury] your selves would be tired out, and not have Patience to hear them."[112] Even without the defendants making a defense, four members of the jury refused to convict. The court sent an officer for those four and, in open court, "The Bench used many unworthy Threats to the four that dissented." Most of the abuse was directed at the jury foreman, Edward Bushel. A commissioner said that "you deserve to be indicted more than any Man that hath been brought to the Bar this Day." London's mayor said, "Sirrah, you are an impudent Fellow, I will put a Mark upon you."

The jury retired to resume deliberations and returned again without a verdict on the "tumult" charge; the jury found Penn guilty of preaching, but preaching was not an offense. According to Penn, the mayor and recorder "resented" the lack of a verdict so deeply "that they exceeded the Bounds of all Reason and Civility."[113] The recorder said that the jury would not be dismissed "till we have a Verdict, that the Court will accept; and you shall be lock'd up, without Meat, Drink, Fire, and Tobacco; you shall not think thus to abuse the Court; we will have a Verdict, by the help of God, or you shall starve for it."

When the jury still had no verdict the next morning, the mayor threatened to cut Bushel's throat and, later, his nose, at which point William Penn said, "It is intolerable that my Jury should be thus menaced: . . . What hope is there of ever having Justice done, when Juries are threatened, and their Verdicts rejected?"[114] The mayor's response was to order "fetters" be brought into court and Penn staked to the floor. The recorder said, "Till now I never understood the Reason of the Policy and Prudence of the Spaniards, in suffering the Inquisition among them."

The jury was once again held overnight without accommodations, and the next morning they gave a verdict. The verdict was, however, not what the court wanted to hear. The eight who had originally agreed that Penn was guilty of "tumult" now had changed their votes to not guilty.[115] And the jury had written out the verdict so that they could not be accused of not returning a verdict. The judge ordered that each juror's name should be called so that all had to give their verdict in open court. All twelve answered "not guilty." At this point, the court gave up and fined the jurors forty marks each and ordered them imprisoned until the fine was paid. Edward Bushel filed a writ of habeas corpus in the Court of Common Pleas.

The issue was joined: Was England going the route of the Spanish to an inquisition, or were the English courts going once again to find answers about justice in the collective wisdom of juries? It was, we know, the latter. *Bushel's Case*[116] held that the trial court lacked the authority to fine or imprison the jury on account of its verdict. Today, *Bushel's Case* is regarded as a watershed that established the jury's independence from the court and thus elevated the jury trial to a fundamental right. While this is true enough, it misses the larger point, which is *why* the jury verdict cannot be impeached.

Chief Justice Vaughan noted that if judges could tell the jury how to decide a case, there would be no point in having juries at all. Vaughan could have stopped there, but he made another, more fundamental, point. He asserted that a jury finding that the evidence was not "full and manifest" is unimpeachable *because it is true*. Noting that two men could infer "distinct conclusions from the same testimony," Vaughan concluded that no reason exists to prefer the court's view of the evidence over that of the jury.[117] This analytical move makes juries the ultimate source of the truth about guilt and innocence. The jury at that moment became the English epistemology of innocence.

The Whig influence steadily increased as the seventeenth century neared its end. After the Glorious Revolution, the Whig theory produced the English Bill of Rights of 1689, guaranteeing free election of members of Parliament, and freedom of speech and debate in Parliament while prohibiting excessive bail and fines and cruel and unusual punishments. The Whig revolution in political theory also produced the Treason Act of 1695, which contained many safeguards that would have provided Raleigh and other innocent defendants a fighting chance. The divine right presumption of guilt had, with remarkable speed, turned into a Whig presumption of innocence.

Matthew Hale wrote his *History of the Common Law* in the 1660s,[118] extolling the virtues of the English jury trial as a way of assessing the truth. Obviously, much had changed in the sixty years between Raleigh's trial and Hale's assessment of the English trial. In Raleigh's trial the truth was already known by the judges and jury. Hale's conception of the trial as a contest seeking the truth and the Whig conception of rights against the sovereign would be instrumental in the developing the American Constitution. A little more than one hundred years after *Bushel's Case,* the Framers of the American Constitution would include the right to a jury trial in two places, first in Article III and later in the Sixth Amendment. The significance of jury trial right was, in large part, that juries were the medium through which the society learned the truth about guilt or innocence.

CHAPTER FIVE
TRUTH FROM JURIES: AMERICA
BEFORE THE TWENTIETH CENTURY

*Why do we love this trial by jury? Because it prevents the hand of
oppression from cutting you off.*

—PATRICK HENRY

During the presumption-of-guilt period that we saw in the last chapter, English monarchs were infamous for housing their enemies
indefinitely in the Tower of London rather than taking a chance on
an acquittal. Lest the reader think, "That is then; this is now," flash
forward three or four hundred years to 2007 and the prison at Guantánamo Bay. While the status of those detained as suspected terror-
ists is, at least formally, different from citizens accused of "ordinary"
crimes, the indefinite detention of "enemy combatants" at Guantánamo paints a vivid, chilling picture of what legal life would be like
without the right to habeas corpus. Some of the prisoners have now
been imprisoned since 2002, without an appearance before a judge,
let alone a jury trial. Of all the rights guaranteed us by the Constitution, this chapter will argue that the right to a habeas corpus hearing
and the right to a jury are the most important. Even the right to
counsel would be meaningless if we could not demand the right to
be heard in court.

Law is nothing if not connected to the past, even the remote past as we saw in the similarities between the use of juries in the Roman republic and modern American juries. By the middle of the eighteenth century, the Whigs and their individualistic view of humans had prevailed. The king still had a huge amount of power in England, but it was beginning to dissipate in the colonies. The opposition to the Stamp Act in 1765 is a good example. Desperate to recover financial losses attributable to the French and Indian War (which, after all, had saved the colonies from French occupation), Parliament enacted the Sugar Act in 1764 and, when revenues were disappointing, the Stamp Act in 1765. The Stamp Act, a tax on every piece of printed material used in the colonies, was seen there as an infuriating attempt to raise money without approval of the colonial legislatures.

Nine colonies sent representatives to the Stamp Act Congress in Philadelphia. The Stamp Act Resolution that was adopted begins by expressing "the warmest sentiments of affection and duty to His Majesty's Person and Government, inviolably attached to the present happy establishment of the Protestant succession, and with minds deeply impressed by a sense of the present and impending misfortunes of the British colonies on this continent. . . ." It then asserts the principle that would become the rallying cry of the Revolution—no taxation without representation—a principle that was "inseparably essential to the freedom of a people." As the colonies had no voice in Parliament, the document concluded, the Stamp Act and other duties imposed on the colonies "have a manifest tendency to subvert the rights and liberties of the colonists."[1]

The Whig influence can be plainly seen, as well as the centrifugal economic forces that would soon tear the colonies away from Great Britain. Given that the dispute was about the divergence of the economic interests of the colonies and the mother country, one seemingly odd provision appears. Paragraph VII states that "trial by jury is the inherent and invaluable right of every British subject in these colonies."[2] What is this doing in a document about economic imperatives? The answer is that in some of the colonies, customs officials were bringing suits for penalties and forfeitures in the courts of vice admiralty, which followed civil law rather than common-law procedures and thus did not use juries.[3] Some colonists thus faced forfeiture of goods and ships without benefit of a jury trial. Paragraph VII was an assertion that these vice-admiralty procedures were contrary to the common-law rights of British citizens. The colonists seized on the right to a jury trial as a central defining right of a free people.

Outside admiralty courts, the common-law right to a jury in criminal cases was flourishing in the colonies. In a sample of Oyer and Terminer records in New Jersey from 1749 to 1757, every criminal trial was decided by a jury of twelve men.[4] The voice of the community was also heard through the grand jury in every case. Goebel and Naughton found a similar robust role for juries and grand juries in New York,[5] and no reasons suggest that the other colonies had drastically different approaches to sorting the guilty from the innocent. The jury trial was a direct transplant from Britain, and the thirteen colonies were, after all, colonies of Britain. The jury trial right was embraced in the Stamp Act Resolution, and was included in all thirteen colonial constitutions.[6]

The value of the community's voice can be seen in the Oyer and Terminer outcomes in New Jersey. In several cases, the grand jury refused to indict, and half of the trials ended in acquittals.[7] An acquittal rate of 50 percent must have been a source of considerable comfort in a world where the king had a prosecutor doing his work and the formal sentence for a felony conviction was death.

The Stamp Act was, of course, followed by the Declaration of Independence, the Constitution, and the Bill of Rights. Each of these documents tells us something about the critical role of people in assessing guilt and innocence.

THE DECLARATION OF INDEPENDENCE AND THE CONSTITUTION

It is easy for us to forget, because history turned out to favor our form of government, that the Declaration of Independence put forth a set of principles for creating a government that was nothing less than revolutionary. It was also an extremely risky experiment. The ideas that all men were created equal, that they had unalienable rights, and that governments drew their "just Powers from the consent of the governed" had their roots in Whig philosophy. But it was America in the late eighteenth century that decided to base a government on those principles.

The Constitution, of course, is the blueprint for realizing the principles that underlie the Declaration. The overarching story here is familiar. From the First and Second Continental Congresses to the Articles of Confederation and, finally, to the Constitution drafted in 1787, a crucial issue was how much authority the states should cede to the central governing authority. Only one aspect of that story concerns us here—the extent to which the Framers of the Constitution sought to protect against excesses of the central government in prosecuting crime.

The power of the king's prosecutors had made the safeguards of the common law appealing to the colonists prior to the Revolution. The new central government created in Philadelphia in the oppressively hot, insect-ridden Philadelphia summer of 1787[8] would raise similar concerns about federal prosecution of crime. The protections that the Framers chose to put in the body of the Constitution must have been what the Framers saw as essential to controlling the prosecutors and judges of the central government. When understood from an eighteenth-century viewpoint, it will become clear why they were viewed as critical.

The Constitution forbids Congress from enacting ex post facto laws.[9] These laws turn conduct, innocent when committed, into a crime by making the crime retroactive. The rule against ex post facto laws has a long and impressive pedigree, going back to Roman times.[10] No abuse of this rule ever seems to have occurred in England or in the colonies, but its inclusion in the Constitution takes away one weapon a government could use to destroy its enemies.

The Constitution both limits the way treason can be proved and the substantive content of any law defining treason. That treason gets so much attention should not be surprising given the terrible history we reviewed in chapter 4 when the English monarchs used treason law to hunt down their enemies and execute them, keep them forever in the Tower of London, or disable them politically. Those memories would have been pretty vivid in the minds of the Framers and surely explain why they essentially copied the Treason Act of 1695 into Article III of our Constitution: "No person shall be convicted of Treason unless on the Testimony of two Witnesses to the same overt Act, or on Confession in open Court."[11]

The Framers extended Parliament's protections by defining the substance of the crime of treason: "Treason against the United States, shall consist only in levying War against them, or in adhering to their enemies, giving them Aid and Comfort."[12] This definition becomes critical in the 1807 Aaron Burr case, which helped develop a criminal process that is resistant to manipulation, as we shall see later in this chapter.

Article III requires trial by jury.[13] The importance of juries to the Framers is manifest in the history of the drafting and ratification of the Constitution and the Bill of Rights. Because all colonies had used juries to decide serious criminal cases, it must have been completely uncontroversial to provide a right to a jury trial. The Framers remembered all too well the royal judges who served at the pleasure of, and owed allegiance to, the king. The fiery Luther Martin, whom we shall get to know better, argued in a pamphlet that the right to a jury trial "is *most essential for our liberty,* to have it *sacredly guarded and preserved*—in *every case* whether *civil or criminal* between *government* and *its officers* on the one part and the *subject or citizen* on the other."[14]

During the North Carolina debate over whether to add a bill of rights to the Constitution, future Supreme Court justice James Iredell noted that "the great instrument of arbitrary power is criminal prosecutions."[15] There is, he continued, "no other safe mode to try these but by a jury," thus avoiding "the control of arbitrary judges." Thomas Tredwell of New York spoke sarcastically of "the tender mercies" of "wicked" federal judges, "(for judges may be wicked;) and what those tender mercies are, I need not tell you. You may read them in the history of the Star Chamber Court in England. . . ."[16]

From all of this, it seems clear that the Framers viewed the jury as the repository of truth in its only relevant sense. What appears odd at first glance, however, is the fuss the Anti-Federalists made over the right to a jury trial. Article III already required a jury trial, and yet the state conventions considering a bill of rights made much of the need for a better right to a jury trial. The Constitution as ratified had no right to counsel, no right against unreasonable search and seizure, no right to subpoena witnesses, no right to be informed of the nature and cause of the accusation, no prohibition of cruel and unusual punishment, no right against excessive bail, no right of free speech or press, and no right to bear arms. Despite this smorgasbord of absent rights, it was the imperfections in the right to trial by jury that dominated the ratifying conventions.

What the Anti-Federalists found missing in Article III was the right to a trial in civil cases, with the jury as ultimate fact-finder, and the right to a criminal jury from the neighborhood where the crime occurred rather than, as Article III provided, in the state where the crime occurred. The concern about the lack of a right to a civil jury was that the new, powerful central government would use civil forfeiture and civil fines to destroy its enemies.[17] That argument led to the Seventh Amendment.

For criminal juries, the debate was over whether to require local juries. Why would the place of trial dominate the debate on amending the Constitution? Part of the concern with the location of the trial was convenience. We should not minimize the problem of travel in eighteenth-century America. In 1776, it took John Adams fifteen days to travel by horseback from his home outside of Boston to Philadelphia,[18] a distance less than that between New York City and Lake Erie. If a crime occurred on a U.S. vessel docked somewhere along the coast of Lake Erie, Article III permitted the federal trial to be held in New York City. And it was not just the defendant who had to make that difficult journey but his witnesses as well. But while convenience was mentioned by the Framers, it was not the principal reason that they wanted a local jury.

Might the goal be to protect the innocent? One could conjure up all sorts of theories about distant juries being easier for powerful federal prosecutors to manipulate but, in truth, any gain for the protection of innocence from local venue seems marginal at best. John Marshall, who would later, as chief justice, help shape American justice, sought to quell the concern about potential abuses of power by federal juries. He asked what we would ask today: Why would a jury of strangers be "the tools and officers of the government"?[19]

So what was different about local juries? As James Wilson of Pennsylvania noted in 1787, local jurors would be "acquainted with the characters of the parties and the witnesses," a "mode of investigation" that cannot be equaled.[20] Patrick Henry was, as usual, more flamboyant:

Why do we love this trial by jury? Because it prevents the hand of oppression from cutting you off. They may call any thing rebellion, and deprive you of a fair trial by an impartial jury of your neighbors. Has not your mother country magnanimously preserved this noble privilege upwards of a thousand years? . . . And shall America give up that which nothing could induce the English people to relinquish? The idea is abhorrent to my mind. . . . This gives me comfort—that as long as I have existence, my neighbors will protect me. Old as I am, it is probable I may yet have the appellation of *rebel*. . . . As this government stands, I despise and abhor it.[21]

The Anti-Federalists preferred a judgment of the community, and the finer the grain of that community, the better. Truth was thus at least partly located in the characters of the accused, the accuser, and the witnesses. In Henry II's day, men were outlawed if they had "a very bad reputation and [were] publicly and scandalously decried on the testimony of many lawful men."[22] In the late eighteenth century, the truth about guilt was not all that different.

To be sure, the Anti-Federalists essentially lost this argument. The Sixth Amendment compromise was that the trial had to be held in the district in which the crime occurred. This is a far cry from "neighborhood"—some states have only one district, and the average number per state is two. This development suggests that the modern conception of the jury's role as a neutral factfinder that sifts evidence was in the ascendancy. But the Framers wanted juries, not judges, to sift facts, there being "no other safe mode" to determine guilt.

Now for the habeas story, which fits neatly into the jury story. An ancient common-law right, a writ of habeas corpus requires the government to produce a prisoner in court and show justification for holding him. Having access to a timely hearing on a writ of habeas corpus had been critically important in England in the century prior to our Revolution. From the Habeas Corpus Act of 1679, we can infer that English monarchs had been keeping arrested prisoners in jail for lengthy periods of time before bringing them to trial. The act sets out the following justifications for requiring habeas corpus:

Whereas great delays have been used by sheriffs [jailers] and other officers, to whose custody any of the King's subjects have been committed for criminal or supposed criminal matters, in making returns of writs of habeas corpus to them directed . . . to avoid their yielding obedience to such writs, contrary to their duty and the known laws of the land; whereby many of the King's subjects have been . . . long detained in prison in such cases where by law they are bailable, to their great charge and vexation. . . .[23]

Article I of the U.S. Constitution provides: "The Privilege of the Writ of Habeas Corpus shall not be suspended, unless when in Cases of Rebellion or Invasion the public Safety may require it."[24] The language appears to recognize a preexisting right, or "Privilege" in the language of the Constitution, and forbids tampering with that right except where necessary to preserve the Union. Why write the habeas clause in this fashion? Perhaps the clause was actually a grant of power to the central government to curtail the preexisting common-law right when the Union was threatened. No one knew at that point how often the writ of habeas corpus would be suspended. The Anti-Federalists opposed the habeas provision on the ground that it offered less than the common law, but the Federalists carried the day on that issue.

The Article I habeas privilege remained a victory for juries. It acknowledges that habeas is a critical right that can be suspended only when the Union is at risk. Habeas, understood in its eighteenth-century context, goes hand in glove with the right to a jury trial. Unlike today, when habeas is almost exclusively a way to test whether a conviction was legally obtained, its historic purpose was to keep the government from imprisoning its enemies without recourse to a court and thus to a jury. If one feared the central government, as did the Anti-Federalists, it would make no sense to require a jury trial and then permit the executive to avoid trial by detaining prisoners forever. The eighteenth-century writ of habeas corpus prevented that form of oppression. Guantánamo Bay reminds us of its value.

The final criminal procedure guarantee to be included in the body of the Constitution is the prohibition on bills of attainder. Unlike ex post facto laws, bills of attainder had been used in England through the end of the eighteenth century and also in the colonies. These were legislative enactments that singled out a person or persons for punishment without benefit of trial. Bills of attainder were obviously inconsistent with the Framers' view that juries determined guilt or innocence.

The criminal procedure protections that the Framers included in the Constitution itself, as opposed to the Bill of Rights, were all aimed at preventing the oppressive hand of government from denying the community a voice in criminal cases. The Constitution prohibits bills of attainder, ex post facto laws, guarantees access to courts through habeas corpus (except when the nation's safety is at stake), strictly limits who can be convicted of treason, and gives juries the final say on guilt and innocence. The Bill of Rights adds procedural protections designed to prevent unjust convictions—for example, the right to counsel, to notice of the charges, to subpoena witnesses, to cross-examine the state's witnesses, and to insist that the jury be impartial. Whether these rights would be given robust application was unknown at the time of the adoption of the Constitution and the Bill of Rights. But John Marshall would set a template for federal judges that would make it more difficult for the government to impose its will through the criminal process.

TESTING THE CONSTITUTION

In retrospect, Aaron Burr's adventures in the southwestern territories look more like a Three Stooges adventure than a real threat to the nation. But President Jefferson, the Senate, and the newspapers viewed it as a crisis that threatened to split the union into two countries. In the words of General William Eaton, Burr had "laid open his project of revolutionising the western country, separating it from the union, establishing a monarchy there, of which he was to be the sovereign, and New-Orleans to be his capital; organising a force on the waters of the Mississippi, and extending conquest to Mexico."[25]

It is difficult for us to appreciate how fragile the Union was believed to be in 1805. We had achieved independence, after a difficult and protracted war, only twenty-two years earlier. Only sixteen years earlier we had, by narrow votes, ratified the Constitution that bound us together. Every major player in the Burr drama was an adult during the Revolutionary War and remembered the debate over how or whether the colonies should join a union. The grand experiment in a federal republic was still that—an experiment that could fail at any moment.

George Washington created a template of a citizen president rather than a royal president. He also had experienced a relatively tranquil presidency. John Adams was not so lucky. At one point, he expected open war with France. When Presidents Washington and Adams refused to join the French war against Britain, the French seized over two thousand American merchant ships in "a retaliatory war of commercial plunder against America."[26]

Even more ominously, word spread in 1798 that Napoleon Bonaparte had assembled an invasion force aimed at the United States. "The Speaker of the House, Jonathan Dayton, speculated publicly that troops already massed in French ports were destined for America. Innumerable others thought a French invasion imminent. To oppose such an invasion, President Adams summoned General George Washington from retirement to command the United States Army."[27] A French émigré wrote in his diary, "People acted as though a French invasion force might land in America at any moment. Everybody was suspicious of everybody else: everywhere one saw murderous glances."[28] Historian David McCullough concluded that in the summer of 1798, "the United States was at war [with France]— declared or not—and there were in fact numbers of enemy agents operating in the country."[29]

In response to this threat, Adams requested, and Congress supplied, the 1798 Alien Act. Considered by President Adams as a war measure, it gave the president the right to expel all aliens "as he shall judge dangerous to the peace and safety of the United States."[30] The companion Sedition Act made it a crime to "write, print, utter, or publish" anything designed "to stir up sedition in the United States."[31] Together, the acts were an example of a government that considered itself in peril and was willing to close its borders and stifle internal dissent. It must have appeared to the Anti-Federalists that their worst nightmares were being realized. But as fear of invasion subsided, the Alien and Sedition Acts were allowed to expire by their own terms in 1800 and 1801.[32]

Six years later, the union was once again threatened. If Jefferson is the villain of the Aaron Burr story, the hero is Chief Justice John Marshall. Blackstone's *Commentaries* were first published in America in 1772, when Marshall was seventeen, and his father was one of the charter subscribers. "For the next several years, father and son . . . studied Blackstone together."[33] As an adult, Marshall "was a naturally gifted leader: humorous, low-key, unpretentious, as outgoing as many of his contemporaries were austere."[34] Justice Joseph Story said that his laugh was "too hearty for an intriguer."[35] "Months before his death, at the age of eighty, the chief justice was still pitching quoits in Richmond on Saturday afternoons, occasionally tipsy from the Quoits Club's powerful rum punch."[36]

When Marshall became chief justice in 1801, the same year the Sedition Act expired, the Court was a sleepy place that proved so boring John Jay turned down President Adams's invitation to serve a second term as chief justice.[37] The Court met but a month a year, had no regular meeting place, and had decided only three cases involving constitutional issues in its thirteen-year history.[38] Prior to Marshall, the Court announced its judgment the way the House of Lords Law Court did: Judges would agree on a judgment but would not join one opinion, instead each writing individual opinions. These seriatim opinions made it harder to know what the law was. Marshall's Court began to issue single opinions, most of the important ones written by Marshall himself. "If George Washington founded the country, John Marshall defined it."[39]

Aaron Burr was one of the most brilliant students who graduated from Princeton College in the eighteenth century. Woodrow Wilson, when president of Princeton, said of Burr, "He had genius enough to have made him immortal, and unschooled passion enough to have made him infamous."[40] The Burr story begins with the presidential elections of 1796 and 1800. The electoral college provisions in the Constitution at the time required each elector to list his top two choices, without indicating a vote for president or vice president. In the 1796 election some of the electors in states won by Adams did not vote for the preselected vice presidential candidate (Thomas Pinckney), producing the odd result that Adams's opponent, Thomas Jefferson, finished second in the balloting and became vice president.

The electors who voted for Jefferson in 1800 did not repeat that mistake, but the 1800 result was even odder. By not "splitting" their votes from the Jefferson-Burr team, all seventy-three Jefferson electors cast one vote each for Jefferson and Burr. Though everyone knew that the country wanted Jefferson, not Burr, to be president, Burr did not withdraw from consideration, throwing the deadlocked election into the House of Representatives. It took six days and thirty-six ballots before Jefferson finally got a majority.[41] Needless to say, Jefferson was not pleased that Burr refused to accept the office that he had campaigned to get.

Shortly before the famous duel with Alexander Hamilton, and while still serving as vice president, Burr was defeated for the governorship of New York. He attributed his defeat to "scurrilous attacks" on him by Hamilton.[42] On July 11, 1804, Aaron Burr killed Hamilton in a duel in Weehawken, New Jersey, across the Hudson River from Manhattan. Unsurprisingly, the combination of these events left Burr outside the corridors of power.

During the winter of 1804–5, Burr had many discussions with his old friend, General James Wilkinson, commandant of the American army and commander of American forces in the southwest frontier, an area that included what is now Louisiana. Burr left Washington in March 1805 on a journey that would eventually take him to New Orleans and to his destiny—a new battle with Jefferson, this time over whether Burr had committed treason against the United States.

On this trip, Burr met many people, including disaffected military men like General Eaton, as he tried to rally support for some kind of expedition into the Louisiana Territory. On December 1, 1805, Jefferson received an anonymous letter warning him of "Burr's intrigues" and comparing Burr to Cataline,[43] a Roman patrician who in 63 BC organized a conspiracy that would first take the surrounding countryside and then move against Rome. By the end of August 1806, Burr was on Blennerhassett's Island in the Ohio River, making final preparations for an expedition, the precise goal of which has eluded historians.

Burr "contracted to purchase fifteen boats capable of carrying 500 men, and a large keel boat for transporting provisions. He made orders for huge quantities of pork, corn meal, flour, and whiskey. Later, in Nashville, he contracted for six more boats, giving $4,000 to Andrew Jackson to pay for them."[44]

Unknown to Burr, General Wilkinson had decided to abandon the conspiracy and to sacrifice Burr to save himself. Burr sent a ciphered letter to Wilkinson that provided details of the conspiracy and said, near the end, "The gods invite to glory and fortune—it remains to be seen whether we deserve the boon."[45] Wilkinson sent Jefferson a translation of the ciphered letter along with a letter from a coconspirator, former Ohio senator Jonathan Dayton (who had been Speaker of the House when Adams was president).

Jefferson responded with a proclamation declaring the existence of a conspiracy against Spain and ordering the arrest of the conspirators.[46] Jefferson did not name Burr (or anyone else), but in a letter to the governor of New Hampshire, Jefferson said:

> Our Cataline is at the head of an armed body, and his object is to seize New Orleans, from there attack Mexico, place himself on the throne of Montezuma, add Louisiana to his empire, and the Western States from the Allegheny, if he can. I do not believe he will attain the crown but neither am I certain the halter will get its due.[47]

The press was not so cautious as to leave Burr's name unmentioned. The *Lexington Gazette*, "a longtime backer of the former vice president," declared a change in its opinion of him."Some weeks ago it was our opinion that Burr's designs were not unfavorable to the interests of our Union. . . . We now declare that opinion changed by the President's proclamation."[48]

In December 1806 Wilkinson arrested the two men who had delivered the ciphered letter, "Erick Bollman, a German doctor caught up in the romance of the western adventure, and Samuel Swartwout, an aristocratic New Yorker who later distinguished himself by stealing several hundred thousand dollars from the New York Port Authority."[49] A territorial court granted their writ of habeas corpus, but Wilkinson ignored the judge's order.[50] We see here events that the Framers had feared and had sought to avoid by writing protections into the Constitution. Would those protections hold now that the president had decided Burr was committing treason?

Though the alleged treason occurred in Ohio, Kentucky, Tennessee, and the Louisiana Territory, arrest warrants for Bollman and Swartwout were sought from, and issued by, the Circuit Court for the District of Columbia.[51] As the men were transported to Washington, news of the alleged conspiracy swept through the capital. Fearful that a writ of habeas corpus might free the two alleged conspirators, the Senate voted, with but a single dissenting vote, to suspend the writ of habeas corpus for three months.[52] The authority for this action, of course, was that this was one of those cases of "Rebellion or Invasion" where "the public Safety may require" suspension of the writ. But the House refused to concur by an overwhelming vote, 113–19.[53] The way thus remained clear for Bollman and Swartwout to have their writ of habeas corpus heard in the U.S. Supreme Court.

Before the Supreme Court heard the Bollman and Swartwout cases, Jefferson once again expressed his view of Burr's guilt, this time naming him. When Congress demanded evidence to support the president's accusation, Jefferson sent a message to Congress "castigating Burr as the 'archconspirator' in a treasonous enterprise to divide the nation," a conspirator whose "'guilt is placed beyond question.'" Burr's guilt was plain to Jefferson even though he admitted in the proclamation that it was "difficult to sort out the real facts."[54]

The Bollman and Swartwout writ of habeas corpus came before the Supreme Court in February 1807. After days of debate, the Court ruled that the Judiciary Act of 1789 gave it jurisdiction to issue a writ of habeas corpus. It then considered whether Bollman and Swartwout could be legally detained pending trial. The question ultimately was whether the acts of Burr and his motley crew created probable cause to believe they were "levying War," and thus committing treason, against the United States.[55]

In an opinion by Chief Justice Marshall, the Court held that the most the government could prove was conspiracy to commit treason. "However flagitious may be the crime of conspiring to subvert by force the government of our country, such conspiracy is not treason."[56] In one fell swoop, the Court rejected centuries of English law that treated a conspiracy to commit treason as treason. That was the theory of the crown's case against Raleigh.

Assembling an army with intent to seize New Orleans is a plausible case for probable cause to believe that the defendants had begun to levy war. But the Court read the evidence narrowly and, in effect, indulged a presumption of innocence in stark contrast to the presumption of guilt that we saw in the seventeenth-century English treason cases. Marshall was aware of the danger in letting the government proceed with a questionable treason case: "As there is no crime which can more excite and agitate the passions of men than treason, no charge demands more [temperance] from the tribunal before which it is made . . . ."[57]

Having lost the preliminary round, Jefferson turned his attention to *United States v. Burr*,[58] the treason case against Burr himself. John Marshall presided over the case, sitting as a federal trial judge. It might strike the reader as remarkable that the president thought he could prove Burr guilty of treason beyond a reasonable doubt when his prosecutors had failed to demonstrate probable cause of a conspiracy in a preliminary hearing. One reason for hope was that, as we will see, the prosecution changed its theory of how Burr had committed treason. Moreover, Jefferson perhaps thought that a jury would be easier to persuade than the crusty Federalist John Marshall. But if that is what the president thought, he had underestimated Marshall's ability to control the evidence that the jury would hear.

The first skirmish in the *Burr* case was over the ciphered letter allegedly written by Burr and now in Jefferson's hands. Burr's lawyers filed a subpoena that required Jefferson to present Burr's letter to the court. Jefferson interposed a claim of executive privilege. Marshall finessed that delicate issue by deferring its resolution until the return of the subpoena.

The president also objected to the scope of the subpoena. Here, Marshall expanded on the literal language of the Sixth Amendment, which provides defendants with the right "to have compulsory process for obtaining witnesses in his favor."[59] What Burr sought was not a witness at all but the letter possessed by the president of the United States. It was a ticklish situation for Marshall. The Supreme Court lacks the power to compel the president to act. Would Marshall risk defiance and order the president to produce the letter? The reporter who was taking down the proceedings noted that the motion to compel production of the letter led to a "protracted debate," which occupied "two entire days, and extending into the third. . . . Much ability and eloquence were displayed on both sides."[60]

One of Burr's lawyers was Luther Martin. Perhaps the most famous lawyer of his day, Martin was an extreme Federalist, indeed was known as the "Federalist bull dog."[61] He was a friend of Burr. He hated Jefferson, and the feeling was entirely mutual. "Having recently defended [Supreme Court justice] Chase for haranguing Jefferson, Martin went on to do a bit of haranguing of his own" during the Burr trial.[62] He accused Jefferson of acting like "some 'kind of sovereign'"when he publicly announced Burr's guilt.[63] "'He has assumed to himself the knowledge of the Supreme Being himself, and pretended to search the heart of my highly respected friend. . . . He has let slip the dogs of war, the hellhounds of persecution, to hunt down my friend.'"[64]

In the end, the president lost. Again. Marshall held that compulsory process included the right to compel a witness to bring a document. He reasoned that if the contents had been communicated orally to a person, the person who heard the contents could be compelled to appear and testify. Why should it matter that the contents were in writing and that the paper had to "speak" for itself? The goal to protect innocence is manifest throughout the opinion. For example, Marshall noted that if Burr's prosecution ended in a conviction, "[A]ll those who are concerned in it should certainly regret that a paper which the accused believed to be essential to his defence . . . had been withheld from him." On a personal note, Marshall said that it would cause him "much self-reproach" if he declared "that the accused was not entitled to the letter in question, if it should be really important to him."[65]

Next was the Burr trial, which was high drama indeed. Though Marshall was not fully aware at the time (or perhaps ever), Jefferson had "assumed control of the prosecution. He devoted several Cabinet meetings to the matter and instructed [Secretary of State] Madison to find additional funds to bring witnesses from great distances."[66] Jefferson sent the chief prosecutor a stack of blank pardons with the president's signature, a means to persuade reluctant witnesses to talk. The president was even willing to give pardons "to the gross offenders" if Burr would "otherwise escape."[67]

The trial began on August 3 and ended in an acquittal on September 1. It was, Newmyer concludes, "a public spectacle. Newspaper coverage was extensive, even national in scope, and highly politicized, which is to say Marshall's every move was reported and scrutinized."[68] Large crowds of spectators wanted to watch the proceedings, causing Marshall to hold the trial in the Virginia House of Delegates, "where galleries were packed for the duration."[69] Great lawyers of the time were arrayed on both sides of the case. "Jefferson was not there in person, but his presence was decidedly felt."[70]

The prosecution "assembled more than one hundred witnesses, many of whom were celebrities and all of whom were prepared to testify about something or other they had heard Burr say or seen him do in his meanderings through the West."[71] But the government's key witness, the "most flamboyant and controversial of them, was archaccuser and chief government witness, James Wilkinson." His first appearance in court was pure theater. He wore a "fantastic military outfit, of his own design . . . almost as outrageous as his testimony, which was so tinctured with lies and contradictions that it nearly got him indicted for treason."

Having failed in the Bollman and Swartwout cases on the theory that treason is committed when a conspiracy to commit treason is shown, the prosecution now relied on the English doctrine of constructive treason—that if the assembling of troops on Blennerhassett's Island was levying war, then Burr was guilty of treason even if his role in that act was minute and remote. Indeed, a passage in Marshall's opinion for the Court in *Bollman* seemed to permit the government's argument.[72]

The prosecution's problem, however was that none of its witnesses could establish any connection between Burr and the assembling of troops on Blennerhassett's Island.[73] The testimony, instead, was about Burr's intention to levy war. Indeed, the first dozen witnesses had shown Burr to be one hundred miles from Blennerhassett's Island when the alleged treasonous acts took place. Burr moved the court to exclude witnesses who could not connect him to the overt acts that occurred on the island. The lawyers argued the motion for days. The defense attacked the government's embrace of the English doctrine of constructive treason. One defense lawyer spent two days on the law of treason.[74]

Luther Martin concluded for the defense, speaking "for fourteen hours over a period of three days and, despite heavy drinking, [Martin] was in perfect command of his faculties. Friends and foes alike conceded that Martin gave a magnificent performance. . . ."[75] His final words were perhaps his most magnificent. He began by noting that it "is easy to do our duty in fair weather."[76] Then speaking directly to the court, he said that when the tempest rages, when the thunders roar, and the lightnings blaze around us—it is then that the truly brave man stands firm at his post. . . . May that God who now looks down upon us, so illuminate your understandings that you may know what is right; and may he nerve your souls with firmness and fortitude to act according to that knowledge.[77]

Luther Martin knew his audience well. On August 31, Marshall delivered a long discourse on the theory of treason, rejecting the notion of constructive treason. Any indications in *Bollman* to the contrary were disavowed. The government had to prove that Aaron Burr played an actual part in the levying of war. It was not enough to be an accessory to those who levied war. Marshall thus ruled that no more testimony could be offered unless it "bore on the events that transpired on Blennerhassett's Island. . . . Left stranded were the dozens of prosecution witnesses, who were prepared to testify about everything about Burr except what counted."[78]

In delivering his judgment from the bench, Marshall spoke to Jefferson and to history:

No man is desirous of placing himself in a disagreeable situation. No man is desirous of becoming the peculiar subject of calumny. No man, might he let the bitter cup pass from him without self-reproach, would drain it to the bottom. But if he has no choice in the case; if there is no alternative presented to him but a dereliction of duty, or the opprobrium of those who are denominated the world . . . who can hesitate which to embrace.[79]

After a brief deliberation, the jury returned a not guilty verdict. "Jefferson was incensed by the acquittal. Rather than acknowledge that the prosecution's case was shaky, the president blamed Marshall for interfering."[80] The Republican newspapers took up that charge. Kent Newmyer, a Marshall biographer, concluded that what "really sank the government's case was not Marshall's prejudgment, but Jefferson's relentless and law-defying pursuit of Burr."[81] Marshall biographer Jean Edward Smith agrees: "Jefferson overplayed his hand" and "convicted Burr before a trial could be held."[82] Perhaps more troubling was that Jefferson made the trial of Burr appear to be "a personal vendetta against the man who had almost snatched the presidency from him in 1800."[83]

History has been kind to Marshall on this point. "Historians rightly celebrate Marshall's clarification of treason doctrine [in the Burr case], a definition that repudiated the English doctrine of constructive treason and thus helped put treason beyond the reason of vindictive politicians."[84] Marshall's "main concern and greatest accomplishment was to move American constitutional law toward a nonpolitical definition of treason and to assure Aaron Burr a fair trial according to prevailing legal standards."[85] Indeed, "It was probably fortunate for Jefferson's reputation as America's champion of human rights that Marshall spared Aaron Burr from the gallows."[86]

For his part, Marshall "could not understand why Jefferson persisted with the treason charge" since the prosecution could easily have convicted Burr of other charges.[87] Marshall made this concern plain in his opinion initially refusing to bind Burr over to the grand jury (Marshall would later change his mind and permit the case to go forward). In explaining why courts must proceed carefully in treason cases, Marshall wrote: "As this is the most atrocious offence which can be committed against the political body, so is it the charge which is most capable of being employed as the instrument of those malignant and vindictive passions which may rage in the bosoms of contending parties struggling for power."[88]

And why not lesser offenses? It appears that Jefferson so hated Burr that nothing short of treason would please him. And so he got nothing.

Taken together these cases involving treason and intrigue stand for the proposition that in the early days of the Republic, even as threats to the nation surfaced, John Marshall stood strongly against government manipulation of the criminal process to convict without regard to guilt or innocence. *Bollman* and *Burr* are thus enduring testaments to the protection of innocence.

THE GUILT OR INNOCENCE QUESTION IS QUIET FOR A CENTURY

The United States had found a resting place for the question of how to protect innocent suspects and defendants. The Constitution guaranteed several rights that benefit innocent defendants—the rights to counsel, to notice of charges, to have a grand jury screen cases, to cross-examine the state's witnesses, and to subpoena witnesses and other evidence (the letter the president initially refused to provide Burr). Most importantly, the whole question of guilt or innocence was to be decided by a jury from the district where the crime allegedly occurred. The Framers, and the colonists before them, had great faith in juries as the place where truth resided.

But as we saw in the Burr case, these rights can be squeezed so as to reduce their importance. The right to present witnesses is less important if the crime is defined in such a way that innocent-looking conduct is relevant. John Marshall did not permit Burr's rights to be narrowed in that way. The right to subpoena witnesses is less protective if subpoenas cannot be issued for what witnesses have committed to writing. Marshall held that documents can be subpoenaed.

As long as juries decided guilt and innocence, and as long as judges were vigilant to prevent government from tilting the process, the system in place was probably as good as any that could have been designed for the nineteenth century. And because judges were appointed or elected from the citizenry, who remained skeptical about the power of government, judges of the time seemed to lean over backward to tilt away from the prosecution. Nineteenth-century judges seemed to take quite seriously Blackstone's adage that it is better that ten guilty defendants go free than that one innocent defendant be convicted.

I will present examples of innocence-protecting approaches from early cases. I do not believe that these approaches can be replicated in cases decided in the modern era. A few samples do not a statistical study make, but I believe that these cases show an attitude that has, sadly, been lost over the last hundred years.

The U.S. Supreme Court did not review criminal convictions in any meaningful way prior to 1889, when Congress first gave the Court power to conduct general reviews of convictions, and then only in capital cases.[89] Thus, to find examples of the Supreme Court reviewing convictions, we must go late in the nineteenth century. An example from 1891 is the murder case of *Hickory v. United States*.[90] A U.S. deputy marshal had a warrant to arrest Hickory, a Cherokee, on the charge of taking whiskey into Indian territory. Several days later, the body of the marshal was found in a ravine; he had been shot and his skull fractured. According to the government's case,

Hickory told three people that he had shot the marshal but that the shot didn't kill him.

In his defense, Hickory admitted killing the marshal in self-defense. A jury convicted but the Supreme Court reversed the conviction on the ground that the judge's instructions effectively decided the self-defense issue rather than leaving it for the jury to decide.[91] A second jury convicted and Hickory appealed again, this time raising twelve errors as to the judge's charge.[92] The Court held that the instructions unfairly implied Hickory's guilt and reversed yet again.

A year later, probably as a result of a plea bargain, Hickory was sentenced to five years and one day.[93] As he was sentenced to death in the first trial, the final result suggests uncertainty about whether his self-defense claim was valid. It appears that the first two verdicts resulted from trials unfairly tilted against innocence, but we would never have known that had the Court not taken painstaking care in its review of the record.

What is striking about both *Hickory* cases is the care with which the Court combed the record when considering the defendant's claims. The Court seemed to be indulging every presumption in favor of innocence. The modern Court takes just the opposite tack.

Because the vast majority of criminal convictions are state cases, the review of state convictions for insufficient evidence is of critical importance in remedying wrongful conviction. In *Jackson v. Virginia,* the Court instructed federal courts that, when reviewing claims of insufficient evidence raised by state prisoners, courts should view the evidence "in the light most favorable to the prosecution" and then ask whether "*any* rational trier of fact could have found the essential elements of the crime beyond a reasonable doubt."[94] It is hard to imagine even innocent defendants winning very many cases under that standard.

To be sure, states are free to fashion their own rules for appeals and could require a more meaningful review of convictions. But the courts that have reached this issue since *Jackson* was decided have, with one exception,[95] either adopted its very low standard for their own review of convictions or insisted that their preexisting standard is equivalent to *Jackson*.[96] One of the odd things about some of the cases here is that *defendants* were usually the party arguing that *Jackson* should apply, as if it were a helpful standard.

Compare the *Jackson* approach to that of the New Jersey Supreme Court in an 1818 case. The issue was whether the confession of a ten-year-old slave to murder was admissible and, if so, whether it would support a conviction.[97] The court held that the confession should not have been used to obtain a conviction. To some extent the decision is based on the youth of the boy, but the court was also concerned that the confession did not contain details that would prove guilt:

> [I]t is a simple naked confession, *disclosing no fact, pregnant with no circumstances to give it authority, or in any way to corroborate it.* It did not even lead to the discovery of the body of the deceased, for it was found before, it opens up *no proof of malice,* or *hatred, or ill will* against the child, *but rather the contrary; . . .*[98]

The lack of corroborating detail created a real possibility that the confession was false. One way to feel confident that a confession is true is if it contains details of the crime that have been "proved independently of, and not coupled with, or explained by, the conversation or confession from which they are derived."[99] This is a splendid idea, but courts today do not scrutinize confessions to see if they are self-verifying. The presumption of innocence has, sadly, weakened over the centuries.

To see how important the presumption of innocence was to courts in the early years of our country, consider a Pennsylvania arson trial from 1792, only five years after ratification of the Constitution.[100] A twelve-year-old boy had confessed to arson, a confession that he never repudiated. Despite his failure to deny the truth of the confession, the court instructed the jury that it must gravely consider the possibility that the confession might be false. The court made nothing of the fact that the boy was twelve. Rather, its concern was whether there was doubt that the prisoner might have "falsely declared himself guilty of a capital offense."

> If there is ground even to suspect, that he has done so, God forbid, that his life should be the sacrifice! While, therefore, on the one hand, it is remarked, that all the stables set on fire, were in the neighborhood of his master's house; that he has, in part, communicated the facts to another boy; that his conduct had excited the attention and suspicion of a girl, who knew him; and that he expressed no wish to

retract the statement, which he has given: the jury will, on the other hand, remember, that if they entertain a doubt upon the subject, it is their duty to pronounce an acquittal. Though it is their province to administer justice, and not to bestow mercy; and though it is better not to err at all; yet, in a doubtful case, an error on the side of mercy is safer, is more venial, than error on the side of rigid justice.[101]

A similar concern with false confessions can be found in hundreds of English and American cases from the nineteenth century.[102] In a New Hampshire case, for example, the defendant was accused of stealing banknotes and offered some unspecified inducement to confess. He then produced a note and said it was one of the ones he had stolen. The Supreme Court of New Hampshire made clear its concern about a false confession: "Influenced by hope or fear, a prisoner might deliver up money of his own, equal in amount and upon the same bank, and bills of the same denomination with those stolen, in order to relieve himself from arrest, or with the hope that he might gain favor. . . ."[103]

Compare these early expressions of concern about false confessions with the attitude of the modern Court in *Colorado v. Connelly*.[104] Decided in 1986, the case involved a confession given by a psychotic with command hallucinations in which God gave him a choice between suicide and confessing to a murder. Little other evidence connected the suspect to the murder, and on appeal the defendant claimed that the Due Process Clause should bar his confession because it was unreliable. The Court was aware that psychotics in Connelly's condition sometimes confess to crimes they did not commit and conceded that Connelly's confession might be "quite unreliable."[105] The Court followed this concession with the remarkable comment that unreliability "is a matter to be governed by the evidentiary laws of the forum and not by the Due Process Clause of the Fourteenth Amendment."

To be sure, when reviewing a state conviction, as in *Connelly*, a federal court might be justified in permitting the states more latitude in how they obtain and review convictions. Even with that concession in place, I find it remarkable that in the early 1800s courts took pains to keep confessions from juries if there was even a slight chance that they might be false, while by 1986 the Supreme Court of the United States seemed indifferent to the possibility that an innocent psychotic would be convicted of murder. And, as we saw, the *Jackson* standard of federal review of state convictions is so low that the chances of reversing a wrongful conviction on appeal are woefully low. Almost two hundred years have passed, and our courts have strayed far from the path of innocence.

CHAPTER SIX

IN GOD'S NAME: IS THAT THE MAN?

In God's name, Miss Taylor, tell us positively—is that the guilty negro? Can you say it—can you swear it?

—*CHATTANOOGA TIMES*, FEBRUARY 9, 1906

The nineteenth century put its faith in juries. The right to a jury trial, hard won in the eighteenth century, was the best mechanism for sorting the innocent from the guilty that had ever been used in Anglo-American law. But evidence of jury failures began to appear early in the twentieth century. Sad to say, but inevitable I suppose, the evidence first became obvious in cases where racism and anti-Semitism moved the jury to convictions that were not justified by the evidence.

Many stories can be told here. I will limit myself to two. We will see that juries, and justice, are no better than the communities in which they exist. This should not surprise us. If asked, the Nazi leadership would probably have said that justice required removal of Jews to the camps. But we will also see that honorable men, in and out of the South, believed in a truth about guilt that exists outside the jury verdict. This Platonic truth about guilt provided a standard by which jury "justice" could sometimes be rejected as a failure.

Chattanooga, Tennessee, in 1906 was a city suffering multiple personalities. Set in mountainous East Tennessee, a region that had never benefited from slavery, Chattanooga was home to many Union loyalists and their descendants. In 1861, East Tennessee voted more than two to one against secession—68 percent voted to remain in the Union—but those votes were swamped by the prosecession votes from West and Middle Tennessee (85 percent in favor of secession).[1] Chattanooga "overwhelmingly favored Lincoln" in the election of 1860 and "strongly supported the Republican Party."[2] Northerners found Chattanooga a relatively hospitable place to move after the war.

But Chattanooga is only a mile or two up Route 27 from Georgia, a state that had no indecision about joining the Confederacy. Thus, in 1906, Chattanooga was very much a city divided between Union and Confederate loyalists. "Confederate loyalists considered Chattanooga 'occupied territory' because there were so many Northern transplants living there."[3] Northerners came to a prospering Chattanooga. It sat astride the navigable Tennessee River, and the railroad companies had "decided to route their north-south lines through the city."[4] More significantly, for my purposes, "black-owned businesses in Chattanooga were thriving."[5] By 1906, "[T]here were an unusually high number of black lawyers, doctors, and other professionals practicing in Chattanooga, compared with other Southern cities."[6]

In 1906, Nevada Taylor "was twenty-one, blond, and beautiful."[7] At 6:00 p.m. on January 23, Taylor left her job at the W. W. Brooks grocery store and paid three cents for a ride on one of Chattanooga's "new electric trolleys, which had replaced the mule-drawn street-cars."[8] Taylor lived with her father, who was the keeper of the Forest Hills cemetery, in a cottage inside the cemetery.[9] The cemetery was at the foot of Lookout Mountain.

The temperature had reached a high of forty-four degrees that morning, but the day had grown steadily clearer and thus colder.[10] Now, with night fallen, the temperature had dropped below freezing. Taylor could see the lights of her cottage when she stepped off the trolley car.[11] "She heard footsteps behind her and turned only to be caught in the powerful arms of a negro man. . . ."[12] When she screamed and tried to fight back, the attacker "warned her not to scream again or to make any noise, threatening to cut her throat if she disobeyed."[13] He "hurled her over the fence into the marble yard" of the cemetery and raped her.[14] Taylor was not able to give the authorities a "lucid description of the fiend who assailed her" but said that "her impression of him was that he was a black negro about her own height."[15]

The Hamilton County (Chattanooga) sheriff was Joseph F. Shipp. He had joined the Confederate army on April 12, 1861, at the age of fourteen, "and served through the war," rising to the rank of captain.[16] In 1890, fourteen years before he was elected sheriff of Chattanooga for the first time, Shipp told the United Confederate Veterans of the Nathan Bedford Forrest Camp about the neglected graves of "their long-sleeping comrades" at a local cemetery.[17] "The ground was purchased and arrangements were made to care for the graves."[18]

Chattanooga had two newspapers at the time. The headlines the next day in the *Chattanooga Times* proclaimed:

Awful Crime At St. Elmo
Girl Attacked by Negro at Gate of Cemetery
Choked Insensible With Leather Strap
Whole Town Joins in Search for Brute, But No Success is Met With
SHERIFF SHIPP AT HEAD OF BIG FORCE OF DEPUTIES
Offers $50 Reward for Capture of Brute—Young Woman Unable to Give Accurate Description of Man and Bloodhounds Lose Trail in Short Order—Every Effort, However, To Be Made to Capture Him Today.[19]

The headlines in the *Chattanooga News* were similar.[20] The story in the *Times* noted that the physician who examined Taylor found a "livid red streak around her neck" as well as "marks on her body that gave proof of rough handling when the negro threw her over the fence." But "worst of all, it was found that the negro had accomplished his devilish purpose."[21]

There were no clues and, apparently, no eyewitnesses.[22] Various groups began to offer rewards, totaling $300, for information leading to capture of the rapist, referred to in the newspapers as a "black brute."[23] A moderate newspaper in a Republican part of a border state, the *Chattanooga Times* predicted without criticism that the perpetrator would be lynched when caught. The following paragraph is a chilling reminder of what it was like to be a black man suspected of raping a white woman in the South of that time:

> It was acknowledged by everybody, including officers of the law, that no power could save the criminal from summary vengeance in case he should be caught. The humor of the citizens of St. Elmo was one of quiet determination to deal punishment to the negro which would be a warning to others of his stamp to abandon the present tendency toward outlawry in this community. Neither is there any likelihood of any dying out of public sentiment along these lines. The crime was so horrible in every particular and the victim so popular in her neighborhood that any mention of the affair, it is stated, will stir up the wrath of the citizens for weeks and months to come.[24]

Ed Johnson was one of two black suspects arrested on January 25. A laborer, he had most recently worked on the St. Elmo church, which would make him familiar with the area where Taylor was raped. The *Chattanooga Times* described him as a "hanger on at various saloons in South Chattanooga."[25] That story was followed by one with a headline that read, "Better Class of Negroes Vigorously Condemn Crime."

Johnson "was subjected to some severe sweating and tested in many ways."[26] One shudders to imagine the "severe sweating" and "testing" that Johnson faced at the hands of a former Confederate officer seeking a confession from a black man accused of raping a young white woman. But Johnson insisted then, as he was to insist many times for the rest of his life, that he was not guilty of Miss Taylor's rape.[27]

It was barely above freezing that evening[28] when a mob of perhaps fifteen hundred men gathered ominously around the county jail, led by "a man fresh from some mill with a face begrimed with soot and dirt."[29] As the *Chattanooga Times* put it the next morning, the mob was "[f]ierce in its determination to wreak vengeance upon some negro, and not caring to any great extent what one." One of the jailers told the mob that Johnson was not in their care, but the mob did not believe him and stormed the jail. Some fired their guns; others threw stones or bricks. The mob was stopped by the big iron door and by two "determined" deputies who stood their ground despite perhaps twenty guns pointed at them. When the mob threatened to kill the deputies, one of them said if "any person tried to pass through the door, it would be over his dead body." These deputies "for three long hours gave unmistakable evidence of nerve, [and] stood there immovable."

Circuit judge Samuel D. McReynolds had, earlier in the day, advised the governor to call out the National Guard "to aid in suppressing the riot and restoring order," and units had assembled at the armory.[30] During the siege of the jail, the courthouse bell began to ring, a signal that the militia was "needed at the jail." At about this time, the judge appeared and made an appeal to the mob "as a friend, and I am sure you are all friends of mine, to quietly disperse to your homes and refrain from violence." He, too, told them that Johnson was not in the jail, that he was in Knoxville. The mob greeted that announcement "with jeers and insulting epithets," and "the crowd again became uncontrollable." The judge responded with a creative proposal: The mob could appoint three men to accompany the judge and the jailers into the jail to search for Ed Johnson. The mob counteroffered that ten men should accompany the jailers, and the judge agreed.

The arrival of a "platoon of police, twenty men strong," combined with the judge's offer to let some men search the jail, had the effect of quieting the mob.[31] But there was still the problem of dispensing at least one thousand men. The police made a "heroic effort to clear the street," but it proved "to be beyond their power." At this point, a "fairly strong force" of National Guard arrived and tried its hand. "Sullenly and slowly the mob began to back away down the street and at about 10:50 the danger point was past."

The police cleared the lobby of the jail so that the mob's "committee" could search the jail.[32] When the men reached the "negro department," the "inmates were found to be in state of abject terror. They were nearly all on their knees praying with upturned, ashen faces, and gave every evidence they believed their hour had come." Ed Johnson was not to be found.

The judge had told the truth, or at least the relevant truth: Johnson was not in the Chattanooga jail. Nor was he on his way to Knoxville—a lie told in case anyone tried to intercept him before he was safely in another jail. Judge McReynolds had ordered Sheriff Shipp to take the prisoner to Nashville.[33] He was "spirited out of town," perhaps disguised, earlier in the afternoon.

From their study of the events of that evening, Mark Curriden and Leroy Phillips conclude: "Even though the leaders of the mob went home disappointed that Thursday night, they had put Sheriff Shipp and Judge McReynolds on notice: convict and punish this Negro quickly or they would be back."[34] The message was communicated in part by the severe damage done the jail: "Every window and lamp was shattered. The assault on the front door had left it in ruins. Bullet holes riddled the building's brick-and-cement walls, as well as the doors and furniture inside."[35]

Because Johnson continued to maintain his innocence, Shipp decided to try an eyewitness identification. The county paid for a train ticket for Nevada Taylor and her older brother on the L & N (Louisville and Nashville) Railroad. They arrived at Union Station in Nashville on the morning of January 27.[36] It is likely that neither Nevada Taylor nor her brother had ever been to Nashville. If not, they were surely awed by Union Station, which was far larger and newer than the station in Chattanooga. Completed only six years earlier, the "magnificent" Richardsonian Romanesque structure featured a clock tower that "soared over 200 feet into the sky, adorned with a modern digital clock and a [copper] statue of Mercury."[37] The waiting room had a sixty-five-foot vaulted ceiling with "an ornate skylight that flooded the room with sunshine. On one end, two young female figures in bas-relief represented the cities of Louisville and Nashville with arms outstretched to one another. Opposite them, two other figures represented Time and Progress."[38]

Sheriff Shipp met them at Union Station. From there, it is about twelve blocks to the Nashville jail. They walked out into the cloudy, cold January day.[39] They had two choices of transportation—horse-drawn carriage over the limestone streets (likely a slimy mud that time of year) or the relatively new electric trolleys. In either case, they had to breathe the fetid Nashville air. Soft coal was the principal fuel for Nashville residences and businesses. During winter, the city was often blanketed by a "dense pall of black smoke" mixed with garbage odors.[40]

At the jail, both suspects were brought into a room where Taylor sat.[41] For more than fifteen minutes Taylor observed the men, heard their voices, and saw them walk around the room. When Shipp asked her opinion "whether either of the two was the guilty party," she said that Johnson "was like the man as she remembered him." She concluded her "scrutiny" with words that would become hauntingly familiar before Ed Johnson was murdered: "it is my best knowledge and belief" that Johnson was the man who raped her.

Shipp telegraphed Judge McReynolds: "Nevada Taylor has identified suspect."[42] The judge convened a grand jury that indicted in two hours.[43] A few days later, still in the Nashville jail, Ed Johnson released a statement to the *Nashville Banner* declaring his innocence and giving the names of several people who could provide him an alibi. Near the end of his statement, he said, "No, sir, I never done what they charged me with. If there's a God in heaven I'm innocent."[44]

McReynolds assigned three lawyers to represent Johnson. As Curriden and Phillips describe the appointment, the judge first appointed Robert Cameron, a young lawyer who had never handled a criminal case and whose only trial experience involved simple divorces and real estate disputes.[45] At some point Lewis Shepherd, "a former judge and possibly the most prominent member of the local bar," told McReynolds, "This is a very important case. You need to have one of the older members of the criminal bar involved."[46] Shepherd named several men who would satisfy these criteria, and McReynolds then asked Shepherd if he would agree to work with Cameron. Yes, he said, on the condition that the judge persuade another seasoned lawyer, W. G. M. Thomas, to join the defense team. After being importuned at length by Judge McReynolds, Thomas very reluctantly agreed.

While I cannot verify the Curriden and Phillips account of how the legal team was assembled, the newspaper stories do show that Thomas was very reluctant to be assigned the case. On the Friday before jury selection was to begin on Monday, Thomas released a statement to the press. He said that he wanted to explain what the defense team was "attempting to do in obeying the hard appointment of Judge McReynolds."[47] He noted that Johnson had been "accused of committing the most awful crime capable of being imagined by the human mind." Then he continued: "I would avoid the task if I could honorably do so. I didn't want it. I didn't ask it." He then pointed out the constitutional right to a lawyer and that Judge McReynolds had the duty "to select some lawyers from the Chattanooga bar, and his lot has fallen on me, and I shall not dodge or shirk the hard duty thus imposed."

He concluded, "I am not a criminal lawyer. I have never sought a criminal practice. . . . What I am trying to do in this case is conscientiously, and as thoroughly as I know how to find out whether the accused man is guilty or innocent."

To their credit, Thomas, Shepherd, and Cameron worked hard to prepare a defense. And they had to do their work in a hostile atmosphere. Chattanooga, population 100,000 in 1900, was hardly a small town. But neither was it New York City (population 3.4 million) or Chicago (population 1.7 million). One can imagine the reaction of the friends, employees, and families of the defense lawyers.

Without citing sources, Curriden and Phillips provide the following account of the hostility that the lawyers faced. One of the best clients of Cameron's law firm withdrew his business; Thomas's secretary quit because she didn't want to work for a man who defended black men who rape white women; and Thomas's mother "refused to cook dinner for him when she learned he was handling the case."[48] It got worse. One night, vandals threw rocks and broke the windows in Thomas's home while he was getting ready to go to bed and his elderly mother was already asleep.[49] I cannot confirm the accuracy of this account, but it fits with Thomas's statement seeking to make plain that the task was thrust upon him.

Judge McReynolds set the trial for a week later. It seems that the judge told the lawyers not to bother making a motion to change venue because he had "already expressed his opinion that he himself will try the negro brute" in Chattanooga.[50] It is not clear that a change of venue would have helped. The entire region was gripped by fury and fear. Seven black men were held in protective custody in the Nashville jail "from various parts of the state, the populace not being trusted to allow the negroes to live in their own counties."[51]

Perhaps seeking to calm Chattanooga, the newspaper story assured readers that Ed Johnson would receive a speedy trial.

Working in a hostile atmosphere, and with only a week to prepare, the defense mounted a powerful defense. No transcript exists of the trial because the Hamilton County courthouse burned after being struck by lightning in 1910.[52] The facts about the trial that follow are drawn from newspaper accounts. The state's case was built on two slender reeds. First, a witness came forward who claimed that he had seen Johnson in the cemetery about the time of the crime. Of greater importance, of course, was Taylor's identification. The defense destroyed the credibility of the witness claiming to have seen Johnson, showing that he cared only about the $300 reward. Taylor's identification never got any stronger than it was in Nashville. "[S]he believed he was the man."[53]

The hardworking defense lawyers presented a detailed alibi defense. On the witness stand, Ed Johnson asserted "his innocence in strong terms" and detailed every moment of the afternoon when the crime occurred.[54] Then the defense presented seventeen defense witnesses. Seventeen. As the relentless attack on the state's case continued, the jurors "became restless, fingers working nervously upon arms of chairs."[55]

Finally, a remarkable moment: "C. E. Bearden, the well-known architect, . . . threw his hands to his head and with tears in his eyes exclaimed: 'I can't stand it any longer: I can't stand it.'"[56] Unsurprisingly, Judge McReynolds immediately called a recess and had the jurors removed from the courtroom. When they returned, an even more remarkable event: the jurors said they wanted Taylor to identify the defendant again. Taylor was recalled to the stand and Johnson was ordered to stand directly in front of her. Then the most remarkable event of all: The jury questioned Taylor.[57] One juror asked if that was the negro who attacked her. Her stock answer followed: "To the best of my knowledge and belief, he is the same man."

> Again the strain proved too much for Mr. Bearden. With tears streaming down his face he leaned forward toward the injured girl and in a voice trembling with emotion, he cried: "In God's name, Miss Taylor, tell us positively—is that the guilty negro? Can you say it—can you swear it?'"[58]

And still she would not swear it. Her voice cracked as she said, "Listen to me. I would not take the life of an innocent man. But before God, I believe this is the guilty negro." She "raised her right hand toward heaven . . . , her tears came, her voice quivered and she was led trembling from the witness stand. The effect was electrical. One of the jurors collapsed from his emotion and leaned forward in his chair choking with sobs. . . . Evidences of weeping were heard on every side."[59]

In closing argument, Lewis Shepherd, the former judge, accused Judge McReynolds of making rulings "biased in favor of the state."[60] Then, for an hour, he "delivered a most impassioned plea to the jury on behalf of the negro." The young lawyer, Cameron, "excoriated" the witness who said he saw Johnson near the scene of the crime, denouncing him as a "liar" and "perjurer." But the final closing argument, by Thomas, was the finest. The *Chattanooga Times* described it as "a most remarkable plea to the jury" that his client was innocent:

> Were I not convinced of the absolute innocence of that negro sitting over there, I would be there silent in my chair or over on the other side aiding the attorney general to fasten the guilt upon him. Log chains couldn't pull me and make me stand before twelve men of my home and say a word for that man if I did not believe in his innocence. . . . In the face of twelve good men from my own home . . . I could not stand here and ask the acquittal of a man I believed to be guilty . . . I could not be so false to the womanhood dear to me and to the mothers, wives and sisters dear to you, as to stand here and ask you to acquit this man if there were any reasonable certainty of his guilt.[61]

The prosecutor responded with an argument that the newspaper called "masterly, almost cruelly denunciatory and most convincing. He plead [*sic*] for the womanhood and girlhood of the country and rebuked the defense for asking the jury to believe the perjured testimony of a lot of 'thugs, thieves and sots—the off-scourings of hell.'"[62] Unspoken, but hanging like the oppressive winter air of Nashville, was the fact that most of the defense alibi witnesses were black.[63]

The jury began deliberating around six o'clock. At midnight, the jury retired without reaching a verdict. Word spread that the jury

stood eight for guilt and four for innocence.[64] Rather than seques-
tering the jury, Judge McReynolds let them go home for the evening.
This decision was fatal to Ed Johnson's chances of avoiding a conviction. As Curriden and Phillips put it, "After a night at home with
their families, their doubt over Miss Taylor's identification and [the
eyewitness'] motives evaporated."[65] The headlines two days later
would scream: "Guilty of Rape and the Punishment—Death By
Hanging. So said each member of the jury. . . ."[66]

What happened to change their minds? Curriden and Phillips
hint darkly that the judge, the prosecutor, and the sheriff—or one or
two of them—might have done something. Without citing a source,
Curriden and Phillips claim that the three actors shared a bottle of
whiskey after the jury was discharged for the night and "all agreed
that a 'not guilty' verdict could not be tolerated, nor could a mistrial—the city could not afford, financially or socially, a second
trial."[67] Did they visit the houses of the dissenters? Did they know
which four voted not guilty?

I suggest an explanation that takes the judge, sheriff, and prosecutor off the hook but is, in a way, even darker. The social pressure
on the four dissenters would have been enormous. It is one thing for
a lawyer to represent a client charged with rape. Representing clients
charged with crimes is part of what lawyers do for a living. It is quite
something else to disbelieve "Miss Taylor" and find the man not
guilty of raping her when she said, to the best of her knowledge, he
was the man. Where southern womanhood was involved, there was
simply no room for doubt. Taylor believed he was the black man
who had raped her. That was enough for the families of the jurors
and, ultimately, I believe, for the four dissenting jurors.

The headlines in the *Chattanooga News* for February 9, 1906, said
all that needs to be said about the atmosphere in which Ed Johnson
was tried and convicted: "The Jury Finds Ed Johnson Guilty; He Will
Hang for His Fiendish Crime; Given the Full Benefit of Law, A Human Brute Is Convicted. Announcement Calmly Received in Court
Room."[68]

There is more to be said about the Johnson case, but I wish to examine the lessons learned to this point. First, even one hundred
years ago in the South there were honorable white men who sought
justice when black men were accused of raping white women. The

defense lawyers—Lewis Shepherd, Robert Cameron, and W. G. M. Thomas—were honorable men. Judge McReynolds might have favored the state in the trial, but he alone prevented the first attempted lynching, and he appointed three able lawyers to defend Johnson.

Indeed, at this stage of the narrative, we can even claim honor for Sheriff Shipp. To be sure, Judge McReynolds ordered him to remove the two rape suspects from the jail. But when Shipp returned from Nashville, he explained that it was his duty to move the suspects. He had been warned, he said, that to save the suspects would cost him a defeat in his race to be reelected sheriff. "I replied then that I did not want an office won at the expense of my sworn duty. One of those negroes is innocent. Had he been here he would have been hanged. . . . In that case I was the one that would have been responsible for innocent blood."[69] Moreover, whatever "severe sweating" Shipp inflicted on Johnson during the interrogations, he did not use brutal torture or physical abuse, as happened all too often in the South of this era.

Honorable, up to a point, were the four jurors who voted not guilty before being sent home for the evening. I would single out the architect who wept and begged Taylor to be more certain. But all four, including the architect, wound up voting guilty. Here is lesson number 1. Jurors cannot accurately discharge their function within a racist culture. When racism rises in the throats of the jurors, it chokes them and denies them the ability to act rationally. When the community believes that blacks are savage brutes who violate southern womanhood or kill white men, juries will convict innocent men far too often.

More troubling, the thirst for vengeance is so powerful that innocence seems not to matter as long as someone pays the price. Early reports suggested that the other suspect arrested in the Taylor case was the guilty party because Johnson had an alibi and he did not. But once Miss Taylor identified Johnson, even in a less than certain way, no need existed to pursue another suspect. Miss Taylor believed Ed Johnson was the black man who raped her. That was enough for the jury, even for the four who went home at midnight with doubts about guilt.

It is not just racism that caused southern men to lose the ability to think clearly. Anti-Semitism seemed to work about as well.

THE SUPREME COURT REFUSES TO SAVE LEO FRANK

In 1913, Mary Phagan was thirteen years old, a brunette, with pretty eyes and mouth.[70] She was employed in a pencil factory in Atlanta.[71] On Confederate Memorial Day, she was viciously raped and murdered. "Both eyes were bruised and her cheeks had been slashed," and she had been choked to death by a strip of her underwear and a rope.[72]

The horrible murder led to sensational newspaper coverage and, a few days later, to the arrest of Leo Frank. Frank was the superintendent of the pencil factory where Phagan worked and where her body was found.[73] From the beginning, the case attracted nationwide attention, in part because Frank was a Jew and anti-Semitism was on the rise in the United States. It seemed to be particularly virulent in the South. "In an 1878 campaign speech Senator John T. Morgan of Alabama referred to a candidate as a 'Jew-dog.'"[74] Anti-Semitic demonstrations in Louisiana culminated in an 1893 wrecking of Jewish stores.[75] "That same year Mississippi night riders burned Jewish farmhouses, and a Baltimore minister preached: 'Of all the dirty creatures who have befouled this earth, the Jew is the slimiest.'"[76]

Many factors contributed to American anti-Semitism and to the particularly harsh strain in the South. At least part of the cause was the same as what fanned the flames of racism. Though little noted today, racism was more muted in the years immediately following the ratification of the Civil War amendments than it would become by the end of the nineteenth century. What made racism get worse? The dire straits of the working class in the South during this period made jobs scarce and led to resentment of free blacks who competed for the jobs. The southern economy, built on slavery and plantations, was never as robust as that in the North, and the war wrecked what economy there was. The South attempted to industrialize after the war but the process was painfully slow. Poverty was profound and widespread. Southerners were literally dying of poverty. Atlanta had, in 1905, the twelfth highest death rate among 389 U.S. cities.[77]

When groups of people feel hopeless and abandoned by the larger culture, they sometimes demonize and seek to subjugate an even more powerless group. We may be poor and unemployed, they think, but at least we're not black or Jewish. Moreover, those who view themselves as failures need to blame someone other than themselves, and it is easy to blame groups who are historically viewed with fear and suspicion. "The most distressed people . . . are aggressively hostile to those outside the pale, and fiercely proud of their own community's accomplishments."[78]

Leo Frank was convicted and sentenced to death based wholly on circumstantial evidence offered in a trial that took place, according to Justice Oliver Wendell Holmes, "in the presence of a hostile demonstration and seemingly dangerous crowd, thought by the presiding judge to be ready for violence unless a verdict of guilty was rendered."[79] After the conviction, the defense made a motion for a new trial, claiming that the evidence did not support a conviction and the charged atmosphere precluded a fair trial. The trial judge overruled the motion. This is hardly surprising. Judges rarely overturn a jury verdict. What does surprise are the judge's comments while overruling the motion: "I am not certain of the man's guilt. With all the thought I have put on this case, I am not thoroughly convinced that Frank is guilty or innocent."[80] Yet the judge did not overturn the conviction or the death sentence.

A series of appeals followed, culminating two years later in the U.S. Supreme Court. Despite Holmes's explicit doubt that Frank had received due process, the Supreme Court voted seven to two to deny his final appeal.[81] The reluctance of the Supreme Court in the early twentieth century to reverse the fact-finding of state courts was powerful indeed. Frank now had only one hope left. His lawyers filed a petition seeking executive clemency with Georgia governor John M. Slaton, who was, at that time, "one of the most popular chief executives in the history of Georgia."[82]

> He had entered office with sixteen years of legislative experience behind him, and the esteem of all who knew him. In 1912 he had been elected Governor, "on a tidal wave of popular enthusiasm unprecedented in Georgia's annals." During his two years in office Slaton fulfilled the expectations of those who had elected him . . . by carrying out his duties with integrity and aplomb.[83]

In 1914, he received the largest number of votes in the Democratic primary for the U.S. Senate, but the nominating convention chose another candidate. It was widely believed that he would receive the nomination for the next available Senate seat and win easily.[84]

Slaton's world would come crumbling down because of the Leo Frank case, though he was near the end of his term "and could have withdrawn gracefully from consideration of the case."[85] Slaton not only reviewed the case but also went to great lengths to uncover the truth. He heard arguments from the defense and the prosecution, visited the scene of the crime, and "secluded himself to consider the evidence."[86] The evidence consisted of a voluminous file and, perhaps most importantly, a letter from the trial judge "asking him to rectify the mistake the judge realized he had made in sentencing Frank to death."[87]

Thousands of pleas for the governor to commute Frank's sentence arrived in the mail. But the mail also contained more than one thousand letters "threatening to kill Slaton, and his wife, if he let Frank live."[88] The governor did just that. After telling his wife what he had decided, he said "it may mean my death or worse." She reportedly replied, "I would rather be the widow of a brave and honorable man than the wife of a coward."[89]

The day before Frank was to be hanged, Slaton announced that he was commuting the sentence to life in prison.[90] The pardon was accompanied by a ten-thousand-word explanation of why Slaton thought Frank innocent, an explanation that made plain that he had given the record an "exhaustive review."[91] If he believed Frank innocent, why only a commutation rather than ordering a new trial? Apparently Slaton thought that further investigation would make Frank's innocence even clearer and that would be the best time to grant a full pardon.[92]

Georgians were furious. His political career ruined, Slaton had to declare martial law and call out an entire battalion of state militia to keep from being lynched himself.[93] He then fled the state.[94] Slaton's brave act did Frank little good either. Two months later, a mob of twenty-five men stormed the prison farm, abducted Frank, and hanged him. "Hordes of people made their way to the oak tree" to view Frank's body and take pictures.[95] Those who planned and participated in this lawless act included a "clergyman, two former Superior Court judges, and an ex-sheriff."[96] The *Marietta Journal and Courier* wrote: "We regard the hanging of Leo M. Frank in Cobb County as an act of law abiding citizens."[97]

How can a lynching be "an act of law abiding citizens"? The answer is an elaboration of lesson number 1 from the Johnson case: When a young southern woman was raped or raped and murdered, and men of that era were whipped to a frenzy by anti-Semitism or racism, they would believe the worst about the Jew or the black, and no rational explanation of innocence would persuade. It is as if some contour in their minds prevented them from seeing and perceiving facts as humans otherwise would.

The Supreme Court of the United States refused to free Leo Frank. But had they done so, the end result would almost certainly have been the same. The power of the mob, driven by blind rage and prejudice, was too strong.

Now for lesson number 2 about justice in the early twentieth century. Unlike the fourteenth century, where the English jury's truth was absolute, unlike the court's view in *Bushel's Case* that the truth manifested by the jury verdict was the only truth that mattered, lawyers and judges by 1906 recognized that there is an empirical truth about guilt. It may be beyond our ability to identify, but it is there. And if it is out there, that empirical truth can be used to criticize, and ultimately reject, jury verdicts. The Frank case gives us a true hero, a man who sacrificed his career—he never held elective office after he left the governorship[98]—and put his life and his wife's life at risk, to save an innocent man. John M. Slaton is an inspiration to everyone who believes that the most important value in a criminal justice process is to protect the innocent.

The U.S. Supreme Court believed that Ed Johnson's verdict might have missed the empirical truth about who raped Nevada Taylor. But the Court failed to save his life.

THE REST OF THE ED JOHNSON STORY

The end of the Ed Johnson story is, in part, a story of John Marshall Harlan, a justice on the U.S. Supreme Court from 1877 to 1911. Known as the Great Dissenter, he strongly believed in individual rights against the government and was also staunchly opposed to racism. He believed that the Court should take steps, even at the expense of state sovereignty, to protect individual rights and remedy racism, and he dissented in many major cases where the Court was unwilling to restrain the power of the states. Ironically, his grandson, also named John Marshall Harlan, became the Great Dissenter on the 1960s Warren Court, though he was on the opposite side of the state sovereignty issue from his grandfather, favoring the retention of state sovereignty in some cases even at the expense of individual liberty.

The first John Marshall Harlan was elected county judge on the Know-Nothing ticket, a party that bridged the gap between the Whig party and the Republican party.[99] He served in the Union Army during the Civil War as a lieutenant colonel, became Kentucky attorney general in 1864, and twice campaigned unsuccessfully for governor of Kentucky. When his law partner ran for president in 1876, the Kentucky delegation to the Republican Convention was committed to him as a favorite son candidate. Harlan led the delegation. His well-timed switch of the delegation to Rutherford B. Haynes gave the nomination to Hayes. A year later Hayes appointed Harlan to the Supreme Court.

Johnson's lawyers for the appeal to the Supreme Court, Noah Parden and Emanuel Hewlett, were black men. Parden would later recall visiting the Supreme Court: "Mr. Hewlett and I were the only Negroes present, except for the man handing out towels in the bathroom. He sure seemed surprised when I walked in."[100] After an entire day spent waiting in an anteroom, they were ushered into chambers where Harlan sat, alone, at the end of a long oak table.[101] A tall, burly man—"six feet two inches and well over 260 pounds"[102]—he had a well-deserved reputation for being bombastic and scathing. He "never hesitated to tell lawyers appearing before the Court that they were doing an awful job and that their clients should demand a refund. . . ."[103] He did not even look up when Johnson's lawyers entered the conference room. "There was no friendly welcome to Washington, D.C. There was no handshake or apology for the daylong wait."[104]

John Marshall Harlan was Ed Johnson's last hope. If Harlan could be persuaded to move the Court to grant the appeal, it would automatically also grant a stay of execution. If Harlan turned down Parden and Hewlett, Johnson would hang in three days. Even if the lawyers could persuade Harlan, the chances of him persuading the Court must have seemed remote. After all, the sovereign state of Tennessee had given Johnson a procedurally fair trial, with the assistance of three able lawyers, and without the mob atmosphere that sometimes dominated trials.

Parden emphasized to Harlan the lack of evidence. Even the victim would not swear that Ed Johnson was the guilty man. "Justice Harlan displayed no opinion," Parden wrote in his notes later that day. But it "is good for Mr. Johnson" that Harlan heard their argument. "He is a fair and honorable judge with regards for the Negro people and his opinion is that the Constitution is colorblind."[105]

While the lawyers skirmished in Washington, Ed Johnson waited to die. "Day of Doom Is Very Near," trumpeted one of the newspapers while assuring the readers that the "Negro Is Apparently Indifferent to Fate."[106] The day after the lawyers met with Justice Harlan, a Sunday, "proved to be a busy one for [Johnson] and was no doubt considered full of events momentous for him. All day long he had visitors and in the afternoon religious services were held for him and he was baptized in accordance with the rites of the Baptist church."[107] After the services, the minister asked Johnson

to say something concerning his religious feelings. The prisoner folded his hands before him in an attitude of devotion and said in the low musical voice that figured in his trial:

"I have had a change of heart and I am ready to die. The change came over me all at once and I can't tell how it was. Before the change I hated the people that were against me. I couldn't eat and could only think of the arrest and the trouble I was in. I didn't want to talk or eat and I didn't want to see any one. All at once I said that I was willing to give up my friends and folks and life itself if I had to and then I felt different. I didn't hate the white people any more, my appetite returned and I am proud now to have anybody come to see me."[108]

The next day, the day before Johnson was to hang, Justice Harlan sent a telegram to Sheriff Shipp: "Have allowed appeal to accused . . . Ed Johnson."[109] The effect of Harlan's order was to stay the official execution of Ed Johnson. It was to no avail. I will describe the events of Monday evening by quoting extensively from Tuesday's, March 20, 1906, *Chattanooga Times*. I think it important for the reader to see the tone and description of reporters and editors intimately connected to the events rather than strained though my mind a hundred years later.

The headlines in the *Chattanooga News* proclaimed: "Johnson Hanged On Bridge With Rope From Trolley Car; Body Of Negro Riddled With Bullets By Frenzied Rioters. Mob's Defiance Of Law's Majesty Was Fierce, Deliberate, And Unflinching."[110]

Protesting his innocence to the last and with the words "God bless you all" on his lips, Ed Johnson, the negro convicted of assaulting Miss Nevada Taylor in St. Elmo on the night of Jan. 23 was shot to death on the county bridge last night. The awful penalty was meted out by a small but determined band of men who stated that the courts had been given all the time due them and that they had made up their minds to take the law into their own hands.

Johnson's life was ended just as the court house clock struck 11. At 7 o'clock the negro was resting calmly in his cell happy over an official order from the United States supreme court which gave him an indefinite time to live. At the same hour the city was quiet and there was but little talk or thought of trouble. A half hour later there were rumors that a few men were getting together to lynch the negro, but nobody seemed to take the report seriously. . . .

At 8 o'clock a dozen men, a few with handkerchiefs over the lower part of their faces and the rest undisguised in any manner, walked into the jail office. A few minutes later another half dozen men came. Close upon the heels of these a few more strolled in. In all there were only about twenty-five, but each man seemed to know just what to do and the twenty-five did the work as efficiently as it could have been done by hundreds. . . .

Then began the work of battering the two heavy doors down. Man after man took his turn with the hammer and axe and rivet after rivet was knocked out. Men streaming with perspiration yielded their implements to others as their strength gave out and the work went on steadily. At 10:30 the first of the two doors was torn out, and the workers began on the second. It took only about five minutes to batter and pry the second door open and then the way to the negro was clear.

The systematic manner in which the mob did its work was shown by the fact that when the doors were broken open only a half dozen men entered the corridor. One of these had the key to cell No. 7 the one in which Johnson was confined and he opened the door slowly and carefully and his helpers in the corridor seized the Negro and bound him with a rope which one of them carried and the doomed man was led outside and down the stairs.

As Johnson was brought out of the corridor and to the head of the stairs there was a cheer from the crowd awaiting him. About half of this crowd was made up of idle spectators who had done no work at all. Some of these became wildly excited at sight of the negro and some of them began howling "Kill him now!" The men from the section where the crime was committed, however, had no intention of permitting a shooting in the jail. "To the county bridge," was the command of the leaders. . . .

When the place chosen was reached two men scrambled up the ironwork and pulled the rope, one end of which was around Johnson's neck, over the beam. The negro was then given a chance to talk and he was urged to make a confession. To all questions and demands for a confession he would only say, "I'm ready to die, but I never done it."

Finally it was decided that time was being wasted, and the order to hoist up the negro was given. Eager hands began to pull, but the rope slipped and more time had to be spent in adjusting it. When the hoisting finally began, the now frenzied lynchers could restrain themselves no longer, and a fusillade of shots was turned loose. One of the first bullets cut the rope and the body came tumbling to the bridge floor. Then the frenzied men from the suburban district, every one of whom had a gun or pistol, gathered around and emptied the contents of their weapons into the prostrate negro. When all the firearms had been discharged the Negro was seen to move his head slightly. "He's not dead!" yelled men close to him, and this was followed up with demands for another gun. Then a big, broad-shouldered man, who had done much of the work, slowly refilled the chambers of his revolver. When his weapon was loaded to his satisfaction, he walked up to the Negro, stood directly over the body and fired five shots into it. This ended the work of the lynchers and they left the bridge so rapidly that the idly curious hardly knew they were going.

Dr. Cooper Holtzclaw reached the bridge a few minutes after the lynching. He said the Negro had been shot fifty times, and any one of the shots was sufficient to produce death. The body lay on the bridge for about an hour.[111]

Ed Johnson's last words were "God bless you all—I am innocent."[112] An innocent man was brutally murdered by a mob that simply could not disbelieve "Miss Taylor" when she said she thought Ed Johnson was the rapist. It took the mob over two hours to secure entrance to the interior of the jail and during that time no man raised a hand in defense of Ed Johnson. He could hear every sound as they battered down the door and approached his cell.

Spring was struggling to make an appearance in Chattanooga, Tennessee, on Sunday, March 25, 1906, six days after Ed Johnson was murdered. It was overcast but the temperature reached a high of sixty-three degrees.[113] Dr. Howard E. Jones, of the white First Baptist Church of Chattanooga, delivered a sermon on Chattanooga's soul.

> "Whatsoever a man soweth, that shall he also reap."
>
> . . . [F]or two hours, [the mob] toiled at the steel bolts which were more loyal to Chattanooga's interest than all of her citizenship. But where are the police and where are the thousands who should have and could have defended us against an unspeakable disgrace?
>
> And so the mob marches [to] a gallows . . . prepared with rope [stretched] within the precincts of the jail. They are not in pursuit of justice, but lawless revenge. Their business is to brutalize a community. Let the curtain fall upon the rest of that unspeakable scene.
>
> The worst elements among the white men of this community took over the reins of government. Was this disgrace ever rebuked? Has any arrest of those men who unsheathed their keen blades and struck deadly blows at the very heart of our civilization ever been effected? Does anyone here know of any attempt? . . .
>
> Ah, no. "Whatsoever a man soweth that shall he also reap."
>
> We had but sown the wind, and were yet to reap the whirlwind. We had cast pearls before the swine, who were presently to trample them in the mire and turn and rend us. We had given the sacred and holy trust of law to dogs, who, despising the holy thing we had compromised, would presently be fixing their vicious fangs in the throat of our civilization. . . .
>
> But let me speak plainly to the man who sees no more in the tragedy on the bridge than that Ed Johnson got what he ought to have had. Admit it, but how about the community? Has it gotten what it ought to have had? I maintain that that mob struck more terrible blows at the heart of our civilization than it inflicted upon Ed Johnson. The beam in our eye has prevented us from seeing this. . . .

Think of the number of people who today only know us as a city where fifty hoodlums can terrify us into passive submission to lawless barbarism. . . .

"Whatsoever a man or a community soweth, that shall he also reap."

Lawlessness begets lawlessness. It always has and always will. Sow an act of lawlessness and you will get a harvest of lawless conditions. If this is not true, civilization is a farce, and anarchy is the best goal to strive for. . . .

I resent the crime on the bridge because of my unspeakable indignation against the crime at St. Elmo. To give over our dealing with this atrocity to lawless procedure means that over and over again, not only the innocent man hangs, but the guilty man remains free, as a threat to the sanctity of our homes. Tell me not, with the pages of history open before me, that a mob ever helps civilization. . . .[114]

Four days after Dr. Jones bravely gave this sermon, his house was set on fire.[115] No arrests were ever made in the arson case. No arrests were made for the murder of Ed Johnson.

CHAPTER SEVEN

TRUTH FROM PROCEDURE:

THE SUPREME COURT TRIES

A NEW TACK

> *Viciousness is not a trait in Chattanooga. Now and then the pas-*
> *sions and prejudices of men predominate and blood-bad temper*
> *claims victory over judgment.*
>
> —*CHATTANOOGA TIMES*, TWO DAYS AFTER ED JOHNSON
> WAS MURDERED

About a year after Ed Johnson was murdered, Nevada Taylor moved with her father to her birthplace in Findlay, Ohio. She died two months later, at the age of twenty-three. News accounts attributed her death to "nervous prostration incidental to the crime committed under the very shadow of the historic Lookout Mountain."[1] One wonders about the effect on her of Ed Johnson's brutal lynching.

In the last chapter, we saw two horrific failures of state criminal processes. This chapter describes the Court's fumbling, tentative—and largely unsuccessful—attempts to avoid future failures in state criminal courts. I begin with the Court's reaction to the failure that culminated in Ed Johnson's lynching.

AFTERMATH: THE SUPREME COURT BEGINS TO INTERVENE IN STATE CRIMINAL JUSTICE

We do not know how Justice Harlan persuaded the Court to agree to hear Ed Johnson's case. It had the potential to be a momentous case. At the time, the Court had never reversed a state criminal conviction because of the unfairness of the trial. The Chattanooga mob made it impossible for the Johnson case to be the first. The Court was naturally outraged that a lynch mob had denied the justices a chance to review Johnson's trial. The *New York Times* carried a story about the Court's reaction, a story that the *Chattanooga Times* also ran. The story begins, "The open defiance of the supreme court of the United States of the mob that lynched the Negro, Ed Johnson, last night has no parallel in the history of the court," and continues:

> The event has shocked the members of the court beyond anything that has ever happened in their experience, on the bench. They have met by twos and threes today and discussed the matter, and the course to be taken to vindicate the power and authority of the court. No justice can say what will be done. All, however, agree in saying that the sanctity of the supreme court shall be upheld if the power resides in the court and the government to accomplish such a vindication of the majesty of the law.[2]

The *Times* story quoted an unnamed justice of the Supreme Court about the failures of the Johnson trial:

> "The fact was," said one of the members of the supreme court tonight, "that Johnson was tried by a little better than mob law before the state court. . . . There was abundant proof that there was intimidation of witnesses and counsel and the reason why the court did not allow an appeal or a plea in abatement was the fear that if any such consideration was shown, the mob would lynch the prisoner. There was reason to believe that the man was innocent. Some of the leading white people of the place gave money for his defense. But be that as it may, whether guilty of innocent, he had the right to a fair trial, and the mandate of the supreme court has for the first time in the history of the county been openly defied by a community."[3]

Justice Oliver Wendell Holmes told reporters, "In all likelihood, this was a case of an innocent man improperly branded a guilty brute and condemned to die from the start."[4] President Theodore Roosevelt said the lynching was "contemptuous of the Court."[5]

Though the lynching was condemned by some in the white establishment in Chattanooga, Sheriff Shipp was reelected in a landslide eight days after Johnson's murder.[6] But he would not completely evade the responsibility for allowing the lynching. Two months later, the Supreme Court of the United States did something it had never done before and has never done since: It held a criminal trial. To be sure, the Court did not sit in a room while witnesses testified. Instead, it authorized a clerk to record evidence from thirty-one government witnesses, testimony that the Court would evaluate to decide whether the sheriff and twenty-five others were guilty of contempt of court for violating the stay of execution.[7]

The case against Shipp could be proved on one simple fact. He knew of the danger of a lynch mob and had previously moved Johnson to protect him. After receiving the telegram from Justice Harlan announcing the stay of execution, Sheriff Shipp not only left Johnson in the Chattanooga jail but also left only a single night jailer to guard the jail. The sheriff did not come to the aid of the jailer "for an hour or more after the mob" began its attack on the jail.[8]

Openly defiant in the face of the contempt charge, Shipp put the blame for the lynching squarely on the Supreme Court:

> The Supreme Court of the United States was responsible for this lynching. I had given that Negro every protection that I could. For fourteen days I had guarded and protected him myself. The authorities had urged me to use one of two military companies in doing so but I told them I didn't need them. . . .
>
> In my opinion the act of the Supreme Court of the United States in not allowing the case to remain in our courts was the most unfortunate thing in the history of Tennessee. I was determined the case should be put in the hands of the law as it was. The jury that tried the Negro Johnson was as good as ever sat in a jury box.
>
> The people of Hamilton county were willing to let the law take its course until it became known that the case would not probably be disposed of for four or five years by the supreme court of the United States. The people would not submit to this and I do not wonder at it.[9]

Shipp's legal defense at trial was that he was set upon by members of the mob and held prisoner while the lynching was done.[10] The cross-examination of Shipp was devastating. First, he conveniently claimed that he could not recognize any of the men who took two hours to batter their way into the jail. Second, he made no effort to obtain help.

> Q. You could have turned, without anybody interfering with you, and gone about three blocks to the police station and got the police?
> A. Yes sir; I could have done that.
> Q. But you did not?
> A. It did not occur to me to do that.[11]

Nor did he resist the mob. After conceding that he was sworn to protect the prisoner, he testified, "I made no effort except that I remonstrated with the mob."[12]

> Q. You used no force?
> A. No, sir.
> Q. You did not pull your gun?
> A. I had no adequate force, and knew that the pulling of a gun would be useless.
> Q. You were sheriff of the county?
> A. Yes, sir.
> Q. And you did not pull your gun?
> A. No.
> Q. You had strength enough to have pulled the trigger, I suppose?
> A. Oh, I guess I could have pulled the trigger.
> Q. You made no effort at all?
> A. No, sir. . . .
> Q. You did not draw your pistol; you did not endeavor to use any force whatever to protect that prisoner? Is that not a fact?
> A. I did not.[13]

When the Court reviewed the evidence, three years after Johnson's lynching, it found Shipp, his jailer, and four members of the lynch mob guilty of contempt of court.[14] They served short sentences in the federal jail in the District of Columbia.[15] When Shipp completed his sentence, he arrived "home to a hero's welcome. 10,000 Chattanooga residents greet Shipp at Terminal Station."[16] After his term as sheriff was over, he spent much of his time "promoting the history of the Confederacy. He was frequently seen wearing his old gray uniform."[17] Sixteen years later, at the age of seventy-eight, Shipp died and was buried "in Forest Hills Cemetery, the same cemetery in which Nevada Taylor was raped."[18]

Sheriff Shipp claimed it was his duty to protect Ed Johnson from the first lynch mob that almost destroyed the jail. If we take him at his word, it appears that the existence of a guilty verdict changed the moral calculation for Shipp. Moreover, it is probably difficult to exaggerate the feeling in the former Confederacy that federal courts had no business interfering with local justice. Indeed, Judge McReynolds and the governor of Tennessee echoed Shipp's sentiments when commenting on the lynching.[19]

THE SUPREME COURT FINALLY SAVES INNOCENT DEFENDANTS

The U.S. Supreme Court, in the early twentieth century, was willing to review a southern case where it appeared an innocent man had been found guilty of a capital crime. When its order to keep Johnson safe provoked a mini-rebellion, the Court acted to save its dignity and to send a message that it was, after all, the Supreme Court. The Court refused, however, to come to the aid of Leo Frank seven years later. It took even more obvious examples of system failures before the Court began, ever so tentatively, to impose controls on southern criminal justice.

Lesson number 1 from the last chapter is that jurors cannot "see" the truth when their minds are warped by prejudice. The lesson from this section will be that a racist system often did not present the truth for the jury to hear. But lesson number 2 from the last chapter holds here as well: Honest men of that time knew that there was an empirical truth about guilt, and if the jury presentation was sufficiently warped, then the defendants deserved a new trial.

If Johnson was denied justice by a white southern jury, there was no chance at all for the nine black defendants in the Scottsboro, Alabama rape case. Accused of raping two white women on a train passing through Alabama, the young men did not know why they had been arrested until the guards lined them up at the jail.

One of the women [who was raped], Victoria Price, pointed to six of them. When the other didn't say a word, a guard said that "If those six had Miss Price, it stands to reason that the others had Miss Bates." The boys protested, insisting they hadn't touched the women, hadn't even seen them while on the train. Clarence Norris called the women liars. One of the guards struck him with his bayonet, cutting to the bone the hand that Norris put up to shield his face. "Nigger," the guard hollered, "you know damn well how to talk about white women."[20]

Twelve days later, the nine defendants were tried in an Alabama court. The defendants were given no opportunity to employ counsel, and the Supreme Court would later characterize the trial court's slipshod "appointment" of counsel as "casual" and "little more than an expansive gesture, imposing no substantial or definite obligation upon any one."[21] Before a packed courtroom, without lawyers committed to their defense, the defendants heard Bates and Price accuse them of repeated rapes.

"There were six to me," Price told the jury in the first trial, "and three to her, and three of hers got away. It took three of them to hold me. One was holding my legs and the other had a knife to my throat while the other one ravished me. It took three of those negroes to hold me. It took two to hold me while one had intercourse. . . ." In what seemed like two or three hours, each of them was raped six times. They begged the Negroes to quit but the men ignored them, and even after they finished they stayed in the [train] car with them, "telling us they were going to take us north and make us their women or kill us."[22]

The defendants denied guilt. They denied touching the women. But what chance did they have? The belief structure was against them. Historian James Goodman writes,

Writers and editors all over the region agreed that it was the most atrocious crime ever recorded in that part of the country, perhaps in the whole United States, "a wholesale debauching of society . . . so horrible in its details that all the facts could never be printed," a "heinous and unspeakable crime" that "savored of the jungle, the way back dark ages of meanest African corruption." . . . Blacks were savages, more savage, many argued (with scientific theories to support them), than they had been as slaves. Savages with an irrepressible sex drive and an appetite for white women. They were born rapists, rapists by instinct; given the chance, they struck. Two white women swore that they had been raped. . . . Most of the boys denied it. There was no question in anyone's mind about whom to believe.[23]

Not much had changed in the South in the twenty-six years since Miss Taylor was raped. But one thing was different. In the Scottsboro case, the authorities protected the defendants throughout the judicial process, and this time the Court had a chance to correct an injustice.

The Supreme Court granted leave to hear the case in *Powell v. Alabama*,[24] and the defendants raised three grounds for reversing their convictions. They claimed that due process prohibited the state from "systematically exclud[ing]" blacks from the jury and that they had been denied a "fair, impartial, and deliberate trial."[25] The Court did not reach the merits of either of these claims, instead holding that the ad hoc provision of lawyers for the defendants did not meet Sixth Amendment standards.

The reasons why the Court went with a procedural solution to the foundational problem of racism cannot, of course, be known. Indeed, it is not clear that the Court could have achieved foundational changes in the southern justice systems. Three years later, one of the Scottsboro cases returned to the Court in *Norris v. Alabama*,[26] and the Court ruled unanimously that the defendant's equal protection rights were violated because of the exclusion of blacks from the jury pool. Once again, a death sentence imposed on a Scottsboro defendant was vacated.

But even the foundational right to have blacks included in jury pools turned out, in the racist South, not to mean very much. Some states drew jurors from voting lists, and blacks were effectively disenfranchised in the Deep South.[27] In other states, the law at the time permitted almost unlimited discretion to choose from the jury pool. If any blacks made it to the jury pool, the prosecutor could use peremptory challenges to remove them. In one of the Scottsboro retrials, twelve blacks were part of the pool of one hundred potential jurors. Seven requested to be excused and the other five were struck by challenges.[28] That Scottsboro defendant was again tried by an all-white jury.

As for why the Court in *Powell* did not grant the due process claim that the trial was unfair, here are two speculations. First, evidence to the contrary in the Johnson and Frank cases notwithstanding, the Court could have believed that over the general run of cases, counsel would help avoid unjust convictions. A second reason could have been fear of the consequences of having federal courts supervise the day-to-day operation of state criminal trials. After all, the Court had seen what happened when they ordered the Tennessee authorities to keep Ed Johnson safe while the Court reviewed his case. As Michael Klarman has observed, "Several southern newspapers warned in connection with Scottsboro that if outsiders continued to assail Alabama after juries had returned guilty verdicts, then there would be little incentive to resist a lynching on future occasions."[29]

Given this hostile environment, the Supreme Court could not be blamed for deciding *Powell* on the ground that demanded the least from state criminal justice. The justices were entitled to hope that good lawyers would make a difference in some, perhaps many, cases. It would not matter to five of the Scottsboro defendants. After the Supreme Court reversed the convictions, five were eventually convicted in a way that withstood appellate review. In all these cases, the defendants "enjoyed outstanding legal representation in their retrials, yet it made absolutely no difference to the outcomes."[30] Even when Bates recanted and testified, in a later trial, that none of the defendants ever touched either her or Price, the jury convicted. With the southern belief structure about white women and black men firmly in place, the jury chose to believe Price and not Bates.

The Scottsboro defendants, in the end, received formal due process—the right to have a trial with competent counsel zealously representing them—even as substantive justice eluded them. That procedural due process victory gave five of them a lot of heartache and long prison sentences. But it saved all nine from the gallows.

The *Powell* Court attempted to send a message to state courts: There is an empirical fact in the universe about whether a defendant is guilty. And the U.S. Supreme Court is looking over your shoulder. If state trials obviously fail to provide a defendant with a fair chance at justice, as in the cases of Ed Johnson, Leo Frank, and the Scottsboro defendants, the state courts should expect federal intervention. It was a brave attempt on the Court's part. But why did the Court not do more in the early part of the twentieth century?

The Court had plenty of evidence that state justice systems were failing in the most obvious ways. The cases presented in this chapter and the last are literally the tip of the iceberg. It was well known throughout the country that lawless mobs lynched almost at will. By some accounts, 4,708 lynchings took place in the United States from 1882 to 1944.[31] That is almost one hundred per year. No judge in the country could have been blissfully unaware of the epidemic of lynching. One reason not to interfere very much with state trials is that the Court feared it might make matters worse if it insisted on greater federal control. But at a deeper level, the Court was also respectful of state sovereignty.

THE STATE SOVEREIGNTY PROBLEM

By the 1930s, state sovereignty had arrived at a sad, sordid place. But it was not always just an excuse for racist trials and lynchings. The tension between federalists, who favor a strong central government, and Anti-Federalists, who prefer more power be retained by the states, has been with us since before the Framing of the Constitution. During the period after the Revolutionary War, many farsighted men thought that the Articles of Confederation did not create a sufficiently strong central government. But the very prospect of that kind of government brought shuddering back the horrid memories of Parliament and King George III. Thus was born the natural enmity between the Federalists, who wanted more government, and the Anti-Federalists, who wanted less.

We know how the first chapter of that story ended. Sent to Philadelphia to revise the Articles of Confederation that loosely bound the states, the Framers staged their own mini-revolution and presented the states with a charter for a brand-new form of government. And while we tend to gloss over this period in our history, it was far from certain that the states would accept what the Framers had wrought. The drafting convention reported out the Constitution on September 17, 1787. The debate in the Congress of the Confederation lasted three bitter days, after which the document was sent to the states without a recommendation.

The first five states were easy. Delaware unanimously ratified on December 7, 1787, and by January 9, 1788, four others had ratified: Pennsylvania, New Jersey, Georgia, and Delaware. Only nine states had to ratify before the Constitution became effective, but three states were considered critical to the success of the fledgling government because of their size and wealth—New York, Virginia, and Massachusetts. As of January 1788, none of the critical three had yet ratified, and the prospects in each were uncertain. The debate in those conventions was tumultuous. The Anti-Federalists eyed the proposed central government as a potential bully or, worse, as a tyrant. We read in chapter 5 Patrick Henry's fiery speech before the Virginia ratifying convention, in which he concluded, "As this government stands, I despise and abhor it."[32]

Ultimately, of course, all three approved the Constitution, influenced to some extent by Madison's promise to provide a bill of rights. Even with the promise of a bill of rights, the vote in Virginia was close, eighty-nine to seventy-nine, and even closer in New York, thirty to twenty-seven. Changing two votes would have meant defeat in New York.

When the Bill of Rights was added, the states felt more comfortable. They viewed the Bill of Rights as a wall between themselves and the central government. It guarantees free expression, forbids a national religion, guarantees a criminal process that is difficult to manipulate, and, in the Ninth and Tenth Amendments, specifically reserves rights and powers to the people and the states. The potential tyrant was hobbled. As we saw in chapter 5, John Marshall's Supreme Court comprehended that the Bill of Rights was meant to be a severe limitation on the powers of the central government, a formidable wall between the citizens and the government. The Court interpreted these provisions to require federal prosecutors to walk through a narrow gate in the wall, a gate hedged with a series of requirements designed to make convictions more difficult to obtain. But the Court was clear that these restrictions do not apply to the states.[33] States thus remained sovereign in the criminal justice context, free to conduct their affairs in most matters as if the federal government did not exist.

But the Bill of Rights could not solve the fundamental political divide between Federalists and Anti-Federalists. Washington and

Adams were Federalists, Jefferson an Anti-Federalist, Madison a Federalist. And so on. Embedded in the divide was the cancer of slavery. The slave states feared a strong federal government because they feared legislation banning slavery. But the argument was made at the abstract level of state sovereignty. Indeed, the secession of the southern states was justified precisely on state sovereignty grounds—states were autonomous entities that could choose to be part of the Union, or not.

When the ordeal of civil war finally ended, most Americans realized that too much state sovereignty is just as hazardous as too little. Once viewed as responsive and protective of rights, the states were now viewed by many with suspicion, particularly in their treatment of the freed slaves. The Fourteenth Amendment arrived.[34] Ratified three years after the end of the Civil War, it was designed to deprive states of power in certain situations as a way of protecting freed slaves, Union loyalists, and other marginal groups in the former Confederacy. It creates U.S. citizenship and state citizenship for every person born in the United States. It then creates three sets of rights for those citizens: the right to the "privileges or immunities of citizens of the United States"; the right not to have the state deprive any person of "life, liberty, or property, without due process of law"; and the right to the "equal protection of the laws."

While these are glorious phrases, they are far from self-defining. The Supreme Court's first attempt to interpret the Fourteenth Amendment produced a narrow ruling that favored state sovereignty. Without troubling the reader with the issue in the 1873 case, which had nothing to do with criminal law, the general dispute was how much power the Fourteenth Amendment took away from states.[35] By a five-to-four margin, the Court held that the Fourteenth Amendment protected only the most fundamental of rights.

Despite this narrow ruling, litigants kept asking the Court to find various activities protected by the Fourteenth Amendment. For the most part, these suits were civil, involving a dizzying array of challenges to state laws. One plaintiff sued to compel the "railroads in Texas to cut the Johnson grass off from their rights of way before it goes to seed," while a barber in Minnesota challenged the state law determination that "running a barber shop" is "the practice of a handicraft for gain."[36] Defendants lost 90 percent of these cases from 1868 to 1911 as the Court sought to stem the tide of due process suits.[37] Few criminal cases were argued under the Fourteenth Amendment, but defendants fared no better than civil plaintiffs. Defendants lost all but one case, and that state law was clearly in violation of the letter and spirit of the Fourteenth Amendment.[38]

Ironically, the country's decision to expand federally protected rights in the Fourteenth Amendment led the Court to adopt a narrow interpretation of due process. After the Court had interpreted the Fourteenth Amendment for half a century, the net effect of the amendment was to provide pretty minimal rights. The framers of the amendment might not have been happy with the Court's interpretation. But the Court's action was evidence of the continuing power of state sovereignty.

There was at least one flaw in the process that gave narrow interpretations to the Fourteenth Amendment. What was the Court to do with cases like Scottsboro, *Frank,* and *Johnson?* Something had to be done. It was all well and good to let Texas decide when and where to cut grass off the rights of way and to let Minnesota decide the status of the job of barbering. But it would not do to let states provide the kind of justice we saw in these cases.

At first, the Court tried a common-law approach, by which I mean the Court sought to reach the right outcome in individual cases, developing over time a fairness doctrine on a case-by-case basis. This approach eschews rules in favor of giving judges a principle that they can apply in their discretion. The Court plainly hoped to shape the rights necessary to achieve basic fairness without burdening the states with too much federal oversight. In the Scottsboro case, for example, the Supreme Court noted the extremely difficult conditions faced by the nine young, black defendants in Alabama, their "ignorance and illiteracy . . . their youth, the circumstances of public hostility, the imprisonment and the close surveillance of the defendants by the military forces, . . . and above all that they stood in deadly peril of their lives. . . ."[39]

In that situation, the Court held that "the failure of the trial court to make an effective appointment of counsel . . . was a denial of due process."[40] But the Court, in the best common-law, case-by-case tradition, was careful to note that it was not embracing any broader rule: "Whether this would be so in other criminal prosecutions, or under other circumstances, we need not determine. All that it is necessary now to decide, as we do decide," is that the trial court's failure in the case before the Court violated due process.[41]

Phrased that way, the parameters of the right to counsel were left open. Would it apply, for example, in *Betts v. Brady* to a "a man forty-three years old, of ordinary intelligence, and ability to take care of his own interests" when the issue for trial was whether his alibi was to be believed?[42] The answer, the Court provided ten years after *Powell*, was no. The defendant asked the Court to create a rule that an indigent defendant, at least in felony cases, had a right to counsel without having to demonstrate that he was uneducated or handicapped in representing himself in some way. It would have made life simpler for judges, and the Court would get there twenty-one years later, but in 1942 the Court stuck to the idea that the defendant had to show some kind of "special circumstance" (as it later became known) before Fourteenth Amendment due process would require the state to provide him a lawyer. That common-law road quickly became narrow and treacherous for defendants.

A somewhat more promising common law developed from *Brown v. Mississippi*,[43] where a deputy sheriff in 1932 tortured confessions from three black men. The common-law principle that evolved from *Brown* was that the state could not use at trial a confession that was involuntary. While that question was easily resolved against the state in *Brown*, it is a fact-specific and difficult question in most cases. Is a confession involuntary when taken after two interrogations totaling over forty hours? Does it matter that the suspect knew that his confederate had blamed him for the crime?

More fundamentally, what does it mean to say that a confession is involuntary in the first place? When I open my mouth and choose to say certain words over other words, in what sense is that involuntary? If you take my hand and, being stronger than I, use my hand to hit someone, that is involuntary. But when I say to the victim, "I'm glad he made me hit you," that is a voluntary choice on my part. As John Henry Wigmore archly noted in his foundational *Treatise on Evidence:* "As between the rack and a false confession, the latter would usually be considered the less disagreeable; but it is nonetheless voluntarily chosen."[44]

As potentially incoherent as the philosophical concept of voluntariness may be, and as malleable a legal standard as it may yield, in the hands of the Supreme Court the involuntariness test produced a set of outcomes that are more or less satisfying. In *Lisenba v. California*,[45] a confession was held voluntary because the accused had withstood thirty hours of questioning and confessed only after his accomplice blamed him for the murder. Compare that case with *Ashcraft v. Tennessee*,[46] holding that a confession is involuntary if taken after thirty-six hours of interrogation when no external cause of the confession could be shown.

The Court elaborated the voluntariness doctrine over the next two decades. A confession is not involuntary merely because the suspect was not provided a lawyer, the Court held, but a confession *is* involuntary when made after the police threaten the suspect with loss of custody of her children.[47] A confession is involuntary if, through no fault of the police, a drug was administered that functioned like a truth serum.[48] A confession of a black man in Alabama is involuntary if he was insane and incompetent when he confessed after an eight- or nine-hour sustained interrogation in a small room where he was surrounded by white law enforcement officials, without friends or legal counsel present.[49]

Whatever the conceptual defects of the voluntariness test, the U.S. Supreme Court applied it to protect racial minorities and the powerless. The problem, as the Warren Court realized in the 1960s, was that lower courts were not so protective of the poor and powerless. For example, the case involving thirty-six hours of relentless interrogation, the case where the police threatened to take the suspect's children away from her, and the "truth serum" case had all resulted in convictions that were affirmed on appeal in state courts. So while the Supreme Court's common law might have been satisfactory if applied with the same rigor that the Court used, the state courts tended to exploit its vagueness to affirm convictions.

And police interrogation was just one manifestation of a deeper justice problem that the Warren Court perceived as the 1950s turned into the 1960s: a fundamental inequality between the rich and the poor when it came to the investigation and prosecution of crime. About half the states did not require the suppression of evidence seized in violation of a citizen's right against unreasonable searches. Police in those states were thus free to conduct suspicionless stops and searches of whomever they pleased. That these suspicion-less stops often targeted blacks cannot be doubted. If police got lucky and found evidence of a crime or contraband, they could arrest the suspect, and the fruits of their illegal search would be admissible to convict. If the police were not lucky, the target of this harassment would be free to go, his perception of the unfairness of the criminal justice system and of his lowly status in that system etched in his memory.

The Warren Court set out to do what it could to remedy this structural inequality as it affected the investigation and prosecution of crime. It is that story to which we turn now.

THE WARREN COURT OF 1961–68

It is traditional to "name" Supreme Courts for their chief justice. One might wonder what is the special significance of the chief justice. He has administrative responsibilities that the associate justices do not have, to be sure, but how does he shape the direction of the Court more than any other justice? To the extent a chief justice has the eloquence or political skill to change votes, the answer is obvious.

But there is another, more subtle and more powerful, force that the chief justice wields. If he can persuade a majority of his colleagues to vote his way, he has the power to assign the opinion to a member in the majority, including, of course, himself. Before the reader dismisses that as ministerial, remember that for centuries we have recognized the power of the pen in arenas as diverse as journalism, politics, and law. Moreover, once John Marshall began the practice of having the majority speak for the Court, the way in which it speaks for the Court is critical.

A good example is *Miranda v. Arizona*.[50] Chief Justice Warren assigned the opinion for the five-justice majority to himself. Had he assigned it to Justice Douglas, well known for short and opaque opinions, the evolution of the *Miranda* rule of warnings and waiver might have been very different. Indeed, one can imagine Douglas writing an opinion reversing the convictions and simply holding that the prosecution has the burden of proving that the defendant knew of his Fifth Amendment right not to answer questions, without specifying the warnings that Warren carefully included.

Thus, it was important, if not critical, to the Warren Court criminal procedure revolution that President Eisenhower named Earl Warren to be chief justice in 1953. Given recent experience with confirmation hearings for federal judges, and particularly Supreme Court justices, it may surprise the reader to know that Eisenhower appointed Warren as a recess appointment when Congress was not in session. When Congress returned, Warren was confirmed ninety-six to zero, and this despite Warren's major role, as California's attorney general, in orchestrating the internment of tens of thousands of Japanese citizens for the duration of the Second World War. He later wrote, "I have since deeply regretted the removal order and my own testimony advocating it, because it was not in keeping with our American concept of freedom and the rights of citizens. Whenever I thought of the innocent little children who were torn from home, school friends and congenial surroundings, I was conscience-stricken."[51] It is quite a comment on the times that his role in internment earned him not a single negative vote or abstention in the Senate.[52]

Warren was a Republican who had over two decades of experience as a prosecutor and attorney general. That record, plus his support for Japanese internment, probably suggested to Eisenhower that he was far from liberal. In any event, like the first John Marshall Harlan, Warren was appointed as political payback. While governor of California, he led the California delegation to the 1951 presidential convention and was instrumental in Eisenhower's first ballot victory over Taft; at some point Eisenhower promised Warren that he would get the first vacancy on the U.S. Supreme Court.[53] When Chief Justice Vinson died unexpectedly, Eisenhower initially reneged, claiming the chief justice's seat was not part of the bargain.[54] Here we can see recognition of the power of the chief justice.

But Warren was not going to give up without a fight. According to Goodwin Knight, lieutenant governor of California under Warren, "Warren gave the president an ultimatum: appoint him to the first vacancy, as promised, or he would resign as governor and stomp the nation, denouncing the president as a liar."[55] Eisenhower relented.

Shortly after joining the Court, Warren accomplished what many thought was impossible: he delivered a unanimous Court in holding that the Constitution did not permit "separate but equal" schools. It was widely assumed that at least two justices would dissent. But there were no dissents and no concurring opinions. While it is easy for us to see the correctness and justice of *Brown v. Board of Education,* it was a brave act at the time, one that created many difficulties for Eisenhower.[56]

Eisenhower's second appointment to the Court was William Brennan, a Democrat and a surprising choice. Part of Brennan's attraction was that he was Catholic but, more importantly, he was one of Judge Arthur Vanderbilt's protégés, and Vanderbilt had helped deliver New Jersey for Eisenhower in 1952. Brennan and Warren became a critical part of several five-justice majorities. According to legend, Eisenhower was asked if he made any mistakes while president, and he responded, "Yes, two, and they are both sitting on the Supreme Court."[57] The reference was understood to be Warren and Brennan.

By 1962, the Warren Court was in place. In addition to Warren and Brennan, it included William O. Douglas and Hugo Black, two liberal "New Dealers" appointed by Franklin Roosevelt; and two Kennedy appointees: Byron White and Arthur Goldberg. Goldberg was a solid fifth vote for the coming criminal procedure revolution. When he was replaced, in 1965, by Abe Fortas, the vote stayed with the Warren bloc. White was harder to classify, sometimes voting with the Warren bloc on criminal justice cases but often voting with the dissenters. Tom Clark, appointed by Truman, was a sometimes-member of the Warren bloc. Of Clark, Truman said, "It isn't so much that he's a *bad* man. It's just that he's such a dumb son of a bitch. He's about the dumbest man I think I've ever run across."[58] When Clark retired in 1967, President Johnson nominated Thurgood Marshall, who became a reliable member of the Warren bloc.

The dissenters were led by John Marshall Harlan, grandson of the man who heard Ed Johnson's petition. Harlan was an Eisenhower appointment who worked out as the president had hoped. Like his grandfather, he was the great dissenter of his time[59] but in the opposite "direction," arguing at almost every turn for less federal involvement in state criminal justice matters. Another Eisenhower appointment, Potter Stewart, was like White, often a swing vote, sometimes joining Warren and sometimes not.

Those nine men constituted the Warren Court, shifting majorities of which would seek nothing short of a revolution in federal regulation of state criminal processes in the 1960s. It was, by Supreme Court standards, a brief but spectacular run. As the rest of the chapter will detail, its gains were mostly cosmetic or formal, without much substance. In some ways at least, defendants were more poorly situated in 1969 when the Warren Court ended than they were in 1960. To be sure, as Craig Bradley has demonstrated, the failure of the Court's doctrine was largely because the Supreme Court is the wrong entity to devise a code of criminal procedure.[60] That job belongs to the legislative bodies. Pizzi agrees, noting that the Supreme Court "has arrogated to itself an institutional role for which it was not designed and for which it is poorly equipped."[61] The Court made critical missteps along the way, errors that left innocent defendants at risk.

THE WARREN COURT REWRITES THE CRIMINAL PROCEDURE "RULEBOOK"

One difficulty in writing history is that it is impossible to tell all parts of the story. Sometimes when scholars write about one aspect of a Court's work, its free speech cases or its search and seizure cases, there is a tendency to forget that the Court was doing many things at once. The Warren Court worked to effect changes that it thought good for America in four categories of cases. The landmark case of *Brown v. Board of Education* struck a blow for racial equality, followed a decade later by the Court affirming long-overdue federal legislation guaranteeing civil rights and voting rights.[62] That the federal courts were ultimately unable to achieve desegregated schools in many parts of the country takes nothing away from the noble attempt to level the playing field.

The 1950s also saw the Cold War, the red scare, and McCarthyism. The Court reviewed various legislative acts, state and federal, designed to fight Communism. The Warren Court does not, in my judgment, get enough credit for its delicate handling of these issues. It could have turned tail and run, simply affirming the right of the legislatures to do what they must to keep us safe from Communism. Or it could have held that the First Amendment protects those who have joined the Communist Party.

The Court avoided both extremes. In a series of cases, the Court upheld the right of Congress to punish those who plotted to harm the country but hedged those opinions with procedural requirements that made successful prosecutions very difficult.[63] Thus, the Court managed to navigate dangerous shoals in American politics in a way reminiscent of John Marshall in the Burr cases.

The third area of concern for the Warren Court was that of participation in democracy and other aspects of American life. In this category are the "one man, one vote" cases that forced legislatures to reapportion to meet changing population growth. Here, too, we can put the cases where the Court subsequently struggled to understand equal protection of the law outside the area of race—concerning sex, age, sexual orientation, national origin, and religious preference—as well as the cases involving free association, freedom of religion, and freedom from government-imposed religion.

The fourth area of concern was the investigation and prosecution of crime. The Court saw its job here as simply a piece of what it was doing in the other areas—seeking a balance between the legitimate needs of governments and the need for equal treatment of those who had been relegated for whatever reason, to second class citizenship. The leveling of the playing field in the interrogation room was no different from the leveling of the playing field for blacks, women, gays, city voters, and Communists.

In the criminal justice context, the Court had grown increasingly troubled by the cavalier attitude of state officials toward suspects and defendants. Underlying these concerns was a belief that state officials were mistreating those with less power—the poor and racial minorities. For almost one hundred years, the Court had lightly regulated state criminal procedures under the Fourteenth Amendment, asking whether they squared with "fundamental principles of liberty and justice which lie at the base of all our civil and political institutions."[64]

As long as fundamental fairness was the Court's polestar, it did not require much in the way of regulation of state justice systems. One fundamental principle of liberty and justice is that defendants should be tried in a way that does not unduly threaten the conviction of the innocent.[65] This explains why the Court got involved in the cases of Ed Johnson and the Scottsboro defendants and why the

Court created a voluntariness doctrine to attempt to regulate police interrogation.

But was it fundamentally unfair, in the sense of risking a false conviction, to permit the states to use evidence seized in searches that would be unconstitutional under the Fourth Amendment? The answer is no, as *Wolf v. Colorado* held in 1949.[66] But if the goal is to have the police give more respect to the Fourth Amendment rights of racial minorities and the poor, the only weapon the Court had in its arsenal was to require states to follow the Fourth Amendment and exclude evidence seized in violation of that Amendment. If police knew that any evidence they found might be inadmissible, perhaps police would be less likely to conduct harassing, suspicionless stops. And so the Warren Court gave us *Mapp v. Ohio*,[67] overruling *Wolf* and requiring the states to suppress evidence seized in violation of the Fourth Amendment.

Was it fundamentally unfair to question suspects, fairly and without coercing them, trying to solve crimes? No, as the Court had held in a series of cases. But if the Court wanted to empower suspects facing police interrogation, then coercion is only a part of the picture. As Yale Kamisar put it, "[R]espect for the individual and securing equal treatment in law enforcement" require the state to make counsel available to suspects facing interrogation and to warn them that they need not answer.[68] He concluded in his characteristically colorful style: "To the extent that the Constitution permits the wealthy and the educated to 'defeat justice,' if you will, *why shouldn't* all defendants be given a like opportunity?"

Was it fundamentally unfair not to provide lawyers for indigent defendants in felony cases? No, the Court held in *Betts v. Brady*,[69] but here the Court was wrong. At a minimum, the Fourteenth Amendment's Due Process Clause should require procedures designed to benefit innocent defendants, and the right to a lawyer is one of those procedures, as the Warren Court recognized when it corrected this misstep of the fundamental fairness doctrine. But, as we will see, implementation of this critically important right has not fulfilled the claim made in *Gideon v. Wainwright* in 1963: A "poor man charged with a crime," the Court told the world, can be made "equal before the law" by providing counsel.[70]

The Court also held that the Due Process Clause requires the states to provide juries to try serious cases.[71] These developments were all designed to impose beneficial *procedures* on state courts. The right to warnings, the right to have evidence suppressed, and the right to a jury do little to protect innocence. While the right to counsel is important in protecting innocence, it was not enough.

I agree with Markus Dubber that the "avalanche of constitutional law" in criminal procedure "buried theorising about the American criminal process" as scholars quit talking about goals, principles, and norms in favor of talking about the latest twist in "a marvelously intricate, and gnarly, construct of precedent."[72] The result is an "unprincipled patchwork."[73] The Court's criminal procedure doctrine is "shot through with arbitrary distinctions."[74] Carol Steiker suggests a reason for the current mess of precedent: later Courts hostile to Warren Court expansions of rights felt constrained by stare decisis and sought ways to leave the rights in place but to allow evidence discovered in violation of those rights to be admissible. Thus were born the intricate rules governing who can claim Fourth Amendment protection and the exceptions to the *Miranda* rule.[75]

From here, I will discuss the failure of the Court's egalitarian procedural doctrine when it comes to protecting the innocent. Chapter 9 will sketch the basic outlines of a due process approach designed to protect innocence.

INTERROGATION AND CONFESSIONS

In its rush to bring standard procedures to the interrogation room, the *Miranda* Court ignored the problem of false confessions. Though I once believed that only a mentally ill person would confess falsely, thanks to Richard Leo I now see the problem as more complicated.[76] Suspects do not have to "confess" the way they do to Columbo or Perry Mason to lead to the introduction of false or misleading evidence of their guilt. An innocent suspect can tell his story in different ways, either because he remembers it differently or because the earlier version did not persuade his interrogators. An innocent suspect can agree with statements, more or less true on their face, that might later be linked to other statements that falsely suggest guilt. An innocent suspect can, out of desperation, claim a false alibi or seek to shift the blame to another innocent person. An innocent person can, out of desperation, agree when police suggest he might have done it but has blacked out the memory.

We saw in chapter 1 the case of Michael Crowe, a young, fearful, exhausted, sleepy fourteen-year-old boy who was accused of the murder of his sister over and over during a ten-hour interrogation that spanned three days. Having waived *Miranda*, his parents absent from the seemingly endless interrogation, he faces his interrogators alone. At some point, he becomes desperate for the interrogation to end. How can it end? Will it ever end? How can he persuade his interrogators to believe him?

To compound the desperate situation described above, the police can heighten the likelihood of a false confession in a variety of ways. They can present the suspect with false evidence of guilt and, once a *Miranda* waiver has been obtained, they can interrogate literally without end as long as the interrogators permit breaks for sleep and food. Some of the false evidence that can be used to confront the suspect can be pretty powerful. In the case of Michael Crowe, the police utilized a "Computer Voice Stress Analyzer" that police told Michael was both scientific and accurate.[77] When Michael accurately stated his innocence again and again, the police told him that he had failed the test and that the failure "established his guilt conclusively. Michael was devastated and began to sob almost uncontrollably."[78] Finally, seemingly out of options, truly desperate, he "began to admit the possibility that he could have done it without remembering."[79] Recall that he was exonerated by DNA but served seven months in detention before his innocence was demonstrated.

Miranda, as interpreted by later Courts, permits all the police techniques described above. How could the Court have been so wrong in believing that a routinized set of warnings, delivered once, would be a powerful antidote to police pressure and trickery? We must remember that *Miranda*, like all of us, was a product of its times. In 1966, Americans believed that we were the masters of our fate. We had played a major role in winning World War II. We had achieved a stable, if tense, stalemate with the Soviet Union. Arab fascism was directed at other Arabs and thus of no concern to us. We were the most powerful, and richest, country on earth. We had yet to discover what a minefield the Vietnam War would become. Watergate and OPEC were years away. We had yet to realize that J. Edgar

Hoover and the Internal Revenue Service were capable of quite un-American deeds.

We believed in government, in the police, in ourselves. Give police the right set of guidelines, give suspects the right set of instructions, and the interrogation problem would be largely solved. But what about the suspects who waive *Miranda* and are subjected to endless interrogation that leaves them hopeless? Why, they are not hopeless at all. The Court in *Miranda* was careful to stress that no waiver was permanent.[80] The suspect could invoke at any time. Hopeless? *Miranda* was an eternal font of hope.

There are, we see now, two profound problems with *Miranda* as a font of hope. First, humans are hardly the masters of their fate. We are much closer to Dostoyevsky's Raskolnikov than Ayn Rand's towering fictional hero, John Galt. The second flaw is in *Miranda* itself: Even assuming free will and actors modeled somewhat along the lines of John Galt, the *Miranda* warnings need be given only once, *and the warnings do not tell the suspect that he can invoke at any time, even after he has waived his rights.* So *Miranda,* the great victory for the powerless in our society, simply whetted the police appetite for better forms of interrogation, which unfortunately are effective against innocent as well as guilty suspects. Richard Leo reports almost three hundred documented cases of false confessions since the late 1980s.[81]

Was there a route other than the quick fix—which turned out to be a mirage—in *Miranda?* Perhaps the question is better asked as follows: Given *Miranda,* is there something else the Court can do now to remedy the situation in which we find ourselves? There are no magic bullets. The magic bullet of *Miranda* was a failure, and the Court should give up the search for a magic bullet that will solve all problems connected to police interrogation.

Due process should have a role to play along with *Miranda,* and chapter 9 will present fresh ideas for making police interrogation more transparent and more fair.

RIGHT TO COUNSEL

The Court has read the Sixth Amendment right to counsel into the Due Process Clause. The problem with this doctrinal move is that the Sixth Amendment invites a procedural focus. The Sixth Amendment, in its entirety, is about procedure. It guarantees a public and speedy trial; notice of charges; confrontation of the witnesses against the defendant; and compulsory process to obtain witnesses. Not much of substance there.

Quite in keeping with the procedural focus of the Sixth Amendment, the Court has developed a series of rules about the structural right to counsel. We know with reasonable precision *who* is entitled to counsel and *when* defendants are entitled to counsel. Indigent defendants cannot be sentenced to jail time unless they were given the right to counsel.[82] Defendants have the right to appointed counsel at the first appeal but not in subsequent appeals or in postconviction proceedings, including federal habeas corpus petitions.[83]

It is tempting to assume that the "right to the Assistance of Counsel" requires only that set of procedures. And the Court has come very close to embracing that view. To be sure, the Court insists that counsel must be "effective," but scholars almost universally view as a failure the Court's attempt to set standards for "effective counsel" in *Strickland v. Washington*.[84] It amounts to little more than insisting that lower courts examine the record and then instructing them to *strongly* presume competent representation. In the Court's words, "[C]ounsel is strongly presumed to have rendered adequate assistance and made all significant decisions in the exercise of reasonable professional judgment."[85]

Strickland's reliance on procedure and its assumption of competent lawyering is the bitter fruit of relying on the Sixth Amendment right to counsel rather than creating a substantive right to counsel under the rubric of due process. What defendants have, in effect, is the procedural right to a licensed lawyer next to them in court (although sometimes a sleeping lawyer works just as well).[86] A due process right to counsel that viewed "justice" as protecting the innocent would not be so easily satisfied by a procedural right to a lawyer. I will make specific recommendations in chapter 9.

EYEWITNESS IDENTIFICATIONS

In 1966, the Warren Court granted certiorari in three cases with the obvious intent to provide protections to suspects who face eyewitness identification procedures. *Wade v. United States* quoted Frankfurter's comment that the "identification of strangers is proverbially untrustworthy"[87] and then proceeded to require defense counsel to observe the procedures. When I first read the Court's counsel solution, it made sense to me. It no longer does.

How does the presence of counsel add substantially to the *reliability* of the identification? Lawyers are not likely to be expert in the methodology of identification procedures. While a lawyer can, presumably, help avoid the most egregious kinds of suggestive procedures, these are not the real problem when police are acting in good faith. I believe police good faith is the norm. If it is not the norm, then we have far deeper problems than unreliable eyewitness identification. Assuming police good faith in most cases, the problems will typically be subtle and unintentional. These will fly undetected past a lawyer's radar.

Indeed, the Court failed to include any discussion of what exactly the lawyer should do at the lineup. Though the briefs and record show that the issue of the role of counsel was discussed by both parties, the Court said nothing. Jim Strazzella concluded that this failure "has been a source of great puzzlement to courts and commentators."[88]

To the extent that it is a good idea to have a lawyer observe the identification process, in whatever role, the Court in *Wade* made a pretty serious error. It permitted the state to argue that even when counsel was not present, the in-court identification can be shown to be independent of the Sixth Amendment violation. If police wish to use a blatantly unfair identification procedure and do not want a defense lawyer present, they might decide it is worth taking the chance that a prosecutor can wiggle out of the *Wade* suppression remedy. To be sure, the Court was clear in *Gilbert v. United States*[89] that the *out-of-court* identification is categorically inadmissible if the right to counsel is violated, but imagine that you are a prosecutor and could get a court to permit the witness to identify the defendant in court. Would you care that the out-of-court identification was suppressed? I can't imagine why you would.

What about the lawyer's value in cross-examination of the eyewitness? The Court clearly assumes in *Wade* and *Gilbert* that the lawyer who saw the procedure will be more effective on cross-examination. But as Cutler and Penrod point out, even when a lawyer is present at the identification procedure, she will lack critical information about the viewing conditions at the scene of the crime.[90] This information can come only from the eyewitness. Moreover, as we will see in a moment, *Wade* and *Gilbert* were quickly reduced to near irrelevance by a later case.

The third case the Court decided with *Wade* and *Gilbert* was *Stovall v. Denno*.[91] While Justice Brennan's opinions in *Wade* and *Gilbert* are unpersuasive and superficial, his opinion in *Stovall* is a disaster. Five police officers and two members of the district attorney's office brought the suspect to the hospital room of the victim. The victim had told police that the perpetrator was a black man. The suspect was the only black man in the room, and he was handcuffed to one of the officers. The victim identified him after he repeated "a few words for voice identification."[92] It is difficult to imagine a more suggestive procedure, and yet the Court affirmed the conviction on the ground that the witness was in the hospital for major surgery.

It is hard to believe that Brennan wrote *Stovall*. The Court did not even insist that the eyewitness be in critical condition. It spoke only of her having to undergo emergency surgery. Moreover, the "test" the Court suggested for future cases looked to the "totality of the circumstances," a flaccid standard that rarely suppresses eyewitness testimony even when the procedure is quite suggestive.

Perhaps Brennan was unresponsive to the reliability problem because he had high hopes for the *Wade-Gilbert* doctrine. If suspects routinely were provided counsel, except when witnesses were severely injured, then counsel would be available to monitor the identification procedure in 99 percent of the cases. Justice Brennan clearly had higher hopes for what lawyer-observers can accomplish than I do. Granting him his premise, he might have thought that he had won a great victory on the counsel front, so why not "throw a bone" to police and prosecutors in *Stovall* and permit some flexibility when there is a risk that a witness might die.

But the *Wade-Gilbert* rule quickly went from a 99 percent solution to a 1 percent solution. Leaving aside whether providing a lawyer is an effective way to monitor the identification procedure, Brennan was unable to avoid an interpretive difficulty with his counsel solution. The Sixth Amendment applies only to "criminal prosecutions." It is difficult to argue that a procedure done shortly after arrest, to see whether the police have the right suspect, is part of a "criminal prosecution." Because the identification in *Wade* had occurred after an indictment, the Court would later distinguish pre-indictment cases.[93]

Wade thus does not apply to preindictment lineups. Almost all eyewitness identifications occur prior to indictment precisely because they are an investigative tool of the police. Thus, the great victory in *Wade* and *Gilbert* turned to ashes, and the losers were innocent suspects who do not need a lawyer but do need a due process protection against unreliable identifications that is more precise and more robust than the vague mess that is *Stovall*.

I believe the Burger Court was right to limit the counsel remedy, but the Court threw out the baby with the bathwater. Perhaps because *Stovall* is such a bad opinion, or perhaps because the Burger Court thought the threat to innocent defendants was not all that great, the Court in the 1970s began to narrow further the already-narrow protection offered by *Stovall*. Because the eyewitness in *Stovall* had been severely, if not critically, injured, one might think that due process would require that any suggestive identification procedure at least be justified by necessity. A severely injured victim might die and the evidence would be lost forever. But the Court has rejected any requirement of necessity.

In 1977, the Court held that an identification procedure that was both suggestive *and* unnecessary did not violate due process. The state conceded that the procedure was suggestive and that it was not justified by any necessity, yet the Court in *Manson v. Braithwaite* held that due process was not violated.[94] Rather than manifest any real concern about the risk of false identification, the Court deferred to *Stovall*'s "totality of the circumstances" test. If a trial court wants to admit an identification that came from a suggestive, unnecessary procedure, it can do so. The chances of being reversed on appeal are slim.

If the Court had used the Due Process Clause as the vehicle for addressing the entire identification problem rather than dumping what it thought was 99 percent of the problem into the right-to-counsel bin, it surely could have devised a better set of procedures or at least written an opinion that would have opened the door to a better set. *Stovall* should have focused on how the "process" of identifying suspects can be improved, rather than speak generally of reliability and then abandon suspects to the lacuna of "totality of the circumstances." Chapter 9 recommends a completely new direction for eyewitness identification procedures.

THE PATH FROM HERE

The procedural rights that the Court found in the Due Process Clause simply miss the point of protecting innocence. As Dripps has demonstrated, the Court's focus on "the specific procedures in the Sixth Amendment leads to the conclusion that *those procedures* are themselves the ultimate value protected by due process. . . ."[95] Jerome Frank concluded that "one imbued with a lively sense of justice will not be satisfied with that minimal [procedural] constitutional test."[96] But the Court seems satisfied with the minimalist procedural test, as Jerry Israel has demonstrated. Today, if a defendant cannot fit his argument into one of the procedural rights, the Court is reluctant to recognize what Israel calls a "free-standing due process claim."[97]

To be sure, Craig Bradley is right that the failure of the Court's criminal procedure doctrine cannot be blamed on the Court: "[B]ecause of the nature of the judicial process, no Supreme Court, no matter how competent and regardless of its political leanings, could have done much better."[98] Creating a coherent criminal procedure doctrine is a task for the various legislatures, and the legislatures in this country have avoided the task. But there were things the Court could have done to focus on the substantive question of whether the defendant is guilty, rather than whether the police misbehaved. The Court has failed to be a friend of the innocent.

For example, a claim of innocence is a freestanding due process claim that the Court should recognize. In 2006, the Court finally took a halting, and too short, step in the direction of recognizing that due process protects innocence. In *House v. Bell,* a bare majority of the Court reiterated dicta in *Herrera v. Collins* that a sufficiently high showing of actual innocence would make an execution unconstitutional.[99] Bravo. The problem with this "baby step"—beyond the narrow five-to-four majority willing to take the step—is that *House* also reiterated language in *Herrera* that the threshold for a successful claim that innocence bars execution is "extraordinarily high." Thus, even though House had "cast considerable doubt on his guilt," his claim of innocence failed to meet the "extraordinarily high" standard that the Court demands.[100]

Why would evidence that a defendant was probably innocent, as in *House*, not be sufficient to bar his execution?[101] The Court offered no explanation. Chapter 9 will recommend several innocence-friendly reforms, including one that would make it easier to get post-conviction relief based on probable innocence.

CHAPTER EIGHT

LOOKING FOR TRUTH IN

UNEXPECTED PLACES

[In France, the] presiding judge is vested with a discretionary power by which he may, upon his honour and his conscience, take any measure he believes useful for the discovery of the truth.

—FRENCH CODE OF CRIMINAL PROCEDURE, ARTICLE 310

Mirjan Damaska concludes that the American criminal justice system has more emphasis on justice-as-contest than any other contemporary criminal process.[1] Because the adversarial, contest system of justice invites a focus on procedure, rather than making the right judgment on guilt or innocence, the American system is more unfriendly to innocent defendants than any Western criminal process. Our claim that the vaunted adversarial system "beats and bolts out the Truth"[2] is far less true than we have long assumed.

David Luban argues that American adversarial advocacy permits lawyers to ignore both truth and moral principle. He also concludes that our system survives because other systems are not demonstrably better.[3] This chapter will seek to show that while Luban's scathing critique is correct, his conclusion is not. Systems that have truth as a goal and that avoid the contest-based framework of the American system—the French system and the American military justice system, for two examples—are more likely to protect the innocent.

The differences in the two criminal systems are, in part, historical. As we saw in chapter 4, after the church forbade clerical participation in the ordeals, English law lurched toward juries while continental law vested power in judges. Erik Luna has persuasively argued that the difference is also in part ideological. The English common-law system developed from a premise that "generally rejected the notion of state paternalism and, in turn, deemed each individual capable of determining the good life for himself." It is better to allow the parties to do battle (literally in medieval times; figuratively today) rather than cede power to a centralized authority. "In contrast, the civil law tradition was not forged in an abiding distrust of centralized authority. . . ."[4]

The ideological and historical differences in the civil and common law play out in many ways, on many stages, but nowhere as starkly as in their approaches to criminal procedure.

A TALE OF TWO CRIMINAL PROCEDURES

This chapter considers criminal procedure systems as they process serious crimes. In American criminal justice, the parties engage in a contest, conducted under rules established by the state. Pizzi concludes that truth has a low formal priority in our system and our judges are weak and passive.[5] To the extent judges play any role in the contest, they are mostly impartial referees. For example, the only role required by the Constitution for judges prior to trial is to decide whether the state has the right to detain a suspect when the prosecutor opposes pretrial release.[6]

If the judge decides that the state can detain the suspect, he can be held for weeks or months while the police seek to build a case against him. The police work only for the state, thus putting the defendant at a radical disadvantage in terms of locating favorable evidence. The investigation of crime is largely in the hands of the police until they decide they have enough evidence to turn it over to the prosecutor.

Once the case is turned over to the prosecutor, she chooses the charge to file. The prosecutor has two incentives to charge the most serious crime that can be justified based on the facts known at the time. First, in most jurisdictions, it is far easier to amend the charge to a lesser one than a more serious one. Second, charging the most serious possible offense or a series of offenses creates pressure on the defendant to plead guilty to a lesser offense. In fact, almost all American cases end in a negotiated plea.[7]

The few cases that make it to trial are governed by rules that are complex, esoteric, and designed to restrict the flow of information.[8] To be sure, most of the rules were developed to control inputs to the jury that might distract or mislead—for example, the evidentiary rules forbidding hearsay and irrelevant testimony. But in the hands of advocates who care mostly about winning, these rules obscure rather than advance truth. Both sides seek to hide evidence from the other and file motions and make evidentiary objections to keep truthful evidence from the fact finder. Feeney and Herrmann conclude: "Convincing the jury and courtroom victory are deemed more important than the discovery of truth."[9]

Testifying in an American court is a "bewildering experience" of being tightly controlled during direct examination and being subject to trickery and cajolery on cross-examination.[10] If a trial were "fundamentally a truth-inquiry," the rules would encourage witnesses to testify in a narrative while observing their demeanor for clues about reliability. "In our contentious trial practice, we do almost the exact opposite," Jerome Frank wrote in 1949.[11] He also observed that when a witness gives testimony that the lawyer believes is both honest and harmful to his client, the "lawyer considers it his duty to create a false impression" of that witness."[12] Three members of the U.S. Supreme Court blessed this tactic when it was engaged in by defense counsel in a criminal trial.[13]

The American system has one lawyer or the other "always supremely interested in misrepresenting, exaggerating, or suppressing the truth."[14] In essence, the American system seeks simultaneously to obscure and highlight the "truth," but in our system, the "truth" is whatever version of the facts is favorable to the lawyer's side of the case. Pizzi's memorable metaphor is that "our adversary system turns witnesses into weapons to be used against the other side."[15] To be sure, prosecutors are formally charged with seeking justice, but the tension between that goal and the goal of winning and preserving convictions is palpable. Consider the Innocence Project data, as of 2002, that prosecutors consented in fewer than 50 percent of the cases to DNA testing that ultimately exonerated convicted inmates.[16] Medwed concludes that numerous institutional barriers appear to dissuade prosecutors, in practice, from being impartial seekers of justice.[17]

At trial, the lawyers decide when the case is over. It then goes to a jury that has been sitting passively while the contest played out in front of them, taking days or weeks of their time. If the jury isn't confused enough by the odd method of simultaneously obscuring and seeking the "truth" about the facts, it will soon be completely bewildered by the judge's instructions about the law. Because technical errors in judicial instructions are the most common basis for convictions to be overturned, judges typically use instructions drawn from appellate courts opinions deciding complicated questions of law. It is no wonder that judicial instructions are long passages of legalese delivered in complex sentences that almost defy comprehension.[18] If the jury requests clarification on the instructions, the judge will typically repeat, word for word, what she said earlier, to avoid the risk of being overturned on appeal.

The law is especially complicated in sentencing hearings in capital cases because of the various aggravating and mitigating factors that can be argued. State capital sentencing schemes require complex instructions about how to identify and weigh these factors. In Governor Ryan's speech announcing the commutation of Illinois death sentences, he cited studies showing "that more than 50 percent of Illinois jurors couldn't understand the confusing and obscure sentencing instructions" given in capital cases.[19]

At no stage in the American process does a judge engage in any meaningful screening of the case against the accused. Why not? The only explanation is the contest culture, where the parties fight it out before an impartial judge or referee. While this makes conceptual sense, and is driven by history, it hardly justifies a hands-off posture by the only person in the process who is both trained in the law and neutral.

To be sure, a preliminary hearing judge decides, very early in the process, whether the state has probable cause to proceed. But probable cause is a low standard, and the hearing comes before the defense has time to marshal its evidence. What prosecutor would bring a case to a preliminary hearing if she did not have some proof of guilt? An erroneous eyewitness identification—and we know that those exist in large numbers—would be enough by itself to send the case beyond the preliminary hearing. The next stage is typically the grand jury, where the prosecutor presents the case, without involvement of the defendant, the defense lawyer, or a judge. The standard here, too, is probable cause. Recall the old saw that a prosecutor can get a grand jury to "indict a ham sandwich."

And what of judicial review after an erroneous conviction? The defendant can ask the judge whether sufficient evidence was offered to justify the conviction, but the standard here is even lower than probable cause. The American system gives the jury the prerogative of deciding the facts, and the judicial review of convictions thus assumes that the jury correctly decided all facts. Once that almost perverse assumption is in place, judicial review is largely pro forma. If the jury decides that the defendant was the one who killed, raped, or robbed, what conceivable basis would there be for an appellate court to find the evidence insufficient? Thus, almost all convictions, of the innocent as well as the guilty, are sustained against claims of insufficient evidence.

The second story is the French story. The story I tell here is of serious crimes that are under the jurisdiction of the Assize Court. As do American justice systems, the French emphasize efficient processing of cases, though the French do so in a very different way. One example that tends to stupefy Americans is that the Assize Court does not contemplate, or accept, guilty pleas. For cases that remain in the Assize Court, no role exists for compromise between the parties because it will have no bearing on the way the magistrates and judges investigate and prosecute the case. If a defendant stands up in the Assize Court and says, "I did it," a trial would still be held.[20]

The key distinction between the two systems is that judges run the show in France. With the exception of a brief period of time if criminal activity is interrupted as it occurs,[21] police are supervised by either the prosecutor or the examining magistrate. The bulk of the supervision of police in France is done by an examining magistrate, who painstakingly assembles a dossier that contains evidence both for and against the accused. His function is explicitly to search for truth. "The investigating judge undertakes in accordance with our law any investigative step he deems useful for the discovery of the truth. He seeks out evidence of innocence as well as guilt."[22] He must grant requests from the accused to interview witnesses, to inspect the scene of the crime, "or for any other step to be taken which seems . . . necessary for the discovery of the truth."[23]

The accused has a right to request a crime scene visit, and the magistrate may do it on his own "to make any useful findings or conduct a search."[24] Continental systems of justice regard visits to the scene of the crime as "superior to all other modes of fact-finding and the best way of reaching true knowledge."[25] The accused has the right to have his lawyer present when the examining magistrate visits the scene or interviews additional witnesses.[26] When the accused is innocent of the charges, the value of having his lawyer present when a neutral judge investigates the case is difficult to exaggerate. Any uncertainty displayed by witnesses or any anomaly at the scene of the crime can be noted and the magistrate can be urged to make further investigation. In the United States, visits to the scene of the crime and interviews of witnesses are the province of the police. Defense counsel are not present.

And what, you may ask, about counsel investigating the case on his own? Is there a role for Paul Drake, Perry Mason's infallible private investigator? In a word, no. In continental justice systems, with their investigative bureaucracy, "Independent investigations by counsel are dramatically curtailed. . . . Incisive early inquiries by private lawyers come close to tampering with informational sources prior to their use by the officials responsible for finding facts."[27] In France, lawyers do not get to coach witnesses to shape their stories to fit the narrative chosen by the lawyer. Hard though it is for American readers to believe, prosecutors and defense counsel are not permitted to talk to witnesses before trial. Defense lawyers can be disbarred for doing so.[28]

In sum, as Mirjan Damaska has demonstrated, continental systems of justice are hierarchical in nature, with professionals at the top setting the goals and directing lower-level officials in how to achieve the goals. "The integrity of a powerful central authority was thought to require strict governance by rules." Judges decide cases "on the basis of orderly documents that [have] screened out 'messy' situational and personal nuances likely to exert pressure toward leeway in decision making."[29]

When the file is assembled, the French magistrate decides whether to send the case to the next stage. In a significant number of cases, the magistrate dismisses the case,[30] which is the same as an acquittal in our country. If the magistrate decides to send the case to the indicting chamber, the magistrate, and not the prosecutor, decides on the appropriate charge.

At the indicting chamber, once again, judicial involvement seeks the truth about guilt. Three judges review the file compiled by the magistrate, and the panel has the authority to conduct its own investigation if it is unsatisfied with the dossier.[31] The state is represented in the indicting chamber not by the local prosecutor who appeared before the examining magistrate but, instead, by the prosecutor general. This is important because it avoids the problem of a prosecutor becoming so wedded to a theory of the case that its weaknesses are obscured. If the three-judge panel decides that the evidence is insufficient, the case is dismissed.[32] There is no presumption in favor of the magistrate's finding of fact. The indicting chamber has the same file the magistrate compiled, after all, as well as the power to collect additional evidence. It can make its own decision.

If neither the magistrate nor the indicting chamber dismisses the case, trial is the next event. As noted earlier, plea bargaining does not exist in the Assize Court. Damaska concludes that it is "truly offensive to Continental ideas on the proper administration of criminal justice" to give the defendant "standing to negotiate with state officials over charges or the sentence to be imposed, as well as to allow the court to sanction such deals."[33] The French criminal process is not tantamount to settling a dispute between parties, as in this country. The French criminal process determines the best outcome for state policy.

The presiding judge runs the trial, rather than being a referee between the parties. The defense counsel, and even the prosecutor, are peripheral figures. The goal is truth: "The presiding judge is vested with a discretionary power by which he may, upon his honour and his conscience, take any measure he believes useful for the discovery of the truth. . . ." These measures include summoning any person or new evidence "which, in the light of developments at the hearing, he deems useful for the discovery of the truth."[34]

It is difficult to overestimate the authority of the presiding judge. In a French murder trial witnessed by Professor Renée Lettow Lerner, the presiding judge "was magnificent in his scarlet and ermine," a robe that is a "symbol of royal authority."[35] The judge "dominated the entire trial from beginning to end, with the sole exception of closing arguments. He controlled the order in which witnesses were presented; he did the lion's share of questioning witnesses. He was responsible for maintaining both the flexibility and dignity of the court."[36]

Witnesses are encouraged to tell what they know in a narrative style. No one—judge, defense lawyer, or prosecutor—seeks to cajole or embarrass a witness who is seeking to testify truthfully. Professor Lerner was called as a witness and found it "a relief to be able to speak without being hemmed in by questions on direct and cross-examination."[37]

What is striking to American viewers is that French lawyers are not busily shaping the evidence. Witnesses are not led through their story on direct examination and then subjected to cross-examination that often implies that they are not telling the truth. In the United States, "lawyers are the stars of the trial process. Almost nothing happens without their initiation or participation."[38] The presiding judge is the star in France. Moreover, consistent with the idea of a free-flowing narrative, France does not have an evidence law labyrinth that causes trials in the United States to move slowly.[39] Witnesses tell what they have to say "and trials move faster."[40]

Three judges sit on a criminal trial in France, two assessors and the presiding judge, along with nine lay jurors. The trial ends when the presiding judge decides, not when the parties decide. The instruction to the jury is the same in all cases, mandated by the French Code of Criminal Procedure. Compared to American instructions, the French instruction is a model of economy and clarity:

> The law does not ask the judges to account for the means by which they convinced themselves; it does not charge them with any rule from which they shall specifically derive the fullness and adequacy of evidence. It requires them to question themselves in silence and

reflection and to seek in the sincerity of their conscience what impression has been made on their reason by the evidence brought against the accused and the arguments of his defence. The law asks them but this single question, which encloses the full scope of their duties: are you inwardly convinced?[41]

This instruction "is also put up in large type in the most visible part of the deliberation chamber" for the jury's benefit during deliberation.

In France, it is not necessary to instruct the jury on the substantive law because the three judges deliberate with the nine lay jurors.[42] One might wonder why judges are part of French juries. The question is better asked the other way. Lay participation in a hierarchical system of justice is an alien concept and appeared only because it was "swept into French law on a tide of revolutionary fervor and anglomania in 1791; philosophers and anglophiles such as Voltaire championed the jury as an excellent English way to free the criminal justice system from improper pressure."[43] But it was just too alien a concept, with too much "potential to destabilize judicial hierarchies" to flourish in France, and, today, juries are controlled by judges who exercise "decisive influence" in reaching verdicts.[44]

After deliberations, the judges and jurors finish this sentence: "Upon my honour and my conscience, my finding is . . ." and put their written verdict in an urn intended for this purpose.[45] French law requires eight votes for a conviction,[46] unlike the unanimity required by federal law and the law of all but two states in the United States. In France, there is no revoting or further deliberation. If fewer than eight guilty votes are found in the urn, the defendant is acquitted. This avoids an intractable problem in our criminal justice system—hung juries. American courts have twisted themselves into knots trying to figure out how best to approach deadlocked juries. There are no deadlocked juries in France. There are either eight or more guilty votes or fewer than eight. Either there is a conviction or an acquittal.

There is no appeal from an acquittal. In this way, the French system parallels ours. Prior to 2000, appeals of convictions in France were roughly like appeals here, though the possible errors were almost exclusively about the formalities in the trial rather than about the judge's instructions or rulings on motions and evidentiary objections. In 2000, however, the French system changed to allow, as an appeal of a conviction in the Assize Court, a second trial before a new jury![47] This, to American eyes, is a very odd procedure. The French in essence say to the convicted defendant: You didn't like your first trial? Here, have a second one. Norway has a similar procedure, though in Norway either side can request a second trial.[48]

The verdict at the second trial ends the case as far as the facts are concerned. As there will be no appeal based on the facts, no reason exists to have a trial transcript and none is kept.[49] An appeal based on legal error is still possible but rarely pursued.[50]

A second trial is possible as an "appeal" of a conviction only because the trial process in the Assize Court is far more efficient than in American courts. Consider a single example: jury selection. In the United States advocates use the voir dire process to seek jurors who might be sympathetic and, at the same time, to try to predispose the jury their way. Voir dire can take days, weeks, or months while advocates maneuver seeking an advantage. Not in France. The lawyers are given, prior to selection, the potential jurors' name, age, address, and occupation. Unlike American voir dire, that is "all the information they ever [get], apart from a juror's appearance. There is no questioning of any kind."[51] The "prosecution and defense have the time the juror stands up until the juror walks to his or her seat to decide whether to use a peremptory strike" to dismiss the juror.[52]

In sum, when serious cases are investigated and tried, France features efficiency, judicial control, and a search for truth. American justice features advocates who seek to present a partisan picture of the case to a jury that they attempted to predispose to favor that partisan picture.

SOME REFLECTIONS ON THE AMERICAN AND FRENCH CRIMINAL PROCEDURE TALES

In the American system when no plea deal is reached, the trial is the main event, where everything important happens. This provides incentives for the parties to hide favorable evidence and spring surprises on each other. The rules of evidence and the process of examining and cross-examining witnesses also reduces the likelihood that the jury will hear the truth. In contrast, the French system (and almost every justice system in the world other than the Anglo-American systems) is a diffuse process, with several inflection points where innocence can be demonstrated. The parties have little incentive to hide evidence—indeed, the police work for the judicial system and thus gather evidence for both sides.

In France, judges control the process. The magistrate, charged with the duty to seek the truth, directs the investigation. The indicting chamber reviews the magistrate's work and can take evidence and modify or dismiss felony cases referred to it. At trial, the presiding judge moves the trial along smartly as he questions the witnesses following the road map created by the magistrate. The role of the lawyers is radically reduced. The evidence is presented naturally by letting witnesses tell their stories, without lawyers seeking to shape the narrative to fit his purposes. Lawyers do not "rehearse" the testimony with the witnesses before hand.

The reliance on judges to discern the truth, and protect the innocent, is a heavy burden. But France utilizes some of its best and brightest lawyers for the ranks of judges and provides them an extra course of study that other lawyers do not receive. To be admitted to training as a magistrate, lawyers must take a "rigorous entrance exam" and then "must finish a special thirty-one month judicial training program."[53] Upon successful completion of that training program, the lawyers must complete "several internships in different courts" and then face another exam that will determine the order in which they can choose a post.[54] Prosecutors are also magistrates and thus, unlike defense lawyers, receive the same training as judges.

The comparison with the American system is not one that should give us pride. The French make judges and prosecutors of lawyers who pass a rigorous entrance exam and then experience extensive training beyond what other lawyers get. In this country, we choose lawyers to be judges and prosecutors mostly because of politics or friendship. If enlisting the best and brightest lawyers for judges and prosecutors is the goal—and why wouldn't that be the goal?—which method would you prefer?

The French system features the magistrate, the indicting chamber, the presiding judge, and the jury in a search for the truth about the guilt of the defendant. And the search is led by judges. Lawyers are almost an afterthought. The American system features lawyers seeking an advantage, one way or the other, for their side of the case. Judges are less important. Which system is superior? It was once fashionable to write that "the American system of criminal justice is armed with more safeguards against wrongful convictions that those of any other nation in the world."[55] After the revelations of the last ten years, I don't know how anyone could say that today.

In France, an innocent defendant has two realistic chances, prior to trial, to have a judge or a panel of judges declare the case insufficient to prosecute. At both stages, the goal is to discover the truth about what happened, not just issue a judgment about the "probable cause" guilt of the accused. In our culture, the term *inquisitorial* has an aura of the Star Chamber and the rack and screw. We imagine relentless judges tricking or coercing false confessions from innocent defendants. But the truth is quite the opposite. The French inquisitorial system is much friendlier to innocent defendants than our vaunted accusatorial system.

The American Uniform Code of Military Justice is wholly a creation of Congress, unlike the federal criminal justice system, which is a patchwork of constitutional law, statutes, and rules. The UCMJ, like the French code of criminal procedure, is explicitly constructed with truth as the goal. No matter may be referred to a general court-martial for trial until "a thorough and impartial investigation of all the matters set forth therein has been made. This investigation shall include inquiry as to the truth of the matter set forth in the charges."[56]

According to Gregory Maggs, here is how the investigation works on the ground in the army. An accusation of criminal misconduct is made to the "convening authority," who is typically the general in command of the division. The convening authority then appoints a subordinate to serve as an investigating officer. For example, the general might appoint a lieutenant colonel on his staff. "This officer is usually not a lawyer, but will have the assistance of a legal advisor from the staff judge advocate's office. The investigating officer investigates and prepares a report for the convening authority."[57]

When the report is complete, the convening authority obtains "advice from the staff judge advocate, and then decides what action to take. The convening authority is not bound by the report, but must consider it. The convening authority might decide to refer charges to a court-martial, to issue a letter of reprimand, to reassign the accused soldier, [or] to take no action."[58] In effect, the convening authority, with help from his delegate, functions roughly as the examining magistrate does in France.

Once charges have been preferred, the accused must "be advised of the charges against him and of his right to be represented [by counsel] at that investigation."[59] This right to be present, and be represented by counsel, at the investigation includes some of the rights the civilian courts reserve for trial: "full opportunity shall be given to the accused to cross-examine witnesses against him if they are available and to present anything he may desire in his own behalf, either in defense or mitigation, and the investigation officer shall examine available witnesses requested by the accused."[60] The results of the investigation must accompany the charges if they are forwarded to the next stage of the process, including "a statement of the substance of the testimony taken on both sides."[61]

It appears that when Congress thinks it has a clear path, it chooses to structure a system that puts the emphasis on involving judges, the defendant, and defense counsel in search of the truth. Truth of course is the best friend of innocent defendants.

CHAPTER NINE

THE HITCH-HIKER'S GUIDE TO

PROTECTING INNOCENCE

Don't panic. You are about to be transported to an alien criminal
justice system. But when you get used to it, you just might like it.

We now know that our adversarial, contest-based system penalizes
the innocent. It is time to change. Valerie Hans notes that "[w]e are
in the midst of a remarkable period in which states appear quite
ready to experiment with and modify some of the traditional features of the adversarial jury trial."[1] Darryl Brown concludes that recent evidence of "weakness of adversarial adjudication is producing
early signs of a new model: a system that depends less on adversarial
process and more on practices that resemble those found in administrative settings."[2] The last twenty years in England and Scotland
have seen a "chipping away at the adversarial system."[3] I wish to
chip away at the American system.

One type of "chipping away" accepts the contours of our contest-
based system and seeks to graft onto it new protections that will help
protect innocence. An American Bar Association monograph published in 2006 is an excellent example.[4] A different approach would
reject some of the principles of the Anglo-American contest-based

process. Rather than graft incremental protections, the revolutionary would replace, root and branch, some of the features of our system. For example, Michael Risinger makes the revolutionary proposal to allow defendants to choose to be tried by "factual innocence" rules.[5] Essentially, Risinger contemplates that the defendant who claims to be innocent would identify the one or two ultimate facts that prove his claim. Everything else could be stipulated. The court under "factual innocence" rules would screen the prosecutor's expert testimony more closely and would permit more freedom to the defense to challenge confessions, jailhouse informants, and eyewitness identifications.[6]

Another revolutionary proposal is Lloyd Weinreb's idea that a French-style examining magistrate replace police investigation, that a presiding judge be responsible for the presentation of the evidence, and that the presiding judge be part of the jury that would also include two lawyers and seven lay jurors.[7] Weinreb's goal is to design a system that will "produce an accurate account of a crime, with the least intrusion on people's lives."[8]

I like Weinreb's system, the French system, and Risinger's "factual innocence" rules at least as well as the system I will propose. But I reject robust revolution for the reason Weinreb himself gives— "opposition to really substantial change is always clamorous."[9] I do not see any legislature adopting "factual innocence" rules. Nor do I see a legislature taking the investigation of crime away from police, letting the presiding judge control the presentation of evidence, and changing the jury in the way Weinreb proposes. Thus, rather than have my proposed reform sink under the same waters that claimed Weinreb's proposal,[10] I will recommend a much more modest revolution. But first I will consider the gradualist solution.

THE GRADUALIST APPROACH TO PROTECTING INNOCENCE

The ABA report, *Achieving Justice,* is a hard-hitting, candid assessment of how our current system puts innocent defendants in jeopardy. It agrees with my assessments in this book, or perhaps I should say I agree with it. The report identifies eight problem areas, one of which—compensation for the wrongly convicted—is outside the scope of my project. The other seven areas concerned me in chapter 1—false confessions, eyewitness identification procedures, bad forensic evidence, jailhouse informants, inadequate defense counsel, flawed investigation procedures, and prosecution practices that jeopardize innocence.

The ABA report makes specific recommendations that seem likely to reduce the jeopardy of innocent defendants. For example, the report recommends videotaping the entirety of interrogations.[11] It considers ways to avoid convictions based on the uncorroborated testimony of jailhouse informants.[12] It calls for the accrediting of crime laboratories and medical examiner offices and the creation of a standard set of procedures "to ensure the validity, reliability, and timely analysis of forensic evidence."[13] It recommends written procedures for the collecting and preservation of evidence in criminal cases, as well as training programs and disciplinary procedures "to assure that investigative personnel are prepared and accountable for their performance."[14] It specifies steps to improve the reliability of eyewitness identifications.[15] It recommends that defense lawyers be required "to investigate circumstances indicating innocence regardless of the client's admissions . . . or the client's stated desire to plead guilty."[16]

In some areas, however, the recommendations seem more like wishful thinking. To facilitate the appointment of "appropriately experienced and qualified appointed or assigned defense counsel in serious criminal cases," the ABA recommends the creation of a "Criminal Defense Plan to be administered by a Responsible Agency."[17] This plan will "establish and publish recommended standards for defense representation." Let me be gracious and assume that a legislature created such a plan and that it had fairly specific requirements. It would also need teeth to enforce its requirements. I cannot imagine the legislative will to create meaningful sanctions for the time when the inevitable budget problems cause funding to sink below what is necessary to sustain the plan.

As for inequality of resources between prosecution and defense, the ABA recommends equalized workloads, comparable rates of compensation, and sufficient resources to investigate cases. The ABA report specifically recommends "adequate funding to prosecutors' offices"[18] to facilitate sorting the innocent from the guilty. Of course. If the ABA could waive its magic wand and make these platitudes come true, the system would work better. It would be fairer. It would be more protective of innocence. But similar recommendations have been made for decades and, while slight progress has been made in a few states, the situation remains dire.[19] State budgets are often in need of tightening. Money for defense lawyers and, to a lesser degree, for prosecutors, judges, and other criminal justice personnel is often seen as a relatively easy target when belt-tightening becomes necessary.

The ABA approach suffers the flaws of all gradualist reforms. A deeply embedded culture, like the adversarial norm, cannot be changed by making changes at the margin. Margaret Raymond notes that, in 1932, Edwin Borchard identified the same basic causes that modern scholars have shown to be causally linked to wrongful convictions.[20] Raymond writes: "Yet we find ourselves, seventy years later, addressing the same problems and the same causes." To Raymond, "The lesson is clear: we do not solve this problem merely by identifying it." I would extend the point and argue that we are not likely to solve the problem with gradualist reform. Proposed changes at the margin are likely to be co-opted by the same powerful forces that have given us the adversarial system that we have today. I recommend more radical surgery.

MORE RADICAL CHIPPING AWAY

We learned from the French that judges can play a critical role in screening innocents out of the system. The French use of judges as screens—the examining magistrate and the indicting chamber—shows how we waste judges. I would have judges actively screening cases, both before and after trial. Prior to trial, I would require judges to make judgments about probable guilt or innocence and not merely whether the state has shown "probable cause" to proceed. Then appellate judges can be required to play a more active role in reviewing convictions.

In addition to a more active role for judges, I will also propose a fundamental change in the way lawyers prosecute and defend criminal cases. I will suggest other, less fundamental, changes, but the centerpiece of my proposed reform is to involve judges in actively screening for innocence and to reorder the way lawyers prosecute and defend criminal cases.

To effect the changes I recommend would require Supreme Court "legislation" on an unprecedented scale. That is not likely or desirable. I agree with Craig Bradley that Supreme Court doctrine, based on individual cases, can never create an adequate criminal procedure.[21] Bradley recommended a national code of criminal procedure, binding on the states as well as the federal system.[22] A national code with a focus on innocence would be the ideal solution, but it is unclear to me in light of recent Court cases (decided after Bradley published his book) how far Congress can go in that direction.[23]

Thus, I imagine my audience as the fifty state legislatures. The mountain of evidence uncovered by the Innocence Project and other researchers should move legislatures to declare that the most important process in "due process of law" (or the state constitutional analog) is the process that protects innocence at a reasonable cost. Legislatures could hold hearings about the best ways to achieve innocence protection and the costs that would be entailed. I offer here some ideas that I believe protect innocence at a reasonable cost.

The Constitution Project begins its recommendations with the right to counsel,[24] presumably because competent defense counsel and vigilant prosecutors are of critical importance to any system. I begin there, too, with a radical recommendation for leveling the playing field between prosecution and defense.

CREATING PARITY BETWEEN PROSECUTORS
AND INDIGENT DEFENDERS

Kay Levine concludes that "the prosecutor has emerged as the empire builder of the American criminal justice system. . . . the principal actor responsible for determining case outcomes and sentences for criminal defendants." In her view, "the imperial role of the prosecutor has reached new heights" in the decade 1995–2005. "[P]rosecutors are more than just advocates in an adversary system; they are social engineers."[25] While having prosecutors, rather than judges, as social engineers is not necessarily a bad idea, Levine's use of the term "imperial" suggests that the new power of the prosecutor's office can be abused.

I will return to the problem of the imperial prosecutor after I explore failures on the defense side of the aisle. These failures are more obvious, and probably more harmful. Lower courts have applied *Strickland v. Washington*[26] to find the Sixth Amendment satisfied when lawyers slept through substantial parts of the trial;[27] failed to interview exculpatory witnesses or the police officer who, according to the defendant, used a gun to coerce the defendant's confession;[28] presented none of the available mitigating evidence at the sentencing phase in a death penalty case;[29] failed to raise the client's best argument on appeal;[30] and failed to transmit a plea offer to his client, perhaps because he was having a sexual relationship with the client's fiancée.[31] It did not matter to courts that these failures, and almost all others in this universe of cases, were the result of inept or corrupt lawyering.

The Illinois Supreme Court has tacitly recognized that, in death cases, *Strickland* does not guarantee a sufficient level of competence. In March, 2001, the state court promulgated a series of rules that create a "capital litigation trial bar" by specifying minimum levels of experience in general and in capital defense, as well as requiring special training in the defense of capital cases.[32] Only members of the capital litigation trial bar may be assigned to defend in death cases.

The Constitution Project's blue-ribbon committee recently called for *Strickland* to be replaced, in death cases, by a standard of "professional competence."[33] That the committee viewed *Strickland* as a lower standard than "professional competence" says volumes about the disrepute in which it is held. Vivian Berger writes about reforms calling for "broad systemic improvements" in the provision of counsel that include "specialization requirements, . . . higher pay and greater auxiliary resources for assigned counsel, and structural changes in the delivery of defense services."[34] Richard Klein calls for the organized bar to step into the breach created by poor funding and exacerbated by *Strickland*'s failure to create a workable standard.[35] Russell Weaver recommends a set of presumptions that would sometimes relieve the defendant of having to prove that his lawyer damaged his chances for an acquittal.[36]

Bruce Green recommends a more rigorous licensure process that would include decertification of lawyers whose work is substandard.[37] In a bold elaboration of the licensure idea, Donald Dripps would require that the trial judge in each criminal case determine before trial "whether the defendant's lawyer can effectively represent him. Because the effectiveness of counsel is relative to the opposition, the test should be whether the defendant is represented by a lawyer roughly as good and roughly as well-prepared as counsel for the prosecution."[38] Another good approach is Darryl Brown's. He recommends rationing scarce defense resources guided by two principles—protecting defendants who are innocent and those who face the most severe penalties.[39]

While all of these proposals are better than *Strickland*, they all share a defect: None is self-executing. Each requires some actor—a judge, in most cases, or the bar—to make a judgment about the quality and ability of defense counsel or the particular need for competent counsel. Any time lawyers or judges sit in judgment of their own, I am doubtful that adequate quality standards will be maintained.

A better approach to indigent defense is that of Schulhofer and Friedman, who recommend a voucher system that permits defendants to choose among the available criminal defense lawyers.[40] This solution is self-executing and does not depend on pie-in-the sky hopes for better funding. Ontario, Canada, has since 1998 used a system in which Legal Aid of Ontario issues certificates to low-income persons, redeemable with participating private lawyers.[41] The implementing regulations are complex, but, roughly, lawyers are paid about seventy-four dollars (Canadian) an hour, with hourly limits for the type of crime and a total compensation limit per lawyer per year.[42] The latter limits are fairly generous; a lawyer with ten or more years of certificate service can earn up to almost $197,000 per year. The voucher system is backed up by "duty counsel" for people who arrive in court without a lawyer.

As good as these proposals are, they miss the real problem of criminal defense. The job itself is the problem. Scholars tend to assume that defense lawyers and prosecutors are mechanical creatures that, if paid the same amount and given the same caseload, would perform at an equal level. But this assumption fails to take account of the psychic toll of representing clients, most of whom are guilty, and some of whom are guilty of truly horrible crimes. Every day brings new clients who have stolen, robbed, mugged, and sometimes raped and killed.

When a prosecutor goes home to her family, she can say, "Today I did what I could to convict dangerous criminals." When a public defender has dinner with her family, the best she can manage in most cases is, "I put the state to its burden of proving my client guilty beyond a reasonable doubt." I have no doubt that the prosecutor's assessment of her workday is, over time, more uplifting for most lawyers—not all, to be sure, but most—than the defender's tale. To spend one's life putting the state to the burden of proving guilt beyond a reasonable doubt must corrode the soul of many lawyers.

Susan Bandes writes of the criminal defense bar, "There may be no other profession whose practitioners are required to deal with so much pain with so little support and guidance."[43] As a result, defense lawyers adopt mechanisms for avoiding the pain, "including avoidance, denial, suppression, repression," and splitting one's personal and professional life.[44] "Feeling too much is painful; not feeling at all is worse, for the attorney and those he loves and perhaps even for his clients."[45] Sometimes there comes "a moment in which the denial stops being possible; the detachment ceases to work. Sometimes this occurs in isolated instances . . . But sometimes it is the result of the cumulative effects of the practice. The time arrives when the lawyer simply can no longer continue to do the work effectively."[46]

The day before opening statements in an armed rape case, a close relative of the defense lawyer was robbed and raped. He asked himself, "What in God's name was I doing here representing this rapist?" He did his job and won an insanity acquittal. "Shortly thereafter, he reports, he left the public defender's office . . . . 'burned out, . . . sick of representing so many bad people, . . . sick of being afraid to walk in my own parking lot yet helping people who mug citizens in other parking lots. I have lost much of the empathy I once had for my clients. It is time to go.' "[47]

It is even worse now that we know that a nontrivial number of the defender's clients are innocent. Because defense counsel will rarely know for certain that her client is innocent, conscientious counsel will approach many of her clients thinking they might be innocent. In those cases, the choices open to the defendant and his lawyer are dismal—plea bargain or face trial where a conviction and longer sentence is always possible. The stronger the lawyer's belief in her client's innocence, the more she is likely to encourage him to face trial. But that very belief in innocence makes the trial a high-stakes gamble indeed.

Imagine the prosecutor who sees a defendant acquitted. She surely feels bad, because she lost and because the defendant, if guilty, is free to prey on society again. Now imagine the public defender who sees an innocent client convicted. There is no second act here. The lawyer failed in what I believe is the most important task in our criminal justice system—keeping the innocent from being convicted of crime. Imagine sitting down to dinner knowing that once the appeals are exhausted (defendants rarely win appeals), an innocent man, or woman, will surrender to prison authorities, will be stripped of clothing and dignity, and will face years in a dank prison where rape, degradation, and death will be constant companions.

It is a testimonial to our system that we find competent, caring lawyers willing to do indigent defense at all. But I agree with Jonakait that "the best and the brightest [of lawyers] often prefer to do other legal work than defending those charged with crimes."[48] The wear and tear of the job is worse for defenders than prosecutors. I cannot imagine that, after a year or two, or ten, most public defenders can get up in the morning and face their job with the same dedication and enthusiasm that prosecutors can muster for their job. We need what Judge Bazelon sought over thirty years ago—a radical rethinking of the role of defense counsel.[49]

Ironically, the uplifting nature of the prosecutor's job can also threaten innocence. Prosecutors can succumb to tunnel vision, ignoring the possibility that the defendant is innocent and using the adversarial system to suppress evidence of innocence. The prosecutor in the Eldon Miller case in chapter 1 failed to disclose that the undershorts were covered mostly in brown paint. The prosecutor in the Ray Krone case relied on a novel and unproven scientific test that he did not even disclose to the defendant until the eve of trial. And Mike Nifong was found to have misled defense lawyers and a judge in the Duke case.

The prosecutor's job in the early twenty-first century invites an imperial attitude, social engineering, and a win-at-all-costs attitude. I want to be clear, at least in part because my brother is a prosecutor, that I do not charge most prosecutors with dangerous tunnel vision. Moreover, all lawyers suffer from at least a mild form of tunnel vision. It is useful in representing clients zealously. But the possibility for dangerous tunnel vision in prosecutors is there, and we have seen enough cases in this book to cause concern.

Is it possible to solve the problem of the imperial prosecutor and the overburdened, burned-out defense counsel? The answer, surprisingly, is that a radical rethinking of both jobs can be implemented rather easily, and in one fell swoop, if we have the political will. I know the lawyers in my audience will be tempted to dismiss my proposal here as unrealistic or, perhaps, insane. I ask your indulgence. Without worrying about the details, or how we get from here to there—issues that can be dealt with if the idea is a good one—imagine a criminal process with a pool of "criminal law specialists." These specialists would work for the district attorney and her assistants in some cases and for the chief public defender and his assistants in other cases.

The specialists will be chosen, or assigned, both to prosecute and to defend criminal defendants. Bingo. We have roughly equal resources because the criminal specialists are paid the same salary, and the legislature must provide enough money to make sure that there are sufficient specialists to prosecute cases. The specialists will draw from the same expert witnesses. The state will still enjoy an advantage because the police work for free as investigators for the state. But even without access to police as investigators, defendants get an advantage over the current system. Having worked with the police when prosecuting cases, the specialists will know which ones might be inclined to cut corners or exaggerate. That knowledge would permit better cross-examination of police and, moreover, should make police more likely to play it straight.

We have instantly created jobs of equal stress, disappointment, dismay, and pride. No longer will there be public defenders who face nothing but an unending stream of mostly lying, guilty clients. No longer will prosecutors overreach because they are always representing the good people of their district. As today's prosecutors will now spend roughly half their time defending, our "social engineers" will not be as tempted to be imperial ones. When public defenders are functioning as prosecutors, they will surely be more likely to open their files when defense counsel request discovery. No longer will prosecutors view defense requests for exculpatory evidence as just an annoyance.

While my "switch-hitting" idea would not entirely solve the problem of perverse incentives for prosecutors noted in chapter 1—a career path that rewards convictions and penalizes dismissals—it should substantially moderate those incentives. Most lawyers would work both sides of the aisle, and promotion to top prosecutorial ranks would likely depend more on organizational skills than "batting average." Hopefully, the time spent defending cases might move all lawyers to care less about convictions and more about getting the right outcome.

Assuming we can solve the problems that I will discuss in a moment, I do not see why this proposal would be dead on arrival in the legislature. It can be sold as achieving equality of resources in a way that makes the dismissal or acquittal of innocent defendants more likely. Of course, some prosecutors will lobby at a radioactive level. Why would they want to join the "other side"—the side that is trying to release dangerous criminals back into our communities? I imagine many public defenders also might not like the idea of switching sides because some view prosecution as an evil business that aids oppression of powerless groups.

To the extent that prosecutors view criminal defense as unethical or inept, that is all the more reason to force them to switch sides on a regular basis. They would have an opportunity to improve the ethics and competence of the defense bar. And it would, I believe, improve their perspective when they are prosecuting cases.

For the reader who is inclined to dismiss this idea as an ivory-tower fantasy, I point to the English system for prosecuting and defending criminal cases. Though it is more haphazard than the system I propose, it recognizes that trial specialists can be hired to do either prosecution or defense. Prior to 1986, individual English police departments decided which cases to prosecute and would then hire a barrister or just use a police officer to prosecute.[50] In 1986, the Crown Prosecution Service, CPS, was set up to create a centralized authority to make decisions about what cases to prosecute and to oversee the actual prosecutions.[51] The CPS continues to hire advocates from private practice to prosecute. Indeed, until recently CPS lawyers could not appear in Crown Court, where the most serious crimes are tried, and CPS hired barristers to prosecute all Crown Court cases.[52] On the other side of the "aisle," criminal defendants can hire from the same pool of barristers; the fee to represent indigent defendants is paid by the government. Thus, it remains true in England that "the barrister who prosecutes one day may defend the next."[53]

The English system appears to work just fine with a pool of lawyers who act as specialists for both the prosecution and the defense. The only difference in my proposed system is that the specialists would be employed full time by the government and would have no civil practice. I see nothing in those differences that would impede the prosecution and defense of routine criminal cases.

But what about prosecutions of vast conspiracies, of organized crime, and of terrorism? Those cases require continuity of prosecutors. I propose creating a group of lawyers who will work exclusively for the prosecution in a discrete category of cases—call it the Criminal Enterprise Task Force. As for the line separating "criminal enterprise" cases from run-of-the mill cases, I would defer to the legislatures to designate which statutes would be under the jurisdiction of the special task force. A legislature could, of course, make the task force jurisdiction so large that it would essentially replace the new system. But a legislature would not adopt my idea in the first place unless it wanted specialists and would thus have no incentive to gut the system, at least initially. If the specialist system were put in place, and worked as well as I think it will, little incentive to defeat its jurisdiction would ever exist.

The typical criminal law specialist's day would include working on the defense of clients and the prosecution of defendants. She would sample both sides. The specialist would be more likely to avoid the hubris that sometimes attends the office of the prosecutor. She would be more likely to avoid the despair and burnout associated with public defenders. Resources would be at more or less parity. What's not to like about this modification, radical though it is?

Now I turn to the process itself.

My book is not about protecting privacy or liberty, except to the extent that protecting innocent suspects and defendants advances those goals. Nor is it about crime control. But I believe the system I will propose is consistent with effective policing. For example, I recommend the French rule that the police must notify the prosecutor "immediately" when they have made an arrest[54] because it creates an opportunity for effective supervision of the investigation.

In France, the examining magistrate supervises the bulk of the investigation. I will recommend a role for a new kind of judge—a "screening magistrate"—but it will entail only limited supervision. Police and prosecutors in my proposed system will largely retain their autonomy to investigate crimes. To protect innocent suspects in police custody, I recommend several reforms. As is generally the case in France, I would give arrestees the right to notify someone of their detention and the right to appear before a magistrate within twenty-four hours of arrest, and would require police to inform arrestees of these rights.[55] The gain in protecting innocence here is, I think, obvious. An innocent person must feel disoriented and abandoned when arrested and placed in custody. To be told he can notify someone and will soon see a neutral judge should provide hope.

To some extent, my screening magistrate will do what magistrates do in the current federal process, though I envision a larger and more formal role. Appointed by the life-tenured district judge, federal magistrates currently assist the district judge in a variety of ways as the judge and the parties find useful. For example, magistrates hear pretrial motions, conduct pretrial conferences, and hold evidentiary hearings.[56]

Magistrates also conduct the initial appearance, where they provide the defendant notice of charges, of the right to counsel, of the availability of pretrial release, of the right to a preliminary hearing, and of the right not to make a statement.[57] The government must also show probable cause that the defendant committed the crime with which he is charged. I recommend these requirements for the states as well, and I add two innocence-friendly requirements. First, the screening magistrate should inquire, on the record, whether anyone has threatened or mistreated the defendant. If the answer is yes, then the magistrate should take the defendant's testimony about the mistreatment.

Second, rather than merely informing the defendant of the right to counsel, as required under current federal law, the magistrate should ask whether the defendant wishes counsel appointed and, if so, take care of that detail during the initial appearance by providing the defendant a roster of criminal law specialists. This roster should contain information about each lawyer—how many years practicing law, how many years as a criminal law specialist, how many cases for the prosecution, how many for the defense, and perhaps some evaluation of performance. Choice of counsel will be permitted as long as the choice does not create administrative difficulties—for example, if the first three choices have full caseloads, the magistrate should assign number four.

This is an innocence-friendly change because most innocent defendants will leap at the chance to confer with a lawyer outside the police interrogation room. Innocent suspects, like guilty ones, are reluctant to request counsel during interrogation because it sends a signal to the police that they have something to hide. But no such signal would be sent by requesting a magistrate to appoint counsel at the initial appearance. To be sure, having the magistrate offer counsel might result in fewer defendants confessing later to the police. But whatever the cost in terms of lost confessions, it is a price we pay for having the Sixth Amendment right to counsel.[58]

I recommend a pretrial release or bail hearing within forty-eight hours after the initial appearance, before the same screening magistrate. Prior to the bail hearing, and afterward if the defendant does not qualify for pretrial release, the police can conduct their investigation as now, with a few exceptions. Interrogations must be recorded—the entire interrogation, not just the confession. The ABA report *Achieving Justice* and many commentators have endorsed this idea, which is critical in reducing the incidence of false confessions.

Solid empirical work shows that taping confessions is "an efficient and powerful law enforcement tool" as well as providing an indisputable record of what occurred during interrogation.[59] Moreover, viewing the tapes would not be a burden for judges. Very few defendants contested confessions in the prerecording days—only

0.16 percent in a study of nine Midwestern counties[60]—and recordings act to "dramatically reduce" defense motions to suppress.[61] That recordings depress motions to suppress suggests, tentatively, that police misconduct is relatively rare. Presumably, defense lawyers would move to supress the recordings in almost all cases where police tricked or intimidated the suspect.

As even *Miranda*-critic Chief Justice Rehnquist recognized in *Dickerson v. United States*,[62] it is too late in the day to overrule *Miranda*. While any benefit of *Miranda* to suspects is ephemeral, it probably does little harm. We can safely leave *Miranda* in place, but we need more regulation of police interrogation, as Richard Leo and coauthors have argued.[63] For example, police interrogators should be trained to be aware of the risk of false confessions, in the hope that this will mitigate the "flat earth" theory of policing. Time limits should also be imposed because the length of interrogation is positively correlated with false confessions—the average interrogation in false confession cases is 16.3 hours, while the average overall is about two hours.[64] Costanzo and Leo suggest a limit of four hours, twice the length of the average interrogation.[65] Special attention should be paid to particularly vulnerable suspects—juveniles and the mentally handicapped and mentally ill.[66]

The issue of police lying to suspects, particularly about evidence of their guilt, should be studied with an eye toward limiting certain types of lies and deception. This is not to say that police should be forbidden to make any kind of misrepresentation. If a police officer gets a confession from a guilty pedophile by feigning sympathy for his sexual attraction to children, society should cheer the deception. Study is needed to identify deception that is more likely to induce a false confession—for example, lies designed to make the suspect's situation appear hopeless.[67]

These regulations can be enforced, of course, by having the screening magistrate view the tape of the interrogation when a defendant seeks to suppress his statements. In addition to enforcing the regulations, the magistrate should be watchful for signs that the statements are unreliable. I agree with Leo and his coauthors that a screening judge should weigh three factors when assessing reliability: (1) whether the suspect disclosed facts that could only be known by the perpetrator and could not easily be guessed; (2) whether the suspect's statements led the police to new evidence; and (3) how well the narrative fits the existing evidence about the crime.[68]

The screening magistrate should also supervise eyewitness identifications. Academics, and a few courts, have offered a wide variety of reforms in eyewitness identification procedures.[69] These proposed reforms include changes in the process—for example, sequential presentation of the participants rather than the traditional line-up—and recommendations about how to select "foils" and how many "foils" to include. The ABA's *Achieving Justice* recommends advising the eyewitness that the perpetrator might not be in the lineup. The State of New Jersey, by executive order of its attorney general, implemented major procedural reforms in 2001.[70] Margery Koosed recommends putting the focus on the procedure used, rather than asking the amorphous question of whether the particular identification was reliable. She would have judges ask whether the procedure lends itself to "irreparable mistaken identification."[71] If so, the identification would not be admissible in court.

We can also learn from the English here.[72] In England, the eyewitness's description of the suspect must be recorded before any identification procedure occurs. The procedure must be conducted by someone who is *not* involved with the investigation. Photographic identifications require a minimum of twelve photos and lineups require eight "foils." Moreover, in-court identifications are rarely if ever permitted in the Crown Court, where serious crimes are tried. I agree with Stanley Fisher and Ian McKenzie that this is a plausible model for the American states.[73]

Beyond problems with the procedure itself, a fundamental jury problem exists when eyewitnesses testify. Cutler and Penrod reach the "truly dismal conclusion" that jurors lack the ability to separate good identifications from flawed ones.[74] Jurors "overestimate the accuracy of identifications."[75] These problems suggest permitting testimony from defense experts about how easily humans make mistakes when identifying others. Cutler and Penrod conclude that "expert psychological testimony can serve as a safeguard" against juror acceptance of mistaken identification.[76] Elizabeth Loftus also endorses expert testimony about human error in making identifications.[77] Cautionary jury instructions might be helpful, though

Cutler and Penrod found "little evidence" that cautionary jury instructions improved the ability of jurors to sort accurate from inaccurate identifications.[78]

Whatever reforms are adopted will work better if the screening magistrate is in charge of the identification process. The police, after all, have a theory of the case and a belief that one of the persons in the lineup is the guilty person. The magistrate has no stake in the outcome of the procedure and can easily be shielded from knowing which person is the suspect.

The screening magistrate should also supervise DNA evidence collection, to standardize the process, to assure testing in accredited laboratories, and to facilitate getting DNA samples from suspects. When police come into possession of DNA evidence, they should be required to turn it over to the magistrate. On motion of the prosecutor or defense lawyer, the magistrate should have the power to compel anyone to submit to DNA testing. Tracey Maclin has argued that routine DNA testing, without judicial authorization, violates the Fourth Amendment.[79] To involve the magistrate in every compelled DNA testing avoids this problem.

Screening magistrate should supervise pretrial discovery. Federal magistrates in our current system do this, though their decisions can be appealed to the district judge. In most state systems, criminal court judges rule on contested discovery matters. It makes more sense to have the screening magistrate rule on discovery requests. The magistrate, after all, will have supervised some of the evidence collection and will know more about the case against the defendant than any other judge.

I agree with Cynthia Jones that reforms in discovery rules should include a requirement that biological evidence be preserved, with sanctions for failure to do so that include vacating the conviction or dismissing the indictment with prejudice.[80] I join Lloyd Weinreb, Bill Pizzi, Susan Klein, and many others in recommending that we liberalize and simplify discovery in routine criminal cases. To Weinreb, the process should not "begin by hiding from the defense the evidence the police have gathered at the scene of the crime until it has been fixed as part of the government's case."[81] To Pizzi, the current American rules resemble "a card game in which the prosecutor and the defense attorney lay individual pieces of evidence on the table but keep the rest of their hands close to the vest."[82] Klein recommends radical, and salutary, changes in the federal rules.[83]

The current federal discovery rules are as complex as calculus and as long as a Hemingway short story.[84] Matters are simpler, and fairer, in France, where "counsel for the defendant has an absolute right to inspect the full *dossier* of the case prior to trial and at certain stages of pretrial procedure."[85] Like Darryl Brown, I would generally follow France.[86] The discovery rules should thus contain a strong presumption in favor of "open-file" discovery in cases outside of terrorism, organized crime, and large-scale criminal enterprises.[87] The presumption could be rebutted only by a showing of a compelling need to keep the information from the defense—for example, to protect witnesses or the identity of confidential informants. The examining magistrate would decide those questions on a case-by-case basis.

PRETRIAL JUDICIAL REVIEW

In France, the magistrate has complete control over the investigation, and innocent defendants have a reasonable chance to have their case dismissed. In 2002–4, examining magistrates dismissed 8 percent of cases for insufficient evidence.[88] In the United States, data for dismissals at the preliminary hearing stage do not seem to exist, but an experienced defense lawyer calculated that "the odds of a magistrate throwing a case out are like 1,000 to 1."[89] Even discounting for hyperbole, the rate of dismissal must be far below the French rate. Data *are* available for dismissals at the grand jury stage. In 2003, federal grand juries failed to return an indictment in 0.2 percent of the cases.[90] Either American prosecutors are much less likely than French prosecutors to bring weak cases, or an awful lot of weak cases survive the preliminary hearing and the grand jury.

The problem is that the preliminary screening processes in the American system are far too narrow in scope to permit an innocent accused to probe the prosecution's case. A preliminary hearing is a carefully scripted presentation of the state's case, where the prosecutor shows just enough to demonstrate probable cause to the judge. The prosecutor would be a fool to put on any weak evidence that may exist. The grand jury is even less effective as a screening mechanism. In most American jurisdictions, neither the defendant nor his lawyer can be present before the grand jury, which hears only the state's side of the case.

We should follow France and create serious judicial review of the state's case prior to trial. Rather than have a trivial judicial screen shortly after arrest, as preliminary hearings now provide; we should require a thorough review after the evidence has been gathered and the defendant has been given discovery of the state's case. The idea behind having the hearing early is to screen out obviously innocent defendants, but there is little evidence that it accomplishes this purpose. To give innocent defendants a realistic chance at dismissal later in the process more than offsets any hardship that results from waiting for a meaningful judicial review of the state's case.

If held after the evidence is gathered and the defense has had discovery, the name *preliminary hearing* does not fit. I suggest *pretrial judicial review*, to make clear that it is a significant hurdle for the state. To make it significant, the state should have to prove guilt to a magistrate by a higher standard than probable cause as it is currently understood. The standing joke in one county where I practiced law was that probable cause existed if the defendant was in the county when the crime took place.

A low standard arguably suffices to justify arrest and detention, but more should be required to bring a case to trial. I suggest *preponderance of the evidence.* This is the standard for a civil verdict, and lawyers and judges are thus accustomed to using it. It demands a "more probable than not" judgment about guilt. But to make it less likely for the guilty to escape, I would follow the current federal procedure and permit the state to use its evidence without regard to whether it will be admissible at trial. If the state cannot meet a preponderance standard after it has had time to marshal its evidence, and without limits on admissibility, two corollaries follow: (1) the defendant might be innocent; and (2) the chance of proving guilt beyond a reasonable doubt at trial is fairly low. To reduce further the risk that the guilty will go free, a dismissal would not be a jeopardy bar to a second trial. If the prosecutor believes in the guilt of a dismissed defendant, she can seek to strengthen the state's case and bring charges again.

The pragmatist skeptic will argue that a pretrial judicial review will make everyone's job more difficult because it will require what amounts to two trials. To the extent the argument is based on wanting to keep trial strategy secret, it reeks of the adversarial mess that we need to leave behind. But to the extent the argument is based on duplication of time and effort, it needs to be addressed. The skeptic notes that many of the witnesses—for both sides—might have to testify at both the pretrial judicial review and the trial.

This valid skeptical argument can be largely finessed by moving the criminal process toward the civil justice process. In civil cases, important witnesses are deposed prior to trial. Darryl Brown has proposed several, somewhat limited, ways in which depositions could aid in uncovering the truth about innocent criminal defendants.[91] But I favor deposing all witnesses, or at least all important witnesses, to the extent permitted by the Constitution.

Florida has for more than forty years provided all criminal defendants the right to take pretrial depositions of most witnesses, and no strain to its criminal justice system has been reported.[92] In 2001, reacting to the same concerns that would later move Governor Ryan to commute 156 death sentences, the Illinois Supreme Court revised its rules to permit defendants in capital cases to take depositions of witnesses "upon a showing of good cause."[93] Both the Florida and Illinois rules are careful to minimize the risk of witness intimidation, which is the greatest harm threatened by depositions in criminal cases. Florida provides for protective orders and forbids the presence of defendants at the deposition unless both parties agree. Illinois denies defendants the right to appear at the deposition but gives judges discretion to permit attendance.

The defendant could not be forced to give a deposition, of course, without running afoul of the Fifth Amendment privilege against compelled self-incrimination. But innocent defendants should be eager to be deposed, with a competent criminal law specialist at their side. Defendants today can be forced to disclose certain defenses, such as alibi and insanity,[94] and it would add nothing to the constitutional burden to require all defense witnesses to be deposed. The Constitution permits deposing of all prosecution witnesses.

Given the broader discovery rights already recommended, defendants would have a good idea what witnesses to depose. The pretrial judicial review is not a trial—no verdict is possible—and most, perhaps all, of the evidence can be presented though depositions. A two-stage process would work nicely here. Based on the depositions, the magistrate could issue a provisional order dismissing the case or retaining jurisdiction. Either side could move for a hearing if dissatisfied with the initial ruling.

I predict there will be few motions for an in-court hearing. If the state has a strong case, and the defendant is guilty, why would he move for a hearing? If the state's case is weak, and the magistrate's provisional order dismisses it, the prosecutor's best avenue is to begin again and build a better case rather than have a hearing at which, presumably, the weakness of the case will be highlighted.

When a hearing occurs, it could be limited to evidence not in the depositions—except to the extent the truthfulness of the deposed testimony is at issue—thus minimizing the problem of witnesses having to testify at two trials. The hearing can be made shorter and more efficient by having the same magistrate who oversaw the eyewitness identification and the DNA collection sit as judge. He would know firsthand about uncertainties of the eyewitness or flaws in the way the physical evidence was collected. Dan Medwed suggested to me that magistrates might be subject to the same "tunnel vision" I noted in chapter 1 with respect to police and prosecutors.[95] I acknowledge the possibility but believe that a judge will, by nature, be more objective, more skeptical, and more aware of the weaknesses in the state's case.

The pretrial judicial review is the best venue for the defense to attack false evidence. Because there is no jury to "protect," no reason exists to exclude defense experts who will challenge the state's science, the eyewitness procedure, the veracity of police testimony, or the truth of the confession. We should have confidence in the ability of the screening magistrate to sort out conflicting testimony to arrive at one simple conclusion. At the end of the review, the screening magistrate either will, or will not, be persuaded by a preponderance of the evidence that the defendant is guilty of the crime with which he is charged.

A research project in England, conducted by McConville and Baldwin, suggests that the pretrial judicial review I have described would be helpful in removing innocent defendants from the process. Police in England prepare written committal papers that describe the case against the accused in some detail, a process that replaced the English grand jury.[96] The researchers asked two "assessors" to examine roughly eight hundred committal papers for cases that had already concluded. The assessors, who worked independently of each other and did not know the actual outcome of the cases, were asked to identify cases so weak that they should not have been brought to trial. The assessors "were asked to act, as it were, as [French] examining magistrates."[97]

Of the cases that the assessors identified as too weak to proceed, 85 percent had resulted in acquittals.[98] There is every reason to believe that many of these defendants were innocent. To be sure, the assessors missed many cases that resulted in acquittal—they identified only 52 of 285 acquittals.[99] This is not troubling for three reasons. First, no screen is perfect. None of the fifty-two cases that the assessors identified as too weak had been screened out by the current system, and any gain in innocence protection is a positive. Second, at least some of the acquittals missed by the assessors were probably guilty but the prosecution lacked proof beyond a reasonable doubt.[100] Finally, the assessors were limited to the committal papers prepared by police. A set of depositions, some taken by the defense, would provide a much more effective screen. Moreover, innocent defendants who lose at the first (provisional order) stage would request a hearing, where the defense could probe the state's case, enhancing the chance of dismissal.

My pretrial judicial review should thus work much more effectively than a screen of committal papers. This kind of pretrial judicial review should have benefits that go beyond screening more innocent defendants out of the system. With most of the case memorialized in depositions, both parties can more realistically judge their chance of a favorable verdict at trial, which is the reason that discovery in civil cases has expanded dramatically in the last half century. And, as I will show in a moment, pretrial judicial review permits a new and much improved form of "plea bargaining."

GRAND JURY

In our current system, the grand jury typically follows the preliminary hearing. But by changing the preliminary hearing to a pretrial judicial review later in the process, where the magistrate will evaluate whether the case is sufficient to take to trial, it would make little sense for the grand jury to screen at that point. Thus, I would make changes in the grand jury process and move it ahead of the magistrate's pretrial judicial review.

In France, if the examining magistrate finds cause to proceed, the case goes to the indicting chamber, where a panel of three judges conducts its own investigation. The indicting chamber is charged with discerning the truth about the accusation. Most American grand juries, by contrast, hear only prosecution witnesses. Truth is not an explicit goal. Indeed, the Court has held that prosecutors are not required to present evidence of innocence to the grand jury.[101]

The French indicting chamber is a much better *screening* tool than our grand jury, but I agree with Peter Henning that the Court's grand jury doctrine seeks to make it an effective *investigative* tool: "The grand jury serves a special role in the investigation of crime, especially white collar crimes in which the authority and presence of a grand jury are the best means of ferreting out information."[102] France has no need for an investigative grand jury because the examining magistrate performs that function. As we lack the French examining magistrate, we do have need for an investigative grand jury.

Is there a way to retain the investigative function and improve the screening function? I believe so. To be sure, the pretrial judicial review will be the most effective screening device, but added screening from the grand jury would be a plus. Susan Brenner recommends following Hawaii and providing independent counsel to the grand jury, rather than relying on the prosecutor who brought the charge. "Statutes could create the office of 'grand jury counsel' and specify the qualifications required of those who would fill this position."[103] Andrew Leipold recommends that grand juries be drawn from the lawyers in the jurisdiction, on the theory that lawyers are more likely to understand the law and are accustomed to doubting and questioning everything.[104]

Both are good ideas to improve screening. The issue is whether either or both would significantly impede the grand jury's investigative function. Though any judgment here is necessarily speculative, any loss in investigative function would likely be slight. Independent counsel would have access to the prosecutor's file and presumably would pursue information as diligently as the prosecutor who brought the charge. Moreover, having the case challenged by a group of testy lawyers would only strengthen those cases that go forward. I think these innovations are worth trying.

If the grand jury refuses to indict, the prosecutor can, as now, begin again if she wishes. When the grand jury indicts, the case stays in the process, heading toward the pretrial judicial review. The parties will take depositions and ask the magistrate to decide whether the state has demonstrated guilt by a preponderance of the evidence. The cases that make it through the pretrial screen will be set for trial.

PLEA BARGAINING

As McConville and Mirsky have observed, something very odd happened to Anglo-American justice on the way to the twentieth century. In the first half of the nineteenth century, the "culture of criminal justice celebrated trial by jury as the fairest and most reliable method of case disposition and then in the middle of the century dramatically gave birth to the guilty plea system or plea bargaining."[105] While the details of this birth are beyond the scope of my project, plea bargaining remains a troubling phenomenon because it is "covert and informal,"[106] and thus we cannot know how many innocent defendants are "sweet-talked" into pleading guilty.

Ron Wright has demonstrated a falling acquittal rate in federal courts since 1971, a fact that is consistent with an increase in the number of innocent defendants who plead guilty and thus avoid trial. In 2002, the acquittal rate was 1 percent, "the lowest level in the history of the federal criminal justice system."[107] More significantly, Wright has shown that two factors completely under the control of prosecutors are statistically correlated with high guilty-plea rates *and* low acquittal rates—the sentencing discounts federal law provides for "acceptance of responsibility" and providing "substantial assistance."[108] These data suggest to Wright that when prosecutors have significant power to offer deeply discounted sentences—as they do in most states—prosecutors have the power to "distort trial outcomes" and to "undercut[] the power of the trial to uncover the truth."[109]

This is not a problem in France, where a defendant who has confessed, and wants nothing more than to be sentenced, must undergo a criminal trial. In my view, that takes formalism too far. If a defendant wants to plead guilty, why force a trial on him? The harder question, for me, is whether to forbid prosecutors from offering plea bargains to obtain guilty pleas. Some wonder whether plea bargaining is illegitimate, either because it induces too many innocents to confess or because it undermines the moral communication to society that a trial provides.[110]

Under the indifferent stewardship of the Supreme Court, plea bargaining in the United States can resemble an ordeal by fire. In *Bordenkircher v. Hayes*,[111] Paul Hayes had been convicted of two prior Kentucky felonies, though neither resulted in even a day's incarceration. When he was indicted for passing a forged instrument in the amount of $88.30, he faced two to ten years in prison. The prosecutor offered to recommend a sentence of five years if Hayes pleaded guilty. The prosecutor said that if Hayes refused to save everyone the "inconvenience" of a trial, "he would return to the grand jury to seek an indictment under the Kentucky Habitual Criminal Act, which would subject Hayes to a mandatory sentence of life imprisonment by reason of his two prior felony convictions."[112]

The contrast with the French system is illuminating and depressing. In France, a trial is judged to be the natural, indeed the only, way to demonstrate guilt. In the United States, it is viewed as an "inconvenience." Hayes chose not to save the prosecutor the "inconvenience" of trial—he refused to plead guilty. The prosecutor did exactly what he threatened: He returned to the grand jury and got a new indictment under the Habitual Criminal Act. The jury found Hayes guilty on the forgery charge, and the judge sentenced him to life in prison.

A defendant who had never been incarcerated was sentenced to life in prison for passing a forged instrument in the value of $88.30. And that sentence was imposed on him *because he chose to exercise his right to a trial.* Moreover, imagine if Hayes were innocent of the forgery. The pressure on this innocent Hayes to plead guilty would be enormous. I know what you are thinking: The U.S. Supreme Court would not tolerate the pale excuse for justice that Hayes received. And, of course, you are wrong.

Because the prosecutor could have brought the Habitual Criminal Act charge in the first place and then bargained down, the Court reasoned, it was no different to bring a lower charge in the first place and threaten the greater charge in an attempt to induce a plea. While as a matter of formal logic, this is indeed true, formal logic misses much here. Trials are not, even under our system, best viewed as an "inconvenience." They should be the default, avoided only if both parties bargain in good faith to reach a deal. Whatever you call the actions of the prosecutor in *Bordenkircher*—"unethical" comes to my mind[113]—it was not a "good faith" bargaining process.

The Court worried that a ruling in Hayes's favor would induce prosecutors to start off charging the maximum and, over a universe of cases, defendants would suffer. I think that assumes, unfairly, that prosecutors are not moved by their ethical duty to seek justice. That duty, as Justice Powell pointed out in dissent, requires the prosecutor to charge what she thinks is deserved under the circumstances of the case, not the maximum allowed by law. And once the prosecutor makes that judgment, she should be stuck with it, unless she discovers additional evidence that shows greater culpability on the defendant's part. This was Justice Powell's view, largely shared by three other dissenting justices.

As much as I disagree with the *Bordenkircher* majority, the Court might be right that it is too difficult for appellate courts to regulate, after the fact, plea deals made between parties of obviously unequal bargaining power. Susan Klein argues for radical changes in discovery law to improve the defendant's bargaining position.[114] I would also involve judges. Courts have been loathe to permit, and have never required, judges to participate in the plea-bargaining process, but this attitude manifests the hoary adversarial approach embraced by Matthew Hale. When the screening magistrate has reviewed the state's case, and found the accused more likely than not guilty of a crime, the magistrate would know far more about the case than judges in our current system would know. Why not authorize the magistrate to decide the proper penalty?

To those who draw back in horror at any greater involvement of the judge in settling criminal cases, I note that Scotland has adopted a process somewhat similar to what I recommend. Prior to trial, the judge in Scotland is required to assess the extent to which the parties agree on facts, whether the accused adheres to a plea of not guilty, and the level of preparation of both sides.[115] Peter Duff notes that thirty years ago, "recommendations of this nature would have been unthinkable" in Scotland.[116] But times are changing.

My proposal that the magistrate be in control of the process leading to a guilty plea avoids the coercion and unequal bargaining power that infects the American plea-bargaining system. Putting the magistrate in control would replace with a transparent process the shadowy, covert, and informal process that now exists. There would be no negotiations. Not being a party, the magistrate would have no incentive to bargain. He would set a fair penalty and if the defendant wanted to accept, he could. If the defendant does not accept the proposed penalty, the case goes to trial.

THE TRIAL

Can we learn something from the French system of trying criminal cases? While I like the idea of the French presiding judge calling and examining the witnesses, I recognize the wrenching change that would be. So I recommend modest changes here, focusing on improving jury instructions, easing the path for the introduction of proof of innocence, and giving witnesses more freedom to tell their story.

A study by Kassin and Wrightsman suggests that jurors who are instructed *before trial begins* that they must find the defendant guilty beyond a reasonable doubt are more likely not to convict.[117] Erik Lillquist concludes that this effect might be because jurors are paying more attention at that stage and because jurors begin forming judgments early in the trial.[118] Lillquist is skeptical that innocent defendants will benefit disproportionately if the reasonable-doubt instruction is given earlier, but my intuition is otherwise. The prosecution gets to present its evidence first and it seems to me that hastily formed opinions about guilt are more likely to incorrectly find guilt than lack of guilt.

The American method of eliciting truth in trials is to have one lawyer ask the witness a series of narrow questions, with the other side prepared to object, thus keeping control of the presentation in the hands of the lawyers. Studies indicate that this method of questioning will not "elicit the fullest information in the least distorted fashion. The preferred method is what we do instinctively—allow a person to give a free, uninterrupted report about the topic of interest and then only ask questions to remove ambiguities, fill in gaps, and test whether knowledge has been exhausted."[119] Once again, the French have a better procedure, with the witness permitted largely to testify in her own words and the presiding judge asking any questions needed to fill in gaps. Adopting the continental system is radical surgery, as Jonakait recognizes, "because the witnesses granted such freedom may too easily say something that the rules of evidence . . . do not permit."[120]

It is unclear to me that we should retain the complex, stultifying rules of evidence that plague our trials. But, in the interest of suggesting the least intrusive reforms that advance the goal of getting to the truth, I offer a modest reform of the way examination and cross-examination are used to construct the facts.[121] The rules of evidence should be amended to require that, at the end of direct and cross-examination, the judge ask the witness, "Is there anything else you would like to say in the interest of helping us uncover the truth about what happened?" If, in answering that question, a witness ran afoul of the rules of evidence, the judge could solve most of those problems by instructing the jury to ignore what violated the rule.

Another reform is to ease the way for evidence of innocence. You might think that even our adversary system would not intentionally preclude evidence of innocence. You would be wrong. In *Chambers v. Mississippi*,[122] the defendant had a strong case for innocence because another man, McDonald, had confessed on three separate occasions to murdering the victim. The state law of hearsay forbade Chambers from presenting the testimony of the witnesses who heard McDonald confess. Most jurisdictions have an exception for hearsay statements against penal interest, which these surely were, but Mississippi did not recognize that exception.

Nor was Chambers permitted to cross-examine McDonald about why he confessed to the murder. The state, naturally, did not call McDonald as a witness. When Chambers called McDonald, he testified that he confessed only because a minister promised him he would not go to jail but would be able to sue the town for damages. As bizarre as that story sounds, McDonald was ripe for a penetrating cross-examination, but the state trial judge trotted out the "voucher" rule and refused to permit cross-examination. This rule holds that when a party presents a witness, it "vouches" for his credibility and thus cannot seek to discredit his testimony. By calling him to the stand, Chambers "vouched" for McDonald and could not challenge his story.

The voucher rule should go the way of the dinosaur. If a witness testifies in a way that counsel did not expect, only gamesmanship or empty formalism justifies denying the lawyer the right to get to the bottom of the difference in the testimony. A system devoted to getting the truth before the jury would insist that both sides be permitted to cross-examine any witness, to "beat and bolt out the Truth." Jenny McEwan has argued that *any rule* that keeps reliable defense evidence from the fact finder should be rejected.[123] Whatever a fair trial entails, we "can be sure that handicapping [defendants] does not represent even rough justice."[124]

Following McEwan, any rule that prevents the introduction of evidence of innocence should give way to the due process interest in protecting innocent defendants. To be sure, this rule will not always be easy to implement. Peter Henning pointed out to me that my use of "innocence" suggests that it is an indisputable fact in the universe. I either killed my enemy or I did not. But what if the issue was my state of mind? Now the fact in the universe about guilt begins to grow fuzzy. What if the issue is not a common-law crime but a white-collar crime? Is there even a fact in the universe about conspiring to restrain trade?

But the judgment about whether a particular rule impedes a defendant from proving his innocence is, I believe, no more difficult than many other evidentiary rulings judges make today. Indeed, one could analogize the innocence objection to the motion to exclude testimony because it is unduly prejudicial. The rule there is, roughly, whether the relevance of the evidence outweighs the prejudicial effect on the jury. The same standard could be used to decide whether an offer of evidence is sufficiently probative of innocence to justify its introduction despite a rule that would otherwise keep it out.

The Court has come close to holding that due process requires the introduction of evidence that is sufficiently probative of innocence. In *Chambers*, the Court held that the state court had deprived Chambers of a fair trial. In *Holmes v. South Carolina*,[125] the defense in a brutal rape and murder was that the state's forensic evidence had been contaminated and that someone else had admitted committing the crime. The state courts rejected the evidence that someone else had confessed, on the state law ground that exculpatory evidence is not admissible if it merely casts "a bare suspicion upon another" or raises "a conjectural inference as to the commission of the crime by another."[126] The Supreme Court held that excluding the exculpatory evidence in *Holmes* violated due process.

Both *Chambers* and *Holmes* are hopeful, though narrow, cases. But the Court has sometimes forgotten the importance of allowing the jury to hear evidence of innocence. In *Taylor v. Illinois*,[127] the defendant offered a witness to testify that someone else shot at the victim. The Sixth Amendment right "to have compulsory process for obtaining witnesses" would seem to give Taylor the right to present this witness. Well, yes, but what if the discovery of the witness was near the time of trial, making it unfair to the prosecution to permit him to testify? It still seems that a court should permit the witness to testify, probably granting a continuance to give the state a chance to prepare its response.

But suppose the defense lawyer knew about the witness in time to give the prosecutor notice but sought an unfair advantage by intentionally hiding his identity, thus violating state disclosure rules. This changes *nothing* about whether Taylor was innocent or whether the witness will offer evidence of innocence. It calls for sanctions against the lawyer for violating the discovery rules. But what if a judge refused to allow the witness to testify as the sanction? Remarkably, the Supreme Court held that the Sixth Amendment permits this sanction. The Court thus permitted the state to punish a defendant, who is presumed innocent, as a way of deterring lawyers from playing games with the disclosure rules. If the presumption of innocence is meaningful, *Taylor* is indefensible.

The trial judge in *Taylor* relied in part on his judgment that the witness was not credible, and the Supreme Court seemed to agree that this was appropriate. What happened to the jury's role as the "conscience of the community?"[128] Matravers argues that in rendering a verdict, the jury "blurs the descriptive and evaluative aspects of judgment" and that this is a vital part of the jury's role.[129] Jonakait concludes that the "practical application of the 'beyond a reasonable doubt' standard should reflect community standards. A jury, once again, can often do that better than a judge."[130]

A jury that reflects the community should hear almost any evidence of innocence, assuming it is sufficiently probative of innocence, and judge credibility for itself. That, in essence, is what the Court held in *Holmes v. South Carolina. Taylor* was a mistake, a moment of amnesia about the value of protecting innocence and the role of the jury in assessing credibility. As *Holmes* is a later case than *Taylor,* perhaps it is part of a new awakening about the critical role of due process in protecting the innocent.

To be sure, the judge must be a gatekeeper of sorts. In addition to judging whether the evidence is sufficiently probative of innocence, the judge should tell the jury if the witness has perjury convictions or other convictions consistent with lack of truthfulness. If the witness has any reason not to be truthful, the lawyer for the other side should be permitted to explore those reasons. For example, recognizing the credibility problem posed by an accomplice who shifts the blame to a defendant, the common law developed a rule forbidding a conviction solely on the testimony of an accomplice.

This brings us to the evidentiary problems posed by jailhouse informants. The ABA report *Achieving Justice* recommends extending the accomplice corroboration rule to jailhouse informants—"no person should lose liberty or life based solely on the testimony of such a witness."[131] Extending this rule to jailhouse informants is a good idea but, as the ABA report concludes, more needs to be done. Better training of prosecutors would certainly help.[132]

As Steven Skurka shows, Canada is far ahead of the United States in recognizing and taking steps to ameliorate the problem of lying jailhouse informants. He concludes that "a clear and sharp warning about concerns with respect to [the informant's] reliability will invariably follow . . . in any jury trial in Canada where a jailhouse informant is called by the prosecution as a witness." Moreover, he is hopeful that "this kind of evidence may simply be a vestige of the past and may rarely appear in a Canadian courtroom."[133]

I agree with Dan Medwed that we should learn from the Canadian experience and "take a similarly expansive and thorough look at the use of informant testimony in American courts."[134] The Oklahoma Court of Criminal Appeals in *Dodd v. State*[135] adopted two innocence-friendly rules of procedure while reversing capital murder counts based largely on the testimony of a jailhouse informant who later recanted his testimony and then recanted the recantation.

Dodd placed a detailed disclosure requirement on the state when jailhouse informants are part of the case, including the criminal history of the informant, any deals made with the informant, the details about the statements attributed to the defendant, other cases in which the informant offered statements, and whether the informant has ever recanted statements. The second *Dodd* rule was to require a cautionary instruction in cases where jailhouse informants testify for the state. Several jurisdictions require cautionary instructions,[136] and the Oklahoma instruction is a good one: "testimony of an informer who provides evidence against a defendant must be examined and weighed by you with greater care than the testimony of an ordinary witness." The instruction also includes a series of considerations to help the jury decide whether to believe the informant.[137]

As much as I like both rules, I was disappointed that the Oklahoma Court of Criminal Appeals withdrew its earlier opinion in *Dodd*, which required a reliability hearing before the judge as an additional safeguard.[138] As with the use of expert witness hearings "to ensure the relevance and reliability of novel scientific expert testimony, this reliability hearing [would] allow the trial court to perform its gatekeeping function and filter out prejudicial jailhouse informant testimony that is more probably false than true."[139]

Using all three procedures—disclosure of information about the informant, a judicial screen, and cautionary instructions for testimony that passes the screen—is the best approach to reducing false convictions due to jailhouse informants. If a judge decides that the informant's testimony is more probably false than true, there is no reason to allow a jury to consider it at all. If a judge finds the testimony more likely to be true than false, we give the testimony to a jury with the cautionary instructions.

As for the general instruction to juries on how to decide the guilt of the defendant, I recommend a variation of the French instruction that is posted in the jury room. Here is my modified version of the French instruction:

> The law does not ask jurors to account for the means by which they convince themselves; it does not charge them with any rule from which they shall specifically derive the fullness and adequacy of evidence. It requires them to question themselves in silence and reflection and to seek in the sincerity of their conscience what impression has been made on their reason by the evidence brought against the accused and the arguments of his defense. The law asks them but this single question, which encloses the full scope of their duties: Are you inwardly convinced beyond a reasonable doubt?

I would not, however, adopt the French secret ballot style of voting. The give-and-take of deliberation, and the requirement that each juror announce her vote during the deliberation, makes clear the solemnity of the task. If you know someone might challenge your vote, you will reflect more deeply on your reasons. If your reasons are illegitimate—based on race or sex, for example—you will have an incentive to change your vote. As Abramson notes, the "give-and-take model" of jury deliberation "defines the democratic ideal."[140] A deliberative vote should make the verdict more the voice of the community than the French secret ballot procedure.

In France, a conviction requires eight of twelve guilty votes. Anything less than eight is an acquittal. I cannot imagine a legislature allowing a seven-to-five verdict for guilt to be an acquittal rather than a hung jury that permits a retrial. Thus, I offer a compromise. A mathematical model that Barry Pollack and I developed shows that the risk of an erroneous verdict with a nine-to-three vote is around 5 percent.[141] While that is far too high a risk if the error is a conviction of an innocent defendant, it seems a tolerable risk level for erroneous acquittals that free guilty defendants. Requiring twelve to zero for conviction but only nine to three for acquittal would be a concrete, formal way to give meaning to the presumption of innocence. Lloyd Weinreb has made a similar proposal.[142]

My system thus contemplates deadlocked juries in a range from eleven guilty votes to four guilty votes. While we are making criminal procedure more rational, we can do something for the arcane, complex law of hung juries. The laws of the states and federal circuits differ substantially on what the judge is permitted to say to a jury to move it toward a verdict. Simple here is better than the current law. If the jury cannot reach a verdict, the judge should say to the jury: "Please return to the jury room and keep trying." This is a radically simplified version of what is known as the "*Allen* charge"— a charge designed to encourage, but not compel, juries to reach a verdict. Mark Greenbaum and I have shown that a simplified "Allen charge" is more likely to produce a verdict and less likely to raise concern about judges coercing the jury to reach a verdict.[143]

If a reasonable number of "please keep trying" instructions fails to produce a verdict, the judge will grant a mistrial. At that point, the judge should poll the jury to determine how it was split. This is a valuable piece of information that should be put on the record. If the vote is eight to four for acquittal, for example, the prosecutor might decide not to reset the case for trial but would surely be inclined to reprosecute if the vote is eleven to one for conviction.

APPEALS

I find much to value in the continental mode of appeals, though here I prefer Germany's approach to the novel French procedure that simply provides another jury trial. In the American system, appeals are almost exclusively about procedural errors: The judge should have granted the motion to suppress, should have sustained defense objections to evidence offered at trial, should have given different instructions, and so forth.[144] A contest-based adversarial system will naturally produce a procedural focus.

A procedural focus on appeal is indifferent to innocence. A substantive review of the evidence that supports the conviction would, of course, favor innocent defendants. But the Supreme Court has never required a meaningful review of the correctness of convictions. The reason for that is found in our contest-based system. Once a fair contest has been held, the system tends to protect the outcome of the contest and thus values, over everything else, stability in judgments. Damaska concludes, "Because substantively correct outcomes are relatively less important [to contest-based systems], it is clear that the conflict-solving style of proceeding is averse to changing decisions—even if they rest on legal or factual error."[145]

Prior to *Jackson v. Virginia*,[146] the standard for federal habeas corpus review of the sufficiency of evidence in state cases was called the "no evidence" rule: Convictions were affirmed unless there was no evidence to support the conviction. This is a robust example of Damaska's notion that a contest-based system values stability even when a conviction is substantively erroneous. Under the "no evidence" rule, defendants rarely challenged the sufficiency of evidence on appeal, and appellate courts spent little time reviewing the record. What would be the point?

The Court in *Jackson*, however, found the risk of erroneous convictions high enough to require a more searching inquiry. Federal courts reviewing state convictions in habeas cases must, the Court said, decide whether "the record evidence could reasonably support a finding of guilt beyond a reasonable doubt."[147] This is a good start, but then the Court flinched. A reviewing court need *not* "ask itself whether it believes that the evidence at the trial established guilt beyond a reasonable doubt."[148] Why not? The Court provided no reason, though it was surely the fear of a crushing burden on appellate courts.

The Court drew the life from its "reasonably support" standard with a test that the state will be able to meet in almost every case: "whether, after viewing the evidence in the light most favorable to the prosecution, *any* rational trier of fact *could* have found the essential elements of the crime beyond a reasonable doubt."[149] The test is whether *any* rational trier of fact *could* (not would) have found guilt beyond a reasonable doubt. And one reaches this extremely deferential standard only after viewing the evidence in the light most favorable to the prosecution.

How many innocent defendants could meet the *Jackson* standard? A precious few, I believe. I offer a real-life example.[150] James Powell was charged with misdemeanor child abuse. Patricia, the mother of the child, testified that James spanked the child on November 2. The physician examined the child on November 8. My theory was that the bruises could not have been caused by that spanking because they were too "fresh." I believed that they had been caused by Patricia in a subsequent spanking. She admitted on the witness stand to a hot temper, to spanking the child on occasion with a switch, and to having been institutionalized for mental illness. She did not report the bruises until her mother angrily demanded an explanation. There was no testimony that James had spanked the child on any other day.

The examining physician's testimony was thus crucial. The physician testified that the bruises were "probably" two or three days old but could have been as much as three to four days old. If the bruises could not have been more than four days old, the state's case would fall apart. When the prosecutor pressed, however, the physician admitted that the bruises "could have been" approximately a week old. The jury convicted.

On appeal, I thought I had an excellent case for reversal on insufficient evidence grounds—"could have been" did not sound like proof beyond a reasonable doubt to me. But I lost under Tennessee's version of the "no evidence" rule. There was *some* evidence—the mother's testimony and the physician's admission that the bruises "could have been" old enough to have been inflicted by James. Notice that *Jackson* changes nothing in the review of the Powell case. Viewing the evidence in the light most favorable to the state, the mother was telling the truth, the physician's testimony about "could have been" must be credited, and the bruises were thus six days old. I would have lost under the *Jackson* standard, too.

The problem is the *Jackson* standard. As I pointed out in chapter 5, states are free to adopt a different standard of review for their own appellate courts. One that has done so is Texas. In a thoughtful opinion recognizing that *Jackson* is the minimum floor, rather than a standard mandated for state courts, the Texas Court of Criminal Appeal (the highest court to hear criminal cases in Texas) adopted a standard of review that

> differs from the *Jackson* standard in two ways: (1) the evidence is not viewed in the light most favorable to the State . . . and (2) the verdict, even if rational and reasonable under *Jackson,* is examined to see if it is so contrary to the overwhelming weight of the evidence, that it is manifestly wrong and unjust.[151]

The Texas approach is a marked improvement on *Jackson,* but I think we can do better.

In the German system, the appeals panel "starts from scratch—hearing the witnesses, considering afresh the evidence and the law, and giving its own independent conclusions."[152] Thus, there is no need for a transcript, a statement of the trial court's errors, or a brief in support of reversing the conviction. Nor is there a retrial. The appeals court judgment is the final verdict. Feeney and Herrmann conclude that "the major functional difference" between the American and German systems of appeal "is the greater opportunity that the German system affords for reviewing mistakes of fact."[153]

Though I like this approach, it is too radical for American courts. An alternative that is more efficient and roughly as protective of innocence would be to require an appellate court to determine, from the transcript, whether the state offered sufficient evidence of guilt. The Constitution Project recently made a similar recommendation for review of convictions in capital cases, calling on appellate courts to reverse convictions "if a reasonable jury could not have found guilt beyond a reasonable doubt."[154] I would permit defendants to seek a transcript review in all felony cases, but I prefer the standard that the Supreme Court already prescribes to decide whether to reverse convictions when a failed procedure threatens a wrongful conviction.

The Court has created two accuracy-related procedural claims: ineffective assistance of counsel and the state's failure to disclose exculpatory evidence. The Court instructs lower courts in these cases to reverse the conviction if the error undermines confidence in the conviction. The failure to turn exculpatory evidence over to the defense, for example, will require an appellate reversal when there is a "reasonable probability that, had the evidence been disclosed to the defense, the result of the proceeding would have been different. A 'reasonable probability' is a probability sufficient to undermine confidence in the outcome."[155]

The Court's explicit goal when structuring the right to effective counsel and the right to exculpatory evidence is to ensure procedures that produce accurate trial outcomes. To apply the same standard for reversing convictions when a defendant makes a substantive claim of innocence simply recognizes the equivalence between procedure and substance. Lower courts are familiar with the standard. It is, to be sure, not very precise, but I trust appellate courts to apply it in a way that benefits innocent defendants who make a substantial showing of innocence. In any event, it is far better than the vacuous *Jackson* standard.

When the appellate judges find their confidence in the conviction undermined, they would have two choices. If the demonstration of innocence is sufficiently powerful, they could simply enter an acquittal—this is the functional effect of a finding of insufficient evidence under current doctrine.[156] Cases with less powerful showings of innocence could be sent back to a magistrate to take new evidence to be reviewed by the court of appeals. The transcript review would have revealed the weak spots in the state's case, and the court of appeals could direct the magistrate to explore those areas. In my Powell case, for example, if the appellate panel were not sufficiently convinced of his innocence from the transcript review, it could direct the magistrate to take expert testimony about the likelihood that James's spanking caused the bruises that appear in the photographs offered at trial.

To make the appellate review less onerous, one could place on the defendant the burden to point out the pages in the transcript that demonstrate innocence, giving the state the chance to rebut that showing of innocence with other pages of the transcript. To reduce the strain even more, I would limit the transcript review to cases where the defendant has made a threshold showing of innocence.

A threshold showing could be made by affidavit detailing evidence that was not presented at trial, or highlighting evidence that was presented but was not weighed appropriately—for example, a confession from someone else or a key piece of evidence that the jury appeared to ignore. In my Powell case, I think the doctor's testimony that it was unlikely that James's spanking caused the bruises reaches the innocence threshold.

Once the innocence threshold has been reached on the doctor's testimony, the appellate court would consider the mother's violent temper, her emotional problems, and the fact that she did not report the bruises until her mother saw them. I believe that those parts of the transcript, along with the doctor's testimony, undermine confidence in the conviction.

One problem with this approach is that the appellate court would not see the witnesses' demeanor or hear their tone of voice. *Jackson* solved this problem by instructing judges to consider the evidence in the light most favorable to the state. The theory here is that the jury must have resolved any conflict in favor of the state. I believe this creates an unfair burden on innocent defendants. I propose, instead, having appellate judges assume that most prosecution witnesses were credible and, when there is a conflict, more credible than the witnesses for the defense.

I would, however, create one exception to the presumption of credible state witnesses. Given the notorious unreliability of eyewitness identifications, and the pervasive role of misidentifications in wrongful conviction cases, I would not extend the credibility rule to eyewitnesses. If the contested issue is what the victim or defendant said or did, I would construe that to favor the prosecution witnesses. But I would not construe eyewitness testimony so that it necessarily defeats a defendant's alibi. I would simply leave it up to the appellate court to determine whether, in light of the eyewitness testimony, the alibi evidence creates a reasonable doubt about guilt.

In the Powell case, the panel would assume that Patricia made a more credible witness than James. But, unlike what *Jackson* requires, the panel would *not* assume that the bruises were a week old given the physician's testimony that they were probably only two or three days old. The panel would assume that the physician was a credible witness and would evaluate his testimony to see whether it undermined confidence in Powell's conviction.

Will some guilty defendants walk free because of this kind of review? Absolutely. But not very many, I believe. In most appeals, guilt is obvious. Prosecutors tend to dismiss or plead out weak cases. I expect that it will be difficult for guilty defendants to make a threshold showing of innocence. The more sophisticated our crime investigation becomes, the more likely it is that solid physical evidence will link the defendant to the crime, thus defeating most attempts by guilty defendants to reach the innocence threshold. I think that most defendants who undermine confidence in their convictions on appeal will be factually innocent.

NEWLY DISCOVERED EVIDENCE

Even a system that values innocence and requires judicial screens both before and after conviction will make mistakes. Some innocent defendants will be convicted and their convictions affirmed on appeal. And in some of those cases, exculpatory evidence will surface after all deadlines for postconviction review have passed. A sticky issue is how (some would say "whether") to permit prisoners to present this evidence to a court.

After surveying the bewildering array of state procedures that potentially remedy unjust convictions, Daniel Medwed in 2005 concluded that states "should abolish the use of statutes of limitations and simplify their mechanisms for presenting newly discovered evidence claims."[157] In addition, "appellate courts should have the authority to review summary dismissals of newly discovered evidence claims de novo."

I have presented, with three coauthors, a proposal that requires courts to hear time-barred claims if the prisoner can show "a strong likelihood of innocence."[158] The reason to require a high standard is that it is not efficient to allow prisoners, who have not much else to do, to relitigate their cases before judges. But what if, rather than require *judges* to decide these cases, we create *an administrative process* to consider any evidence that creates doubt about guilt?

The inefficiencies of hearing more claims would not be as high in an administrative process. It could be structured much like the appellate review I just described, with the burden on the prisoner to point to specific evidence that reaches a threshold of innocence. Only in those cases would the administrative law judge demand a response from the state. If, after the state's response, the administrative judge needed more information, he could investigate the evidence offered by the prisoner. If, for example, the innocence threshold is reached by providing a transcript of a confession from someone else, the judge could interview the confessor and order a DNA test or lie detector test.

The prisoner should have the burden of proving by a preponderance of the evidence that he is innocent. Charles Lugosi believes that new evidence creating a reasonable doubt is sufficient to give federal courts the authority to overturn a conviction.[159] I am not willing to go that far because it risks freeing many guilty prisoners. But federal habeas courts should vacate convictions in all cases where the new evidence shows the prisoner more likely than not to be innocent.

I envision the administrative judge gathering and evaluating evidence much as the examining magistrate does in France. I don't see the need for a formal hearing, though I would create the right to counsel for the prisoner for those cases that make it past the initial screening stage, and counsel could petition the judge for a hearing. In the end, I would entrust the case to the administrative law judge with the same standard that I proposed for the pretrial judicial review: If the judge believes it more probable than not that the prisoner is innocent, he should void the conviction and order his release. That order would be appealable to the court of appeals, but in no cases would there be a retrial. The administrative procedure either releases a probably innocent defendant or dismisses the petition.

English law roughly approximates this system. The English Court of Appeal hears very few appeals—186 of 2,318 filed in 1997, for example.[160] Prior to 1995, defendants who claimed wrongful conviction could petition the Home Secretary, who had the power to refer the case back to the Court of Appeal for further review.[161] A perception arose that "various Home Secretaries were too reluctant to use this power and also perhaps that the whole procedure was insufficiently independent. . . ."[162] In 1995, the Home Secretary's role was transferred to the Criminal Cases Review Commission, which can send the case back to the Court of Appeal if "there is a 'real possibility' that the conviction may not be upheld" because of insufficient evidence.[163]

The CCRC "real possibility of insufficient evidence" standard is similar to a requirement that the prisoner prove by a preponderance that he is innocent. Robert Schehr concludes that the CCRC "has been considered a model worthy of replication by many in the United States" as a way to improve due process.[164] My proposal is better because the commission has no power to reverse the conviction but must send it to the Court of Appeal. My system would give authority to vacate the conviction to the party who decides that the prisoner is probably innocent. Efficiency is served.

Will this idea flood the streets with guilty prisoners? I doubt it. Lissa Griffin reported in 2001 that the new English review process produced reversals in just 1.6 percent of the cases of claimed innocence.[165] As many of these will be wrongfully convicted innocent prisoners, the rate of released guilty prisoners in England is likely to be far less than 1 percent. And that is far less than 1 percent of those who claim to be innocent, not of the general prison population. I expect roughly the same numbers in my administrative system. The burden is on the prisoner. He must produce evidence that he is probably innocent. I do not believe that very many guilty defendants can meet that standard years after conviction or will even attempt to do so. Indeed, I believe the greater problem is that many innocent defendants will not be able to prove that they are probably innocent.

However many innocent prisoners my administrative law process leaves in prison, it is far friendlier to innocent prisoners than the current regime. As I was finishing this chapter, I read in the newspapers of the execution of a prisoner who claimed he was innocent and asked only for a DNA test to prove his innocence. A web site noted flaws in the trial evidence that, if true, would have made it very unlikely that this prisoner had killed the victim.[166] If those facts turned out to be true, the administrative law judge in my system would grant the request for a DNA test. And we would know whether the prisoner was guilty. It is a tragedy, in my view, that he went to his death without conclusive proof of guilt when it was easily available.

I have sketched in fairly broad strokes a system for investigating crime and adjudicating guilt that is, I believe, far more protective of innocence than the current system. It is now time to ask: What will all this cost?

THE COST OF PROTECTING INNOCENCE

The day-to-day operation of the police will not change much, though police must record interrogations and will face other regulations in how they interrogate. The screening magistrate will require a showing of probable cause at the initial appearance, will advise the defendant of various rights, and will ask whether the defendant has been mistreated and whether he wants a lawyer appointed from a list of criminal law specialists. The magistrate will be in charge of eyewitness identification procedures, of discovery, and of DNA collection. The cost of adding magistrates to the system is more than offset, I believe, by gains in protecting innocent defendants and in the efficient processing of cases.

The grand jury can be retrofitted by giving it independent counsel and by using lawyers as grand jurors. The pretrial judicial review that follows the grand jury indictment, unlike the current preliminary hearing, will be a serious test of the state's case. It will come after the evidence has been gathered, discovery has been granted, depositions have been taken, and the case is ready for trial. If the screening magistrate finds probable innocence, he will dismiss the case without prejudice to the state. If, on the other hand, he finds it more likely than not that the accused is guilty of an offense, he will transfer the case to trial and also determine a fair penalty that the defendant can accept by pleading guilty.

The defense and prosecution of routine crimes will be done by criminal law specialists. I have not attempted to calculate the cost of a "criminal law specialist" system over the current patchwork approach to indigent defense and the current highly centralized prosecutor's offices, but lawyering that is more protective of innocence, on both sides, would justify even a substantial additional cost. Having better defense lawyers and more neutral prosecutors would, for example, reduce the number of appeals substantially.

Trial in my proposed system will look much like trials today, but any rule or procedure that keeps sufficiently probative evidence of innocence from the jury will be ignored in the name of due process. Witnesses will be permitted to testify in a narrative at the close of direct and cross examination. Special rules will govern the testimony of jailhouse informants. All of these changes favor innocent defendants without sacrificing many convictions of guilty defendants.

If nine or more jurors vote not guilty after deliberations, that is an acquittal. If the jury unanimously votes guilty, a conviction is entered. All other outcomes are not a verdict. To give the jury every chance to reach a verdict, the judge should send deadlocked juries back to the jury room two or three times with the simple instruction: Please keep trying to reach a verdict.

Appeals of procedural errors will proceed as in the present system. The defendant also has the right to ask an appellate court to review the record and make an independent judgment of whether it has confidence in the conviction. If necessary to render a judgment on whether the state introduced sufficient evidence of guilt, the appellate court can have the magistrate take new evidence. If the appellate court finds that the state failed to prove guilt beyond a reasonable doubt, it will enter an acquittal. If the appellate court rules against the defendant, the conviction stands. In either case, when the issue is sufficiency of the evidence rather than procedural error, the case will not be sent back for a second trial. If the error is a procedural one, such as erroneous jury instructions, it will, as now, require a new trial unless the error is harmless beyond a reasonable doubt.

Though I cannot prove it, I believe appellate courts often reverse convictions on procedural grounds, and remand for a retrial, when they are not convinced that the state met its burden of proof. My process provides an opportunity for appellate judges to address honestly their concerns with sufficiency of the evidence. This will result in fewer retrials, perhaps many fewer retrials, another benefit of my proposal. The time consumed in a more searching inquiry into the sufficiency of evidence will, I suspect, be more than repaid by having fewer retrials.

Finally, I propose an administrative law judge system to hear prisoner claims of newly discovered evidence. Here I would require written proof of the claim of innocence, along with supporting details, and a response from the state in all petitions that survive initial screening. The administrative law judge would decide whether to proceed with an investigation of the claim of innocence. If there is a hearing, the administrative law judge will question the witness and run the proceedings, much as the presiding judge runs the Assize Court trial in France. If the judge decides that it is more likely than not that the prisoner is innocent, he would void the conviction and release the prisoner.

Hiring administrative law judges would be an added cost. Moreover, both the administrative law system and the new appellate system will release guilty defendants or prisoners along with innocent ones, a cost of my system. But as most defendants are obviously guilty, we are dealing with a relatively small pool that contains many innocent defendants. Letting a few guilty people walk free to save substantial numbers of innocents is, I think, a good bargain.

I have presented an idea for a criminal process that has protecting innocence as its most important value. I realize that many parts of it are, at first blush, revolutionary. I have sought to show that the effects, if not the change in hallowed procedure, are anything but revolutionary. We would just be replacing a tired system that functions far less well than we once believed with a new one that has a chance to function more efficiently as it screens out innocent defendants more often.

Andy Taslitz gently suggested that I end with a set of proposals about how to implement some or all of my ideas. In light of his work, this suggestion is unsurprising. Consider, for example, his article examining how the deliberative process can be influenced to improve the eyewitness identification process, and his service as a reporter for the Mandatory Justice Initiative on the Death Penalty and as a member of the American Bar Association Innocence Committee.[167]

I'm not much of a tactician. So I end, instead, with a final story to illustrate how my system would be an improvement.

KELLY MICHAELS AND 235 COUNTS OF CHILD SEXUAL ABUSE

In 1985, New Jersey prosecutors suspected that Kelly Michaels was sexually abusing the four-year-old children under her supervision in a day care center. They interrogated Michaels for nine hours. She denied any wrongdoing and passed a lie detector test. Yet the prosecutors proceeded to build a case against her by interviewing the children. The techniques used, the state supreme court later held, were flawed because "a substantial likelihood exist[ed] that the children's recollection of past events was both stimulated and materially influenced" by the questions that the investigators asked.[168]

In our current system, there is no screening mechanism that might have uncovered those flaws. The prosecutors almost certainly did not disclose to the grand jury the techniques used to elicit incriminating testimony from the children, and it is unlikely in any event that a grand jury would be capable of perceiving problems with suggestive interrogation techniques used on young children. State grand juries returned three indictments that contained a total of 235 counts. Prior to trial, the prosecutor dismissed 72 counts and proceeded to trial on the remaining 163 counts. Yes, 163 counts were tried to a jury.

The trial lasted nine months. At its conclusion, 32 counts had been dismissed, and the jury was instructed to return verdicts on 131 counts. After twelve days of deliberation, the jury convicted on 115 counts, and the judge sentenced Michaels to an aggregate term of forty-seven years. A college senior when the investigation began, by 1988 she faced the prospect of spending most of her life in prison without any screening that might have exposed the flawed investigative techniques.

In my proposed system, the screening magistrate at the pretrial judicial review would be charged with the responsibility of determining whether the investigative techniques passed muster. While there is no guarantee that the screening magistrate would have reached the same conclusion that the New Jersey Supreme Court later reached, he would be in a much better position than a preliminary hearing judge or grand jury. The magistrate could draw from the research that shows the suggestibility of children in sex abuse cases.[169]

To be sure, the American system worked—sort of—in the Michaels case. After living for six years with 115 convictions and a forty-seven-year prison sentence hanging over her head, Michaels finally prevailed when the New Jersey Supreme Court vacated all the convictions.[170] The court held that the interrogations "were improper" and that there was "a substantial likelihood that the evidence derived from them is unreliable."[171] The prosecutors declined to reprosecute, and New Jersey finally got it right. But wouldn't it have been better for everyone if a pretrial judicial review had exposed the flaws in the interrogation techniques? Consider the children who had to testify; the parents whose emotions were wrung out during a nine-month trial and five-year appeals process; the prosecutors who could have reallocated the enormous amounts of time to other cases; and, most importantly, the defendant who had to endure an agonizing ordeal.

Could an overzealous screening magistrate overlook flawed evidence and send the case to trial? Of course. But ask yourself which actor is more likely to be overzealous—a prosecutor whose job it is to prosecute criminals or a magistrate whose job it is to uncover the truth?

And there is something else to be said about the Michaels case. When it became clear that the French system had falsely accused defendants of child sex abuse in the year 2000, the minister of justice and the prime minister met with the defendants to apologize for the mistakes made by the magistrate. A parliamentary commission was created to investigate the failure.[172] In the Sophonow case in Manitoba, Canada, an apology was offered and a commission created to investigate that single failing of Canadian justice.

The Kelly Michaels case occasioned a *Sixty Minutes* episode but no formal investigation and no commission to look into this ghastly miscarriage of justice. There was no public apology. It seems we just don't care that much when a probably innocent defendant is put through the modern version of an ordeal. I think that is partly because American prosecutors often can't or won't admit when they have caused the innocent to suffer. Our indifference may also be because we have gotten used to news stories about innocent prisoners. But what does *that* say about American justice in the twenty-first century?

The system that convicted Kelly Michaels, Jimmy Ray Bromgard, Ray Krone, and thousands of other innocent or probably innocent defendants is more than flawed. It is broken. We have no way of knowing how many innocents are in prison, are on death row, or have already been executed. To those who resist revolutionary change, what I have proposed is not an abandonment of the adversarial system. Criminal law specialists acting as prosecutors will still control the bringing of charges and the presenting of the evidence to the jury. Criminal law specialists acting as defense lawyers will still present a defense. But the pretrial judicial review that functions as a judicial screen and the various changes in how evidence of innocence is discovered and presented should make it far harder to convict the innocent. The changes in appellate review and the review of prisoner claims should make it far more likely that mistakes can be corrected.

We should recall Jerome Frank's wise words that began chapter 1, "Our mode of trials is often most unfair. It will . . . continue to be, until everything feasible has been done to prevent avoidable mistakes."[173] I hope my book makes plain that not everything feasible is being done. I close with Blackstone's wise words: "[T]he law holds, that it is better that ten guilty persons escape, than that one innocent suffer."

NOTES

Introduction

1. Mirjan R. Damaska, *The Faces of Justice and Authority* (New Haven: Yale University Press, 1986), 160.

2. Id.

3. See U.S. Const. amend. XIV (limiting states); U.S. Const. amend. V (limiting the federal government).

4. Donald A. Dripps, *About Guilt and Innocence: The Origins, Development, and Future of Constitutional Criminal Procedure* (Westport, Conn.: Praeger, 2003), 139.

5. *Achieving Justice: Freeing the Innocent, Convicting the Guilty; Report of the ABA Criminal Justice Section's Ad Hoc Innocence Committee to Ensure the Integrity of the Criminal Process* (American Bar Association Criminal Justice Section, 2006); William T. Pizzi, *Trials Without Truth* (New York: New York University Press, 1999).

6. William Blackstone, *Commentaries on the Laws of England, Book the Fourth* (Oxford: Clarendon Press, 1769), 352.

7. Benjamin Franklin, letter to Benjamin Vaughn (March 14, 1785), in *The Writings of Benjamin Franklin*, vol. 9 (Albert Henry Smith, ed., New York: Haskell House, 1907), 293.

8. Jerome Frank, *Courts on Trial* (Princeton: Princeton University Press, 1949), 35.

9. Id. at 88.

10. Erik Luna, "System Failure," *Am. Crim. L. Rev.* 42 (2005): 1207.

11. See George H. Ryan, Governor of Ill., "Commutation Address," Northwestern Center for Wrongful Convictions (January 11, 2003), available at http:// www.law.northwestern.edu/depts/clinic/wrongful/RyanSpeech.htm.

12. David Rose, *In the Name of the Law: The Collapse of Criminal Justice* (London: J. Cape, 1996), ix.

13. Royal Commission on Criminal Justice, *Report to Parliament July, 2003*, par. 20, p. 6 (1993). For a critical view of the response to the finding of professional incompetence, see *Criminal Justice in Crisis* (Mike McConville & Lee Bridges, eds., Aldershot: Hants, 1994).

14. Province of Manitoba, Manitoba Justice Publications, Thomas Sophonow Inquiry, available at http://www.gov.mb.ca/justice/publica tions/sophonow/ (last visited July 9, 2007).

15. Pizzi, *Trials Without Truth*, at 2.

16. Ryan, "Commutation Address."

17. Luna, "System Failure," at 1203.

18. Andrew M. Siegel, "Moving down the Wedge of Injustice: A Proposal for a Third Generation of Wrongful Conviction Scholarship and Advocacy," *Am. Crim. L. Rev.* 42 (2005): 1222.

19. Pizzi, *Trials Without Truth*, at 6.

20. William J. Stuntz, "The Uneasy Relationship Between Criminal Procedure and Criminal Justice," *Yale L.J.* 107 (1997): 44.

21. *Herrera v. Collins*, 506 U.S. 390, 400 (1993).

22. To be sure, the Court assumed, for the sake of argument, that "a truly persuasive demonstration of 'actual innocence' in a capital case" would "warrant federal habeas relief if there were no state avenue open to process such a claim." Id. at 417. But why make the barrier for a successful showing of innocence higher than for a reversal based on a procedural error? A system that cared about innocent defendants would care more about convicting innocent defendants than whether they got the right procedure.

23. Michael Graczyk, "Man Executed for Killing Police Officer," *Dallas Morning News*, May 13, 1993. For three critiques of *Herrera*, see Susan Bandes, "Simple Murder: A Comment on the Legality of Executing the Innocent," *Buff. L. Rev.* 44 (1996): 501–25; Vivian Berger, "*Herrera v. Collins:* The Gateway of Innocence for Death-Sentenced Prisoners Leads Nowhere," *Wm. & Mary L. Rev.* 35

(1994): 943–1023; George C. Thomas III, Gordon G. Young, Keith Sharfman, & Kate Briscoe, "Is It Ever Too Late for Innocence? Due Process, Finality, Efficiency, and Claims of Innocence," *U. Pitt. L. Rev.* 64 (2003): 263–302.

Chapter 1

The opening epigraph is from Jerome Frank, *Courts on Trial* (Princeton: Princeton University Press, 1949), 88.

1. *State v. Krone*, 897 P.2d 621, 622 (Ariz. 1995).

2. Id.

3. Id.

4. Id. at 624–25.

5. Innocence Project, case of Ray Krone, available at http://www.inno cenceproject.org/know/Browse-Profiles.php (last visited July 8, 2007).

6. Matthew Hale, *The History and Analysis of the Common Law of England: Written by a Learned Hand* (1713), 252 (reprinted, Birmingham, Ala.: Legal Classics Library, 1987).

7. Id. at 258.

8. Samuel R. Gross, et al., "Exonerations in the United States, 1989–2003," *J. Crim. L. & Criminology* 95 (2004): Appendix, 555–60.

9. Northwestern Law, Center on Wrongful Convictions, the Exonerated, Exonerations in All States, United States, available at http://www.law.north western.edu/depts/clinic/wrongful/exonerations/States.htm.

10. Email from The Innocence Project to George Thomas, September 18, 2007.

11. Gross, et al., "Exonerations," at 528–29.

12. See 18 U.S.C.A. § 115 (A) (1).

13. Sourcebook of Criminal Justice Statistics 2002, table 5.44, available at http://www.albany.edu/sourcebook/pdf/t5442002.pdf.

14. Id. at table 5.10, available at http://www.albany.edu/sourcebook/pdf/ 5102005.pdf.

15. Email from Richard Coughlin, Federal Public Defender, New Jersey District, to George Thomas, September 14, 2007.

16. Bureau of Justice Statistics, Prison Statistics, "Summary Findings," available at http://www.ojp.usdoj.gov/bjs/prisons.htm (last visited July 8, 2007).

17. Frank, *Courts on Trial*, at 35.

18. Id. at 85. See generally id. at 81–102.

19. Darryl K. Brown, "The Decline of Defense Counsel and the Rise of Accuracy in Criminal Adjudication," *Calif. L. Rev.* 95 (2005): 1608.

20. John H. Langbein, *The Origins of Adversary Criminal Trial* (Oxford: Oxford University Press, 2003), 343.

21. All the data in this paragraph are drawn from Barry Scheck, Peter Neufeld, & Jim Dwyer, *Actual Innocence: Five Days to Execution and Other Dispatches from the Wrongly Convicted* (New York: Doubleday, 2000), app. 2. For thoughts on causes of false confessions, see Richard J. Ofshe & Richard A. Leo, "The Decision to Confess Falsely: Rational Choice and Irrational Action," *Denver U. L. Rev.* 74 (1997): 979–1122.

22. Gate Germond, "The Reasons for the 'Wrong-Man' Cases," in *Convicting the Innocent: The Story of a Murder, a False Confession, and the Struggle to Free a "Wrong Man"* (Donald S. Connery, ed., Cambridge, Mass.: Brookline Books, 1996), at 115.

23. Andrew D. Leipold, "How the Pretrial Process Contributes to Wrongful Convictions," *Am. Crim. L. Rev.* 42 (2005): 1123–65.

24. Id. at 1128.

25. Brown, "Decline of Defense Counsel," at 1613.

26. Id. at 1612.

27. Siegel, "Wedge of Injustice," at 1223.

28. Richard A. Leo, "Rethinking the Study of Miscarriages of Justice: Developing a Criminology of Wrongful Convictions," *J. Contemp. Crim. Just.* 21 (2005): 213.

29. Edward Connors, Thomas Lundregan, Neil Miller, & Tom McEwan, *Convicted by Juries, Exonerated by Science: Case Studies in the Use of DNA Evidence to Establish Innocence After Trial* (Washington, D.C.: U.S. Dept. of Justice, Office of Justice Programs, National Institute of Justice, 1996).

30. Samuel H. Pillsbury, "On Corruption and Possibility in LA," *Loy. L.A. L. Rev.* 34 (2001): 657–64.

31. *United States v. Wade*, 388 U.S. 218, 228 (1967) (quoting Felix Frankfurter, *The Case of Sacco and Vanzetti: A Critical Analysis for Lawyers and Laymen* 30 (1927)).

32. Innocence Project, case of Clark McMillan, available at http://www.innocenceproject.org/know/Browse-Profiles.php (last visited July 8, 2007).

33. John Shiffman, "DNA Test Clears Man in '79 Rape," *Nashville Tennessean*, April 30, 2002.

34. Ronald L. Cohen & Mary Anne Harnick, "The Susceptibility of Child Witnesses to Suggestion," *Law and Hum. Behav.* 4 (1980): 206, tables 1 & 2.

35. See Innocence Project, case of Jimmy Ray Bromgard, available at http://www.innocenceproject.org/know/Browse-Profiles.php (last visited July 8, 2007).

36. Jennifer Thompson, "I Was Certain, but I Was Wrong," *New York Times*, June 18, 2000.

37. Michael L. Radelet, Hugo Adam Bedau, & Constance Putnam, *In Spite of*

Innocence: Erroneous Convictions in Capital Cases (Boston: Northeastern University Press, 1992), 19.

38. Deborah Davis & Richard Leo, "Strategies for Preventing False Confessions and Their Consequences," in *Practical Psychology for Forensic Investigations and Prosecutions* (Mark R. Kebbell & Graham M. Davies, eds., West Sussex, England: Wiley, 2006), 124.

39. See Province of Manitoba, Manitoba Justice Publications, Thomas Sophonow Inquiry, "Investigation of Terry Arnold as a Suspect, Recommendations," available at http://www.gov.mb.ca/justice/publications/sopho now/ (last visited July 9, 2007).

40. Michael Crowe's case is discussed in more detail in Welsh S. White, *Miranda's Waning Protections: Police Interrogation After Dickerson v. United States* (Ann Arbor: University of Michigan Press, 2001), 172–79.

41. Id. at 172.

42. Mark Costanzo & Richard A. Leo, "Research and Expert Testimony on Interrogations and Confessions," in *Expert Psychological Testimony for the Courts* (Mark Costanzo, Daniel Krauss, & Kathy Pezdek, eds., Mahwah, N.J.: Lawrence Erlbaum Associates, 2007, at 71).

43. See id. 69–70.

44. See, e.g., Richard A. Leo, "From Coercion to Deception: The Changing Nature of Police Interrogation in America," *Crime, Law, and Soc. Change* 18 (1992): 35–59. See also David Simon, *Homicide, A Year on the Killing Streets* (Boston: Houghton Mifflin, 1991), 193–207; Martin Yant, *Presumed Guilty: When Innocent People Are Wrongly Convicted* (Buffalo, N.Y.: Prometheus Books, 1991), 76–90.

45. The facts about the Burch case come from *Burch v. State*, 343 So.2d 831 (Fla. 1977).

46. Alex Wood, "Lying Accepted Investigative Tool," in Connery, *Convicting the Innocent*, at 41.

47. White, *Miranda's Waning Protections*, at 173.

48. Richard A. Leo, *Police Interrogation and the American Process of Justice* (Cambridge: Harvard University Press, forthcoming 2008), ch. 6 (manuscript on file with author).

49. Id.

50. Costanzo & Leo, "Interrogations and Confessions," at 82–83, drawing from Ofshe & Leo, "Decision to Confess Falsely"; and Richard J. Ofshe & Richard A. Leo, "The Social Psychology of Police Interrogation: The Theory and Classification of True and False Confessions," *Stud. in Law, Pol., and Soc'y* 16 (1997): 189–251.

51. See Susan Bandes, "Tracing the Pattern of No Pattern: Stories of Police

Brutality," *Loy. L.A. L. Rev.* 34 (2001): 665–80; Susan Bandes, "Patterns of Injustice: Police Brutality in the Courts," *Buff. L. Rev.* 47 (1999): 1275–1341.

52. Richard Ofshe, "I'm Guilty If You Say So," in Connery, *Convicting the Innocent*, at 96.

53. Gerard E. Lynch, "Our Administrative System of Criminal Justice," *Fordham L. Rev.* 66 (1998): 2117–51.

54. Mary Sue Backus & Paul Marcus, "The Right to Counsel in Criminal Cases, a National Crisis," *Hastings L.J.* 57 (2006): 1123.

55. ABA report, *Achieving Justice*, 87.

56. Backus & Marcus, "Right to Counsel," at 1099 (reporting data and citing source).

57. Kent Roach, "Wrongful Convictions and Criminal Procedure," *Brandeis L.J.* 42 (2003–4): 365.

58. See Innocence Project, case of Jimmy Ray Bromgard, available at http://www.innocenceproject.org/know/Browse-Profiles.php (last visited July 8, 2007).

59. Gerald B. Lefcourt, "Responsibilities of a Criminal Defense Attorney," *Loy. L.A. L. Rev.* 30 (1996): 59–60 (emphasis added).

60. *Gideon v. Wainwright*, 372 U.S. 335, 344 (1963).

61. Corinna Barrett Lain, "Countermajoritarian Hero or Zero: Rethinking the Warren Court's Role in the Criminal Procedure Revolution," *U. Pa. L. Rev.* 152 (2004): 1390 (quoting Ed Cray, *Chief Justice: A Biography of Earl Warren* [New York: Simon & Schuster, 1997], 405).

62. Backus & Marcus, "Right to Counsel," at 1054 (quoting source).

63. Id. at 1045.

64. See Adam Liptak, "County Says It's Too Poor to Defend the Poor," *New York Times*, April 15, 2003 (naming, at A15, Mississippi, Pennsylvania, South Dakota, Utah, and Wyoming).

65. Susan Bandes, "Repression and Denial in Criminal Lawyering," *Buff. Crim. L. Rev.* 9 (2006): 380.

66. Michael A. Mello, *Dead Wrong* (Madison: University of Wisconsin Press, 1997), 12.

67. Michael McConville & John Baldwin, *Courts, Prosecution, and Convictions* (New York: Oxford University Press, 1981), 211.

68. Mike McConville, Andrew Sanders, & Roger Lang, *The Case for the Prosecution: Police and the Construction of Criminality* (London: Routledge, 1991), 6.

69. Mike McConville, Jacqueline Hodgson, Lee Bridges, & Anita Pavlovic, *Standing Accused: The Organisation and Practices of Criminal Defense Lawyers in Britain* (New York: Oxford University Press, 1994), 281.

70. Robert Hermann, Eric Single, & John Boston, *Counsel for the Poor: Crim-*

inal Defense in Urban America (Lexington, Mass.: Lexington Books, 1977), 153–66.

71. Alan M. Dershowitz, *The Best Defense* (New York: Random House, 1982), xxi. There are eleven more rules, but Rule I and Rule II are most relevant to my project.

72. Andrew Taslitz, email to the author, August 30, 2006.

73. Roach, "Wrongful Convictions," at 360.

74. Frank Belloni & Jacqueline Hodgson, *Criminal Injustice: An Evaluation of the Criminal Justice Process in Britain* (New York: St. Martin's Press, 2000), 110, citing McConville, Sanders, & Lang, *Case for the Prosecution.*

75. Susan Bandes, "Loyalty to One's Convictions: The Prosecutor and Tunnel Vision," *Howard L.J.* 49 (2006): 479.

76. See, e.g., Daniel S. Medwed, "The Zeal Deal: Prosecutorial Resistance to Post-conviction Claims of Innocence," *B.U. L. Rev.* 84 (2004): 133.

77. Bandes, "Loyalty to One's Convictions," at 493.

78. Article VIII, Illinois Rules of Professional Conduct, Rule 3.8, as amended October 22, 1999.

79. Id. at Committee Comments, March 1, 2001.

80. McConville, Sanders, & Lang, *Case for the Prosecution,* 131.

81. Bandes, "Loyalty to One's Convictions"; Medwed, "The Zeal Deal"; Fred C. Zacharias, "Structuring the Ethics of Prosecutorial Trial Practice: Can Prosecutors Do Justice?" *Vand. L. Rev.* 44 (1991): 45–114.

82. Siegel, "Wedge of Injustice," at 1225.

83. Renée Lettow Lerner, "The Intersection of Two Systems: An American on Trial for an American Murder in the French Cour D'Assises," *U. Ill. L. Rev.* 2001:810 (quoting Maurice Ribert, "Le Systeme franeais actuel de recrutement des juges" 38 (1944) (thesis, Paris), quoted in Anne Boigeol, "Les Transformations des modalités d'entrée dans la magistrature: De la nécessité sociale aux vertus professionnelles," in *Pouvoirs* no. 74 (Les Juges) at 33 (1995)).

84. Michael Tonry, *Thinking about Crime* (New York: Oxford University Press, 2004), 208–10.

85. *Berger v. United States,* 295 U.S. 78, 88 (1935).

86. Duff Wilson & David Barstow, "Duke Prosecutor Throws Out Case Against Players," *New York Times,* April 12, 2007.

87. Duff Wilson, "Prosecutor in Duke Case Disbarred by Ethics Panel," *New York Times,* June 17, 2007.

88. Id.

89. Radelet, Bedau, and Putnam, *In Spite of Innocence,* at 152.

90. "Cab Driver Is Hunted in Girl's Slaying," *Canton Daily Ledger,* November 28, 1955.

91. Id.

92. Willard J. Lassers, *Scapegoat Justice: Lloyd Miller and the Failure of the American Legal System* (Bloomington: Indiana University Press, 1973), 6.

93. Edward R. Lewis, Jr., *Reflections of Canton in a Pharmacist's Show Globe: A Comprehensive History of Canton, Illinois, and the Important Events in Fulton County* (self-published, 1967).

94. Lassers, *Scapegoat Justice*, at 157 (quoting from later hearing to determine whether Miller should be retried).

95. Id. at 25.

96. Id. at 28.

97. Id. at 69.

98. Id. at 67.

99. Id. at 29–30.

100. Id. at 166–67.

101. Id. at 73.

102. *Miller v. Pate*, 386 U.S. 1, 6 (1967).

103. See Note, "The Vindication of a Prosecutor," *J. Crim. L. & Criminology* 59 (1968): 335.

104. The prosecutor contended that the difference in stains was "apparent," id., but the commission carefully avoided making any finding to that effect.

105. Lassers, *Scapegoat Justice*, at 201–2.

106. Susan W. Brenner, "The Voice of the Community: The Case for Grand Jury Independence," *Va. J. Social Pol'y & L.* 3 (1995): 121.

107. Tom Wolfe, *Bonfire of the Vanities* (New York: Bantam, 1987), 629.

108. "Atomic Nucleus," Wikipedia, at http://en.wikipedia.org/wiki/ Atomic_nucleus (stating that the radius of the nucleus of an atom is less than 0.01 percent of the radius of the atom) (last visited July 9, 2007).

109. Mark Twain, "Fourth of July speech, 1873," at http://www.twain quotes.com/Jury.html (last visited July 9, 2007).

110. Frank, *Courts on Trial*, at 124 (not providing source of quotation).

111. Jeffrey Abramson, *We the Jury: The Jury System and the Ideal of Democracy* (New York: Basic Books, 1994), 250.

112. Scott E. Sundby, *A Life and Death Decision: A Jury Weighs the Death Penalty* (New York: Palgrave Macmillan, 2005), 177.

113. See Randolph Jonakait, *The American Jury System* (New Haven: Yale University Press, 2003), 221–32.

114. Valerie P. Hans & Neil Vidmar, *Judging the Jury* (New York: Plenum Press, 1986), 119–20.

115. See Harry Kalven, Jr. & Hans Zeisel, *The American Jury* (Boston: Little, Brown, 1966), 429, table 112.

116. Pizzi, *Trials Without Truth,* at 209.

117. Morgan Cloud, "The Dirty Little Secret," *Emory L.J.* 43 (1994): 1348.

118. Pizzi, *Trials Without Truth,* at 68.

119. R. Michael Cassidy, "'Soft Words of Hope': Giglio, Accomplice Witnesses, and the Problem of Implied Inducements," *Nw. U. L. Rev.* 98 (2004): 1130.

120. Stephen S. Trott, "Word of Warning for Prosecutors Using Criminals as Witnesses," *Hastings L.J.* 47 (1996): 1383.

121. Saul M. Kassin, "Effective Screening for Truth Telling: Human Judges of Truth, Deception, and Credibility: Confident but Erroneous," *Cardozo L. Rev.* 23 (2002): 809–16.

122. Paul Ekman & Maureen O'Sullivan, "Who Can Catch a Liar?" *Am. Psychologist* 46 (1991): 913–20.

123. Ellen Yaroshefsky, "Cooperation with Federal Prosecutors: Experiences of Truth Telling and Embellishment," *Fordham L. Rev.* 68 (1999): 917–64.

124. Province of Manitoba, Thomas Sophonow Inquiry, Introduction, "Trials and Appeals of Thomas Sophonow."

125. Richard J. Wolson & Aaron M. London, "The Structure, Operation, and Impact of Wrongful Conviction Inquiries: The Sophonow Inquiry as an Example of the Canadian Experience," *Drake L. Rev.* 52 (2004): 683.

126. Id. at 682.

127. Province of Manitoba, Thomas Sophonow Inquiry, "Jailhouse Informants," "Douglas Martin."

128. Province of Manitoba, Thomas Sophonow Inquiry, Introduction, "The Facts Giving Rise to the Inquiry, the Authorizing Order in Council, Its Nature and Scope." When Terry Arnold later committed suicide, leaving a note that denied murdering anyone, he was still the lead suspect in the killing for which Sophonow was twice convicted. See Mike D'Amour, "Last Words Deny Killing," *Calgary Sun,* March 30, 2005, available at http://www.injusticebusters.com/05/Arnold_Terry.shtml (last visited July 9, 2007).

129. *Hoffa v. United States,* 385 U.S. 293, 318 n. 2 (1966) (Warren, C.J., dissenting).

130. Id. at 317–18.

131. Id. at 320.

132. Peter W. Huber, *Galileo's Revenge: Junk Science in the Courtroom* (New York: Basic Books, 1993), 4.

133. Stanley Cohen, *The Wrong Men: America's Epidemic of Wrongful Death Row Convictions* (New York: Carroll & Graf, 2003), 221.

134. Associated Press, "FBI Apologizes to Lawyer Held in Madrid Bombings," May 25, 2004, available at http://www.msnbc.msn.com/id/5053007/ (last visited July 9, 2007).

135. See Innocence Project, case of Jimmy Ray Bromgard, available at http://www.innocenceproject.org/know/Browse-Profiles.php (last visited July 8, 2007).

136. Backus & Marcus, "Right to Counsel," at 1099 (reporting data and citing source).

137. Belloni & Hodgson, *Criminal Injustice*, at 127.

138. Id.

139. *In re Investigation of West Virginia State Police Crime Laboratory, Serology Division*, 438 S.E.2d 501, 502 (W. Va. 1993).

140. Id.

141. Jeralyn Merritt, "Death of Lying Chemist Fred Zain," quoting December 4, 2002, obituary in Newsday, available at http://www.talkleft.com/new_archives/001077.html (last visited July 9, 2007). He died in 2002, under indictment, but without having faced the consequences of condemning hundreds of innocent defendants.

142. Sheila Martin Berry, "When Experts Lie," available at http://www.truthinjustice.org/expertslie.htm (last visited July 9, 2007).

143. See Jonakait, *The American Jury System*, at 282.

144. Radelet, Bedau, and Putnam, *In Spite of Innocence*, at 272.

145. Alan E. Gelfand & Herbert Solomon, "Considerations in Building Jury Behavior Models and in Comparing Jury Schemes: An Argument in Favor of 12-Member Juries," *Jurimetrics J.* 17 (1977): 310–11.

146. Baldwin & McConville, *Jury Trials*, at 86.

147. See Bureau of Justice Statistics, *Criminal Sentencing, 2002 data,* available at http://www.ojp.usdoj.gov/bjs/sent.htm (last visited July 9, 2007).

148. Belloni & Hodgson, *Criminal Injustice*, at 141, quoting Royal Commission on Criminal Justice, *Report to Parliament*, at 110.

149. McConville & Baldwin, *Courts, Prosecution, and Convictions*, 66.

150. See Bureau of Justice Statistics, "Felony Convictions in State Court," 2002, http://www.ojp.usdoj.gov/bjs/glance/tables/felcovtab.htm (last visited July 9, 2007).

151. No data on nationwide misdemeanor convictions appear to exist, but we can construct an estimate. Begin with roughly 12,500,000 arrests for misdemeanors each year. If we assume a 65 percent conviction rate, that gives us 8,000,000 misdemeanor convictions. I will supply more details of how I arrive at these figures on request.

152. Leipold, "Wrongful Convictions," at 1162–63.

153. David L. Faigman, *Laboratory of Justice* (New York: Times Books, Henry Holt, 2004), 364.

154. Except as indicated otherwise, the facts in this paragraph come from Robert Bartels, *Benefit of Law: The Murder Case of Ernest Triplett* (Ames: Iowa State University Press, 1988), 77–79.

155. Ernie Triplett, interview by the author, Iowa City, May 1975.

156. Bartels, *Benefit of Law*, at 31.

157. Id. at 13.

158. Triplett, interview.

159. Bartels, *Benefit of Law*, at 5.

160. Id. at 21.

161. Id. at 77.

162. Id. at 134.

163. Id. at 30.

164. Id. at 103.

165. Id. at 47.

166. Id. at 53–55.

167. Id. at 53.

168. Id. at 125.

169. Id. at 136.

Chapter 2

The opening epigraphs are from Richard A. Leo, "False Confessions: Causes, Consequences, and Solutions," in *Wrongly Convicted: Perspectives on Failed Justice*, 47 (Saundra D. Westervelt & John A. Humphrey, eds., New Brunswick, N.J.: Rutgers University Press, 1996); and Lloyd Weinreb, *Denial of Justice: Criminal Process in the United States* (New York: Free Press, 1977), 5.

1. John D. Jackson, "Managing Uncertainty and Finality: The Function of the Criminal Trial in Legal Inquiry," in *The Trial on Trial: Truth and Due Process*, vol. 1 (Antony Duff, Lindsay Farmer, Sandra Marshall, & Victor Tadros, eds., Oxford: Hart, 2005), 124.

2. See U.S. Const. amend. V & amend. XIV.

3. Dripps, *About Guilt and Innocence*, at 145.

4. Blackstone, *Commentaries*, vol. 4, at 352.

5. Herbert L. Packer, *The Limits of the Criminal Sanction* (Palo Alto: Stanford University Press, 1968), 165.

6. The Warren Court's exclusion road began with *Mapp v. Ohio*, 367 U.S. 643 (1961). *Mapp* has been limited in various ways by the Courts that followed the Warren Court, but these limitations are not important for my point in the text.

7. *Miranda v. Arizona,* 384 U.S. 436 (1966).

8. Belloni & Hodgson, *Criminal Injustice,* at 24.

9. *Hudson v. Michigan,* 126 S.Ct. 2159 (2006).

10. Id. at 2180 (Breyer, J., dissenting).

11. See *Ashcraft v. Tennessee,* 322 U.S. 143 (1944).

12. See *Arizona v. Fulminante,* 499 U.S. 279 (1991) (held involuntary by five-to-four vote).

13. Richard A. Leo, "Inside the Interrogation Room," *J. Crim. L. & Criminology* 86 (1996): 282–83.

14. George C. Thomas III, "Stories About Miranda," *Mich. L. Rev.* 102 (2004): 1975, table 6 & 1987–91.

15. 479 U.S. 157 (1986).

16. See Richard A. Leo, "The Third Degree and the Origins of Psychological Interrogation in the United States," in *Interrogations, Confessions, and Entrapment* (Daniel Lassiter, ed., New York: Kluwer Academic, Plenum Publishers, 2004), 37–56.

17. Wickersham Commission, *Report on Lawlessness in Law Enforcement,* available at www.heinonline.org, under Legal Classics, Library, U.S. Wickersham Commission Reports.

18. Frank, *Courts on Trial,* at 100.

19. Tricks can be causally linked to false confessions, to be sure, but usually only if combined with threats or offers of leniency. Recall the Crowe case from chapter 1.

20. See, e.g., *Ashcraft v. Tennessee,* 322 U.S. 143 (1944); *Chambers v. Florida,* 309 U.S. 227 (1940).

21. 372 U.S. 335 (1963).

22. Id. at 345 (quoting *Powell v. Alabama,* 287 U.S. 45, 69 (1932)).

23. *Caplin & Drysdale v. United States,* 491 U.S. 617 (1989).

24. James J. Tomkovicz, *The Right to the Assistance of Counsel: A Reference Guide to the United States Constitution* (Westport, Conn.: Greenwood Press, 2002), 63.

25. *Hoffa v. United States,* 385 U.S. 293, 321 (1966) (Warren, C.J., dissenting).

26. Kent Roach, "Four Models of the Criminal Process," *J. Crim. L. & Criminology* 89 (1999): 673.

27. Sherry F. Colb, "What Is a Search? Two Conceptual Flaws in Fourth Amendment Doctrine and Some Hints of a Remedy," *Stan. L. Rev.* 55 (2002): 119–89.

28. See Damaska, *Faces of Justice,* 47–70; John Rawls, *A Theory of Justice* (Cambridge: Harvard University Press, 1972), 86.

29. Antony Duff, "Introduction: Toward a Normative Theory of the Criminal Trial," in Duff et al., *Trial on Trial,* at 22.

30. See, e.g., George C. Thomas III, "When Constitutional Worlds Collide: Resurrecting the Framers' Criminal Procedure," *Mich. L. Rev.* 100 (2001): 174–80.

31. ABA report *Achieving Justice,* at 1.

32. Erik Lillquist, "The Capital Jury: False Positives and False Negatives in Capital Cases," *Ind. L.J.* 80 (2005): 47–52.

33. Frank, *Courts on Trial,* at 88 (emphases added).

34. Duff et al., *Trial on Trial.*

35. Dripps, *About Guilt and Innocence,* at 102.

36. Heike Jung, "Nothing but the Truth? Some Facts, Impressions and Confessions About Truth in Criminal Procedure," in Duff et al., *Trial on Trial,* at 156.

Chapter 3

The opening epigraph is from Aeschylus, *Eumenides,* lines 621–28 (Ian Johnston, trans., 2003).

1. Id. at lines 320–22.

2. Id. at lines 362–66.

3. Id. at lines 622–23, 626.

4. Id. at lines 627–28.

5. John V. A. Fine, *The Ancient Greeks: A Critical History* (Cambridge: Harvard University Press, 1983), 182.

6. Id. at 386.

7. Id. at 390.

8. Id.

9. O. F. Robinson, *The Criminal Law of Ancient Rome* (Baltimore: Johns Hopkins University Press, 1996), 1.

10. Id. at 14.

11. Wolfgang Kunkel, *An Introduction to Roman Legal and Constitutional History* (Oxford: Clarendon Press, 1966), 15.

12. Id. at 23.

13. Id. at 24.

14. Id. at 26–27.

15. Id. at 27.

16. Id. at 29.

17. James. L. Strachan-Davidson, *Problems of the Roman Criminal Law* (Oxford: Clarendon Press, 1969), vol. 1, 61.

18. Id.

19. A. H. M. Jones, *The Criminal Courts of the Roman Republic and Principate* (Totowa, N.J.: Rowman and Littlefield, 1972), 51.

20. Id. at 48.

21. Id.

22. Robinson, *Criminal Law of Ancient Rome*, at 4.

23. Id.

24. Id. at 6.

25. Id.

26. Strachan-Davidson, *Roman Criminal Law*, vol. 2, at 114.

27. Anthony Everitt, *Cicero, The Life and Times of Rome's Greatest Politician* (New York: Random House, 2003), 158.

28. Cicero, ad Quintum Fratrem, II, 4. 1, available at http://www.thelatin library.com/cicero/fratrem2.shtml#4 (last visited July 9, 2007).

29. Strachan-Davidson, *Roman Criminal Law*, vol. 2, at 114.

30. Id. at 129.

31. Robinson, *Criminal Law of Ancient Rome*, at 6.

32. Id. at 6.

33. Id. at 14.

34. Id. at 9–10.

35. Id at 12.

36. Strachan-Davidson, *Roman Criminal Law*, vol. 2, at 156–58.

37. Id. at 158.

38. Digest of Justinian, Book 48.1.8 (Alan Watson, trans., 1998).

39. Strachan-Davidson, *Roman Criminal Law*, vol. 2, at 156.

40. Kunkel, *Roman Legal History*, at 69–70.

41. Strachan-Davidson, *Roman Criminal Law*, vol. 2, at 205, 209.

42. Id.

43. Everitt, *Cicero*, at 79. Despite the bribes, Cicero outmaneuvered opposing counsel and won a conviction and heavy fine. Id.

44. Strachan-Davidson, *Roman Criminal Law*, vol. 2, at 211.

45. Sir Frederick Pollock & Frederick William Maitland, *The History of English Law Before the Time of Edward I* (Cambridge: Cambridge University Press, 2d ed., 1898), vol. 1, 141.

46. Id.

47. To be sure, the king could "lend" the right of inquest to others, usually to a church to litigate who owned lands claimed by the church. Id.

48. Id.

49. Id.

50. Id. at 141.

51. Pollock & Maitland, *History of English Law*, vol. 2, at 579.

52. *The Laws of the Salian Franks* (Kathleen Fischer Drew, trans., Philadelphia: University of Pennsylvania Press, 1991), 34.

53. Blackstone, *Commentaries*, vol. 4, at 337.

54. Id. at 340.

55. Id. at 341–42.

56. Stanley N. Katz, "Introduction," *William Blackstone's Commentaries on the Laws of England* (Chicago: University of Chicago Press, 1979), at iii.

57. Blackstone, *Commentaries*, vol. 4, at 338.

58. *English Lawsuits from William I to Richard I* (R. C. Van Caenegem, ed., London: Selden Society, 1990), vol. 2, 556 (case 502).

59. *Salian Franks*, at 34.

60. Norman F. Cantor, *Imagining the Law: Common Law and the Foundations of the American Legal System* (New York: HarperCollins, 1997), 62.

61. Id.

62. Trisha Olson, "Of Enchantment: The Passing of the Ordeals and the Rise of the Jury Trial," *Syracuse L. Rev.* 50 (2000): 156.

63. Id. at 156 (referring to the accused himself falsely swearing an oath of innocence).

64. Van Caenegem, *English Lawsuits*, vol. 2, at 622 (case 576).

65. Pollock & Maitland, *History of English Law*, vol. 2, at 601.

66. Van Caenegem, *English Lawsuits*, vol. 1, at 161 (case 193).

67. See, e.g., id. at vol. 1, 244 (case 291) (oaths given that the land belonged to Holy Trinity since the time of King Edward).

68. Id. at 135 (case 167).

69. See, e.g., id., vol. 2, at 501 (case 464).

70. Olson, "Of Enchantment," at 149–52.

71. Id. at 152.

72. Id. at 127.

73. Id. at 161–64.

Chapter 4

The opening epigraph is from the Assize of Clarendon, ch. 1, Sources of British History, available at http://britannia.com/history/docs/assize.html (last visited July 9, 2007).

1. W. L. Warren, *Henry II* (Berkeley and Los Angeles: University of California Press, 1973), 319.

2. "How Was it Compiled?" available at Domesday Book Online, http://www.domesdaybook.co.uk/compiling.html#how (last visited July 9, 2007).

3. Victoria King, "The Domesday Book," *History Magazine*, October–November 2001, available at http://www.history-magazine.com/domesday .html.

4. Van Caenegem, *English Lawsuits*, vol. 1, at 52 (case 22).

5. Id. at 65 (case 61).

6. Id. at 135 (case 167).

7. Id. at 185 (case 219).

8. Id. at 242 (case 242).

9. See, e.g., id. at 268–69 (case 320) (Stephen granting exemption from the authority of a bishop based on "charters and supporting evidence containing the assent of the great King William"); id. at 166–67 (case 202) (Henry I confirming ownership of a particular church); id. at 112 (case 140) (king ordering one abbot to allow another to "take a sufficient amount of stone for his church").

10. Id., vol. 2, at 602 (case 551).

11. Id., vol. 1, at 126 (case 157).

12. Id. at 288–91 (case 331).

13. See, for example, the reference to "confession of robbery, murder, theft" made "in the presence of lawful men" in chapter 13 of the Assize of Clarendon.

14. Van Caenegem, *English Lawsuits*, vol. 2, at 570 (case 519).

15. Id., vol. 2, at 649 (case 611).

16. Warren, *Henry II*, at 8.

17. Id. at 323.

18. Medieval Sourcebook, *Charter of Liberties of Henry I, 1100*, ch. 1, available at http://www.fordham.edu/halsall/source/hcoronation.html (last visited July 9, 2007).

19. Henry I: Ordinance on Local Courts, *Sources of English Constitutional History: A Selection of Documents from A.D. 600 to the Present* (Carl Stevenson & Frederick George Marcham, eds. & trans., New York: Harper & Brothers, 1937), 49.

20. *English Historical Documents* (David C. Douglas, ed., London: Oxford University Press, 1955), vol. 2, 433.

21. See, e.g., Van Caenegem, *English Lawsuits*, vol. 2, at 588–91 (cases 534, 535, 536, 537, 538, 539). Sometimes the scribe taking down the case used the word *settled*. See, e.g., id. at 559 (case 507); id. at 579 (case 523). *Agreed* or *agreement* also shows up in the case reports. See, e.g., 530 (case 488); 565 (case 514).

22. Warren, *Henry II*, at 11–14.

23. Id. at 49.

24. See Per Akesson, "The Danzig Cog," at http://www.abc.se/~m10354/mar/danzig.htm (last visited July 9, 2007).

25. A cog thought to date from the period was discovered when the port of Danzig was being rebuilt in 1872. See id. It was seventeen meters long and six meters wide. Could forty men with weapons squeeze into a ship of that size? Possibly. If so, it would have taken seventy-five ships.

26. See Arms and Armor in Medieval Europe, available at http://www.met museum.org/toah/hd/arms/hd_arms.htm (last visited July 9, 2007).

27. Warren, *Henry II,* at 78–79.

28. Id. at 263.

29. Van Caenegem, *English Lawsuits,* vol. 2, at 331 (case 369).

30. Id. at 122 (case 150).

31. Robert Bartlett, *England Under the Norman and Angevin Kings, 1075–1225* (Oxford: Clarendon Press, 2000), 183.

32. Pollock & Maitland, *History of English Law,* vol. 2, at 599 n. 1.

33. See, e.g., Van Caenegem, *English Lawsuits,* vol. 1, at 51 (case 19) (recounting case from the late eleventh century in which a monk had "formerly been the reeve of" a lord).

34. Paul Hyams, "Trial by Ordeal: The Key to Proof in the Early Common Law," in *On the Laws and Customs of England: Essays in Honor of Samuel E. Thorne* (M. Arnold, T. Green, S. Scully, & S. White, eds., Chapel Hill: University of North Carolina Press, 1981), 93–94.

35. Robert Bartlett, *Trial by Fire and Water* (New York: Oxford University Press, 1996), 78 .

36. Warren, *Henry II,* at 97 n. 1.

37. Bartlett, *England,* at 283 (quoting from the *Anglo-Saxon Chronicle,* a contemporary historical account compiled by English monks).

38. Id.

39. Van Caenegem, *English Lawsuits,* vol. 1, at 244 (case 290).

40. Id. at 290 (case 331).

41. Warren, *Henry II,* at 97.

42. Pollock & Maitland, *History of English Law,* vol. 2, at 604.

43. Cantor, *Imagining the Law,* at 66.

44. Olson, "Of Enchantment," at 166–67.

45. Id. at 166.

46. Id. at 169.

47. Warren, *Henry II,* at 97.

48. Id.

49. Id. at 98.

50. Id.

51. Id.

52. Bartlett, *England,* at 56.

53. Assize of Clarendon, 1166, ch. 11.

54. Id. at ch. 9.

55. Id. at ch. 1.

56. Roger D. Groot, "The Jury of Presentment Before 1215," *Am. J. Legal Hist.* 26 (1982): 22.

57. Assize of Clarendon, at ch. 12.

58. Id. at ch. 13.

59. Van Caenegem, *English Lawsuits,* vol. 2, at 466 (case 432).

60. *The Treatise on the Laws and Customs of the Realm of England Commonly Called Glanvill* (G. D. G. Hall, ed. & trans., London: Thomas Nelson & Sons, 1965), 171 n.1.

61. Assize of Clarendon, ch. 5.

62. Doris M. Stenton, *English Justice Between the Norman Conquest and the Great Charter, 1066–1215* (Philadelphia: American Philosophical Society, 1964), 71.

63. Id. at 74.

64. The Canons of the Fourth Lateran Council, ch. 18, in Medieval Source-book, "Twelfth Ecumenical Council," available at http://www.fordham.edu/halsall/basis/lateran4.html (last visited July 9, 2007).

65. Pollock & Maitland, *History of English Law,* vol. 2, at 599.

66. Sir William Holdsworth, *A History of English Law* (London: Sweet and Maxwell, 1903), vol. 1, at 311.

67. Assize of Clarendon, ch. 2.

68. Holdsworth, *History of English Law,* vol. 1, at 315 (speaking only of France).

69. *Glanvill,* 171.

70. Id. at 172.

71. Groot, "Jury of Presentment."

72. Id. at 22.

73. Holdsworth, *History of English Law,* vol. 1, at 323.

74. Id. at 326–27, citing *The Mirror of Justices,* V i, secs. 19, 126, 127. That a work written in the middle of the thirteenth century would discuss defendants offering to defend an accusation "by their bodies" suggests that trial by battle did not disappear as quickly as trial by ordeal.

75. Pollock & Maitland, *History of English Law,* vol. 2, at 627.

76. Holdsworth, *History of English Law,* vol. 1, at 317.

77. Anthony Musson, "Twelve Good Men and True? The Character of Early Fourteenth-Century Juries," *Law & Hist. Rev.* 15 (1997): 117.

78. Holdsworth, *History of English Law,* vol. 1, at 317.

79. Pollock & Maitland, *History of English Law,* vol. 2, at 624–27.

80. See, e.g., Van Caenegem, *English Lawsuits,* vol. 1, 50 (case 19).

81. Musson, "Twelve Good Men," at 133–34.

82. Holdworth, *History of English Law,* vol. 1, at 343–44.

83. Id. at 344, citing William Hudson, *A Treatise on the Court of Star-Chamber* (1625).

84. Alexander H. Shapiro, "Political Theory and the Growth of Defensive Safeguards in Criminal Procedure: The Origins of the Treason Trials Act of 1696," *Law & Hist. Rev.* 11 (1993): 215.

85. Id. at 217.

86. See id. at 218; Gerald P. Bodet, "Sir Edward Coke's Third Institutes: A Primer for Treason Defendants," *U. Toronto L.J.* 20 (1970): 471.

87. Bodet, "Coke's Third Institutes," at 471.

88. Id. at 471.

89. Shapiro, "Political Theory," 222 (noting difficulty of assessing "the validity of these claims").

90. Bodet, "Coke's Third Institutes," at 471.

91. Shapiro, "Political Theory," at 217.

92. Id. at 222.

93. Edward Coke, *The Third Part of the Institutes of the Laws of England: Concerning High Treason and Other Pleas of the Crown and Criminal Causes* (London: W. Clark and Sons, Law Booksellers, 1817), 137.

94. The Trial of Sir Walter Raleigh, knight at Winchester, for High Treason, 2 How. St. Tr. 1–5 (1603). All the facts in this paragraph are drawn from these pages.

95. Id at 18.

96. Id. at 18–19.

97. Id. at 19.

98. Id. at 19.

99. Id. at 24.

100. Id. at 15.

101. Id. at 26.

102. Id.

103. Id. at 29.

104. Raleigh Trevelyan, *Sir Walter Raleigh* (New York: Henry Holt, 2002), 427.

105. Id. at 515.

106. Id. at 537 & 552–53.

107. Alan Harding, *A Social History of English Law* (London: Penguin Books, 1966), 267.

108. Shapiro "Political Theory," at 240 (quoting Trial of Richard Grahme, 12 How. St. Tr. at 662) (emphasis added by Shapiro).

109. William Penn, "The Peoples Liberties Asssrted [*sic*] in the Tryal of William Penn and William Mead, 1670," at 6, available at http://tarlton .law.utexas.edu/lpop/etext/penntrial.html (last visited July 6, 2007).

110. Id. at "Additional endnotes," following page 23.

111. Id. at 13.

112. This paragraph is drawn from id. at 15.

113. Id. at 17.

114. Id. at 20.

115. Id. at 22.

116. 6 How. St. Tr. 999 (1670).

117. Id. at 1006.

118. Edmund Heward, *Matthew Hale* (London: Robert Hale, 1972), at 151.

Chapter 5

The opening epigraph is from *The Complete Bill of Rights: The Drafts, Debates, Sources, and Origins* (Neil H. Cogan, ed., New York: Oxford University Press, 1997), 438 (June 20, 1788, proceedings of Virginia Convention).

1. Resolutions of the Stamp Act Congress, October, 1765, introductory paragraph, par. III, and par. VIII, respectively, available at http://www.his toryplace.com/unitedstates/revolution/stamp-res.htm (last visited July 9, 2007).

2. Id. at par. VII.

3. Leonard W. Levy, *Origins of the Fifth Amendment* (New York: Oxford University Press, 1968), 395.

4. See George C. Thomas III, "Colonial Criminal Law and Procedure: The Royal Colony of New Jersey 1749–57," *NYU J. L. & Liberty* 1 (2005): 671–711.

5. Julius Goebel & T. Raymond Naughton, *Law Enforcement in Colonial New York: A Study in Criminal Procedure (1664–1776)* (1944; reprinted, Montclair, N.J.: Patterson Smith, 1970), 337 (grand jury) & 609 (jury trials).

6. See *Duncan v. Louisiana*, 391 U.S. 145, 153 (1968).

7. Thomas, "Colonial Criminal Law," 680 & 706, table 2.

8. "Few delegates to Congress ever became accustomed to the bustle and noise; or to the suffocating heat of a Philadelphia summer; or to the clouds of mosquitoes and horseflies that with the onset of summer rose like a biblical scourge." David McCullough, *John Adams* (New York: Simon & Schuster, 2001), 82.

9. U.S. Const. art. I, sec. 9.

10. See *The Civil Law: Including the Twelve Tables, the Institutes of Gaius, the Rules of Ulpian, the Opinions of Paulus, the Enactments of Justinian, and the Constitutions of Leo* (S. P. Scott, trans. & ed., originally published 1932, reprinted Union, N.J.: Lawbook Exchange 2001), vol. 1, XIV, sec. 7.

11. Compare U.S. Const. art. III, sec. 3 with 6–7 William & Mary, ch. 2 (1696) (forbidding treason conviction "but by and upon the oaths and testimony of two lawful witnesses . . . , unless the party indicted and arraigned or tried shall willingly, without violence, in open court confess the same").

12. U.S. Const. art. III., sec. 3.

13. Art. III, sec. 2, clause 3.

14. Cogan, *Complete Bill of Rights*, at 465 (February 1, 1788, "Genuine Information").

15. Id. at 426 (July 29, 1788, proceedings of North Carolina Convention).

16. Id. at 422 (July 2, 1788, proceedings of New York Convention).

17. See, e.g., id. at 434 (June 14, 1788, proceedings of Virginia Convention) (Patrick Henry).

18. McCullough, *John Adams*, at 76.

19. Cogan, *Complete Bill of Rights*, at 439 (June 20, 1788, proceedings of Virginia Convention).

20. Id. at 428 (December 11, 1787, proceedings of Pennsylvania Convention).

21. Id. at 438 (June 20, 1788, proceedings of Virginia Convention).

22. Assize of Clarendon, ch. 14.

23. 30 Charles II, st. 2, ch. 1 (1679).

24. U.S. Const. art. I, sec. 9.

25. *Ex parte Bollman* & *Ex parte Swartwout*, 8 U.S. 75, 1807 Lexis 369, **21 (1807) (prior history appearing in Lexis version).

26. Gregory Fehlings, "Storm on the Constitution: The First Deportation Law," *Tulsa J. Comp. & Int'l. L.* 10 (2002): 64 (citing S. Rep. No. 41–10 (1870), reprinted in 46 Cong. Rec. 366, 377 (1910) (calculating the total at 2,290)).

27. Id. at 66.

28. Id. at 67 (quoting from Mederic Louis-Elie Moreau De Saint-Mery, *Moreau De St. Mery's American Journey, 1793–1798*, 252 (Kenneth Roberts & Anna M. Roberts, eds. & trans., 1947)).

29. McCullough, *John Adams*, at 505.

30. Fifth Congress, Sess. II, ch. 58, § 1, 1 U.S. Statutes at Large 570–72 (1798).

31. Fifth Congress, Sess. II, ch. 75, § 1, 1 U.S. Statutes at Large 596–97 (1798).

32. See Fifth Congress, Sess. II, ch. 58, § 6 (1798), 1 U.S. Statutes at Large 572 (1798) (Alien Act to expire); Fifth Congress, Sess. II, ch. 75, § 4, 1 U.S. Statutes at Large 597 (1798) (Sedition Act to expire).

33. Jean Edward Smith, *John Marshall: Definer of a Nation* (New York: H. Holt, 1996), 75.

34. Id. at 3.

35. Id. at xi.

36. Id. at 5.

37. Id. at 278.

38. Id.

39. Id. at 1.

40. Alexander Valentine, prepared partly from a text by Alexander Leitch, "Aaron Burr, Jr.," Information from the Princeton Companion, available at http://www.let.rug.nl/usa/B/aburr/burr.htm (last visited July 5, 2007).

41. Joanne B. Freeman, "The Presidential Election of 1800: A Story of Crisis, Confrontation, and Crisis," *Historian's Perspective* 1 (2004), available at http://www.historynow.org/09_2004/historian4b.html (last visited July 6, 2007).

42. Valentine, "Aaron Burr, Jr."

43. Joseph J. Ellis, *American Sphinx* (New York: Vintage, 1998).

44. Doug Linder, "The Treason Trial of Aaron Burr," (2001), available at http://www.law.umkc.edu/faculty/projects/ftrials/burr/burraccount.html (last visited July 7, 2007).

45. Smith, *John Marshall,* at 353.

46. Id.

47. Id. (quoting Jefferson to Langdon, December 22, 1806, *The Writings of Thomas Jefferson,* vol. 19 ([Andrew A. Lipscomb, ed., Washington, D.C.: Thomas Jefferson Memorial Association, 1903], 157–58).

48. Id.

49. R. Kent Newmyer, *John Marshall and the Heroic Age of the Supreme Court* (Baton Rouge: Louisiana State University Press, 2002), 182.

50. Smith, *John Marshall,* at 354.

51. *Bollman,* 8 U.S. at 76.

52. Smith, *John Marshall,* at 355.

53. Id.

54. Id. at 354.

55. *Bollman,* 8 U.S. at 130–31.

56. Id. at 127.

57. Id. at 125.

58. 25 Fed. Cas. 30 (C.C.D.Va 1807).

59. U.S. Const. amend. VI.

60. *Burr,* 25 Fed. Cas. 30, 31.

61. Newmyer, *John Marshall,* at 191.

62. Id. at 196.

63. Id.

64. Id.

65. *Burr,* 25 Fed. Cas. 30, at 37.

66. Smith, *John Marshall,* at 360.

67. Id.

68. Newmyer, *John Marshall,* at 190–91.

69. Id. at 191.

70. Id. at 192.

71. The source for this entire paragraph is id.

72. *Bollman,* 8 U.S. at 126.

73. Smith, *John Marshall,* at 368–69.

74. Id. at 369.

75. Id. at 370.

76. Id.

77. Id. (quoting *Reports of the Trials of Colonel Aaron Burr* (David Robertson, ed., Philadelphia: Hopkins & Earle, 1808), 378).

78. Newmyer, *John Marshall,* at 201.

79. *Bollman,* 1807 Lexis 369, Appendix at *** 219–20.

80. Smith, *John Marshall,* at 372.

81. Newmyer, *John Marshall,* at 202.

82. Smith, *John Marshall,* at 354.

83. Id.

84. Newmyer, *John Marshall,* at 189.

85. Id. at 196–97.

86. Id. at 202.

87. Smith, *John Marshall,* at 359.

88. *Burr,* 25 Fed. Cas. at 13.

89. Act of January 25, 1889, sec. 6, 25 Stat. 1889. To be sure, in 1874 Congress gave the Court power to hear criminal appeals from the Supreme Court of the Territory of Utah as the controversy over polygamy heated up. Act of June 23, 1874, sec. 3, 18 Stat. 254. So there are a few scattered Supreme Court cases hearing criminal appeals prior to 1889.

90. *Hickory v. United States,* 151 U.S. 303 (1894) & 160 U.S. 408 (1896).

91. 151 U.S. 408 (1894).

92. 160 U.S. 408 (1896).

93. Barbara Rust, Archivist National Archives-Southwest Region, email to the author, March 24, 2003.

94. *Jackson v. Virginia,* 443 U.S. 307, 319 (1979).

95. The exception is Texas. I will explain the Texas approach in chapter 9.

96. See, e.g., *Mills v. State,* 626 S.E.2d 495 (Ga. 2006) (following *Jackson*); *State v. Goble,* 126 P.3d 821 (Wash.App. 2005) (same); *People v. Mata,* 611 N.E.2d 1235 (Ill.App. 1993) (same); *Hale v. State,* 31 S.W.3d 850 (Ark. 2000) (finding equivalence with prior state standard); *Norris v. State,* 419 N.E.2d 129 (Ind. 1981) (same).

97. *State v. Aaron, slave of L. Solomon,* 4 N.J. L. 231 (N.J. 1818). Readers might be surprised that New Jersey was a slave state. It was but by 1818, New Jersey had adopted an act "for the gradual abolition of slavery," which bound the defendant to his master until he reached the age of twenty-five. Id. at *3.

98. Id. at *7 (emphasis in original).

99. Id. at *6.

100. *Commonwealth v. Dillon,* 4 U.S. 116 (Pa. 1792).

101. Id. at **5.

102. See John Henry Wigmore, *A Treatise on Evidence*, vol. 2 (Boston: Little, Brown, 2d ed. 1923), 927 (noting that, by the beginning of the 1800s, there was "a general suspicion of all confessions, a prejudice against them, and an inclination to repudiate them upon the slightest pretext").

103. *State v. Due*, 27 N.H. 256, at *4 (1853).

104. *Colorado v. Connelly*, 479 U.S. 157 (1986).

105. Id. at 167.

Chapter 6

The opening epigraph is from "Ed Johnson Jury Stands 8 to 4 for Conviction," *Chattanooga Times*, February 9, 1906.

1. See Orville J. Victor, *The History, Civil, Political, and Military of the Southern Rebellion* (New York: J. D. Torrey, 1861), vol. 2, 295–98, partly available as "East Tennessee Anti-Secession Resolutions," available at http://alpha.furman.edu/~benson/tennres1.htm (last visited July 9, 2007).

2. Mark Curriden & Leroy Phillips, Jr., *Contempt of Court: The Turn-of-the-Century Lynching That Launched a Hundred Years of Federalism* (New York: Faber & Faber, 1999), 21.

3. Id.

4. Id. at 23.

5. Id. at 24.

6. Id.

7. Id. at 24.

8. Id. at 25.

9. "Brutal Crime of Negro Fiend," *Chattanooga News*, January 24, 1906.

10. Email, Chattanooga-Hamilton County Library to George Thomas, September 24, 2007.

11. "Negro Fiend," *Chattanooga News*, January 24, 1906.

12. Id.

13. "Awful Crime at St. Elmo," *Chattanooga Times*, January 24, 1906.

14. "Negro Fiend," *Chattanooga News*, January 24, 1906.

15. "Awful Crime," *Chattanooga Times*, January 24, 1906.

16. Douglas Linder, Famous American Trials, "The Trial of Sheriff Joseph Shipp, et al., 1907, Transcript Excerpts," available at http://www.law.umkc.edu/faculty/projects/ftrials/shipp/shipp.html (last visited July 9, 2007).

17. Zella Armstrong, *The History of Hamilton County and Chattanooga Tennessee* (Chattanooga: Lookout Publishing, 1931), 257–58, available at "The Chattanooga Confederate Cemeteries, The Silverdale Cemetery," http://www.utc.edu/Academic/Communication/ConfCem/ConfederateCem.html (last visited July 9, 2007). Nathan Bedford Forrest made a fortune

from slave trading, enlisted in the Confederate Army as a private, and rose to the rank of lieutenant general. Known for his military genius leading a battalion of calvary and for his hatred of blacks, Forrest was, and remains, a polarizing figure. "Nathan Bedford Forrest," available at http://www.civilwarhome.com/natbio.htm (last visited July 7, 2007) (source: "Who Was Who In The Civil War," by Stewart Sifakis).

18. Id.

19. *Chattanooga Times,* January 24, 1906.

20. "Negro Fiend," *Chattanooga News,* January 24, 1906.

21. "Awful Crime," *Chattanooga Times,* January 24, 1906.

22. Id.

23. "Feeling at High Pitch," *Chattanooga Times,* January 25, 1906.

24. Id.

25. "Suspect Arrested and Rushed to Knoxville," *Chattanooga Times,* January 26, 1906.

26. Curriden & Phillips, *Contempt of Court,* 39 (quoting an unidentified newspaper account).

27. Id.

28. Email, Chattanooga-Hamilton County Library to George Thomas, September 24, 2007.

29. The rest of the facts in this paragraph come from "Law and Order Victorious over Overwhelming Odds," *Chattanooga Times,* January 26, 1906.

30. The facts in this paragraph come from id.

31. The facts in this paragraph come from id.

32. Id.

33. Id. The news account said that the sheriff and suspect were headed to Knoxville. We know, because they arrived in Nashville, that this story was planted to enable the party to reach its destination safely.

34. Curriden & Phillips, *Contempt of Court,* at 50.

35. Id. at 51.

36. "Wheels of Justice Turn Fast in St. Elmo Assault Case," *Chattanooga Times,* January 28, 1906.

37. Don H. Doyle, *Nashville in the New South, 1880–1930* (Knoxville: University of Tennessee Press, 1985), 27.

38. Id.

39. *Nashville Banner,* January 28, 1906.

40. Doyle, *Nashville,* at 84.

41. This paragraph draws from "Wheels of Justice Turn Fast in St. Elmo Assault Case, Almost Positive Identification," *Chattanooga Times,* January 28, 1906.

42. Curriden & Phillips, *Contempt of Court,* at 55.

43. "Wheels of Justice, Jury Returns True Bill," *Chattanooga Times*, January 28, 1906.

44. "Says He Is Not Guilty," *Chattanooga Times*, February 2, 1906.

45. Curriden & Phillips, *Contempt of Court*, at 60.

46. Id. at 61–62.

47. "Court Will Do Its Part, Attorneys Make Statement," *Chattanooga News*, February 2, 2006.

48. Curriden & Phillips, *Contempt of Court*, at 70.

49. Id. at 71.

50. "Will Hold Trial Here," *Chattanooga News*, January 29, 1906.

51. "Court Will Do Its Part," *Chattanooga News*, February 2, 1906.

52. James W. Livingood, "A History of Hamilton County, Tennessee," partly available at http://www.hamiltontn.gov/courthouse/Default.aspx (last visited July 13, 2007).

53. "Law Taking Its Course, State Presents Its Case," *Chattanooga Times*, February 7, 1906.

54. Id., "Defendant on the Stand."

55. "Ed Johnson Jury Stands 8 to 4 for Conviction, Jurors Unable to Stand Terrible Nervous Strain," *Chattanooga Times*, February 9, 1906.

56. Id.

57. Although recent jury reforms in many states permit juror questioning, it remains a very unusual occurrence. See Nicole L. Mott, "The Current Debate on Juror Questions: 'To Ask, or Not to Ask, That Is the Question,'" *Chi.-Kent L. Rev.* 78 (2003): 1099–1125.

58. "Ed Johnson Jury, Jurors Unable to Stand," *Chattanooga Times*, February 9, 1906.

59. Id.

60. This paragraph is drawn from "Ed Johnson Jury, Lawyers' Warm Arguments Make Most Exciting Finish," *Chattanooga Times*, February 9, 1906.

61. Id.

62. Id.

63. "Law Taking Its Course, Others for the Defendant," *Chattanooga Times*, February 7, 1906.

64. "Ed Johnson Jury, Lawyers' Warm Arguments," February 9, 1906.

65. Curriden & Phillips, *Contempt of Court*, at 118–19.

66. "The Jury Finds Ed Johnson Guilty; He Will Hang for His Fiendish Crime," *Chattanooga News*, February 9, 1906.

67. Curriden & Phillips, *Contempt of Court*, at 118.

68. *Chattanooga News*, February 9, 1906.

69. "Wheels of Justice, Sheriff's Thrilling Story," *Chattanooga Times*, January 28, 1906.

70. Leonard Dinnerstein, *The Leo Frank Case* (New York: Columbia University Press, 1968), at 12 (showing a drawing of Mary that appeared in an Atlanta newspaper); at 11 (her age).

71. Id. at 1.

72. Id. at 2.

73. Id.

74. Id. at 68.

75. Id.

76. Id.

77. Mortality Statistics 1905, Sixth Annual Report (G.P.O., 1907), available at http://www.cdc.gov/nchs/data/vsushistorical/mortstatsh_1905.pdf (last visited July 9, 2007).

78. Dinnerstein, *Leo Frank Case,* at 69.

79. Id. at 109.

80. Id. at 79.

81. *Frank v. Magnum,* 237 U.S. 309 (1915).

82. Dinnerstein, *Leo Frank Case,* at 122.

83. Id.

84. Id. at 122–23 (quoting Lucian Lamar Knight, *A Standard History of Georgia and Georgians,* vol. 2 [Chicago: Lewis Publishing, 1917], 1168).

85. Id. at 123.

86. Id. at 125.

87. Id.

88. Id.

89. Id. at 126.

90. Id. at 127.

91. Id.

92. Id. at 129.

93. Id. at 132.

94. The New Georgia Encyclopedia, Tammy H. Galloway, "John M. Slaton (1866–1955)," available at http://www.georgiaencyclopedia.org/nge/Article.jsp?id=h-2137 (last visited July 9, 2007).

95. Dinnerstein, *Leo Frank Case,* at 143.

96. Id. at 139.

97. Id. at 145.

98. Galloway, "John M. Slaton."

99. All the facts in this paragraph are drawn from Constitutional Law, Supreme Court Justices, "John Marshall Harlan," available at http://www.michaelariens.com/ConLaw/justices/harlan.htm (last visited July 9, 2007).

100. Curriden & Phillips, *Contempt of Court,* 5.

101. Id. at 9.

102. Id.

103. Id. at 10.

104. Id. at 9.

105. Id. at 17.

106. *Chattanooga Times,* March 18, 1906.

107. "Justice Harlan Allows Appeal of Ed Johnson," *Chattanooga Times,* March 19, 1906.

108. Id.

109. Id.

110. " 'God Bless You All—I Am Innocent,' Ed Johnson's Last Words Before Being Shot to Death by a Mob Like a Dog, Majesty of the Law Outraged by Lynchers, Mandate of the Supreme Court of the United States Disregarded and Red Riot Rampant, Terrible and Tragic Vengeance Bows City's Head in Shame," *Chattanooga News,* March 20, 1906.

111. Id.

112. Id.

113. Email, Chattanooga-Hamilton County Library to George Thomas, September 24, 2007.

114. Linder, "Trial of Sheriff Shipp, A Chattanooga Sermon, Is Lawlessness a Cure for Crime?" available at http://www.law.umkc.edu/faculty/projects/ ftrials/shipp/shipp.html (last visited July 9, 2007).

115. Id.

Chapter 7

1. Findlay, Ohio, *Morning Republican,* May 15, 1907.

2. "Supreme Court Shocked," *Chattanooga Times,* March 21, 1906.

3. Id.

4. Linder, "Trial of Sheriff Shipp, Chronology," available at http://www .law.umkc.edu/faculty/projects/ftrials/shipp/shipp.html (last visited July 9, 2007).

5. Id.

6. Id.

7. Id.

8. "God Bless You All—I Am Innocent, Statement of Sheriff Shipp," *Chattanooga Times,* March 20, 1906.

9. Linder, "Trial of Sheriff Shipp, Newspaper Accounts, Shipp Interviewed, Quoted as Laying Blame on the Supreme Court," Associated Press, May 28, 1906, available at http://www.law.umkc.edu/faculty/projects/ftri als/shipp/ shipp.html (last visited July 9, 2007).

10. Linder, "Trial of Sheriff Shipp, Transcript Excerpts," available at

http://www.law.umkc.edu/faculty/projects/ftrials/shipp/shipp.html (last visited July 9, 2007).

11. Id.

12. Id.

13. Id.

14. Linder, "Trial of Sheriff Shipp, Chronology," at http://www.law.umkc .edu/faculty/projects/ftrials/shipp/shipp.html (last visited July 9, 2007).

15. Id.

16. Id.

17. Curriden & Phillips, *Contempt of Court,* at 338.

18. Linder, "Trial of Sheriff Shipp, Chronology."

19. *Chattanooga News,* March 21, 1906.

20. James Goodman, *Stories of Scottsboro* (New York: Random House, Times Book 1994), 5.

21. *Powell v. United States,* 287 U.S. 45, 56 (1932).

22. Id. at 13–14.

23. Id. at 15–16.

24. 287 U.S. 45 (1932).

25. Id. at 50.

26. 294 U.S. 587 (1935).

27. Michael J. Klarman, "The Racial Origins of Modern Criminal Procedure," *Mich. L. Rev.* 99 (2000): 80.

28. Id. at 81.

29. Id. at 57.

30. Id. at 80.

31. Emily Yellin, "Lynching Victim Is Cleared of Rape, 100 Years Later," *New York Times,* February 27, 2000.

32. Cogan, *Complete Bill of Rights,* at 438 (June 20, 1788, proceedings of Virginia Convention).

33. *Barron v. Baltimore,* 32 U.S. 243 (1833).

34. U.S. Const. amend. XIV.

35. *Slaughter-House Cases,* 83 U.S. 36 (1873). The perceptive reader will infer from the title of the case that it was civil in nature. The precise issue was whether Louisiana had the right to order butchers to slaughter meat only in slaughterhouses designated by the state. The Court held that the Fourteenth Amendment did not deprive the state of that power.

36. Charles Wallace Collins, *The Fourteenth Amendment and the States: A Study of the Operation of the Restraint Clauses of Section One of the Fourteenth Amendment to the Constitution of the United States* (New York: Da Capo Press, 1974 reprint of original Boston: Little, Brown), 29.

37. See id. (noting that of 604 cases, the state won 549).

38. See *Strauder v. West Virginia,* 100 U.S. 303 (1879) (holding that a West Virginia statute that explicitly excluded blacks from serving on grand juries violated the Fourteenth Amendment).

39. *Powell v. Alabama,* 287 U.S. 45, 71 (1936).

40. Id.

41. Id.

42. *Betts v. Brady,* 316 U.S. 455, 472 (1942).

43. *Brown v. Mississippi,* 297 U.S. 278 (1936).

44. Wigmore, *A Treatise on Evidence,* vol. 2, § 824, p. 145.

45. *Lisenba v. California,* 314 U.S. 219 (1941).

46. *Ashcraft v. Tennessee,* 322 U.S. 143 (1944).

47. Compare *Crooker v. California,* 357 U.S. 433 (1958) with *Lynum v. Illinois,* 372 U.S. 528 (1963).

48. See *Townsend v. Sain,* 372 U.S. 293 (1963).

49. See *Blackburn v. Alabama,* 361 U.S. 199 (1960).

50. *Miranda v. Arizona,* 384 U.S. 436 (1966).

51. Roger M. Grace, "Great Norwegians, Earl Warren," at http://www.mnc .net/norway/ (last visited July 9, 2007).

52. The United States had forty-eight states in 1954, and ninety-six to zero thus represented the vote of every senator.

53. Grace, "Great Norwegians, Earl Warren."

54. Id.

55. Id. Roger Grace was a young volunteer in two Knight campaigns for governor in the 1960s. Grace "heard Gov. Knight tell the story [about Warren's ultimatum] several times." Email to George Thomas, April 3, 2008.

56. For thoughts on the legal and political difficulties caused by *Brown,* see George C. Thomas III, "Islands in the Stream of History: An Institutional Archeology of Dual Sovereignty," *Ohio State J. Crim. L.* 1 (2003): 345.

57. Congressional Quarterly, "The Selection and Confirmation of Justices: Criteria and Process, Policy Preferences," available at http://www.cqpress .com/incontext/SupremeCourt/the_selection.htm (last visited July 9, 2007).

58. Merle Miller, *Plain Speaking: An Oral Biography of Harry S. Truman* (New York: Berkley Paperback Books, 1984), at 225–26.

59. For an excellent biography of John Marshall Harlan II, see Tinsley Yarbrough, *John Marshall Harlan: Great Dissenter of the Warren Court* (New York: Oxford University Press, 1992).

60. Craig M. Bradley, *The Failure of the Criminal Procedure Revolution* (Philadelphia: University of Pennsylvania Press, 1993) at 62–87.

61. Pizzi, *Trials Without Truth,* 155.

62. See, e.g., *Katzenbach v. McClung,* 379 U.S. 294, 304–5 (1964) (holding

that Congress may legitimately compel restaurant owners to serve blacks under its Commerce Clause powers if a substantial portion of the restaurant's food has moved through interstate commerce).

63. Yarbrough, *John Marshall Harlan*, at 190–97.

64. *Palko v. Connecticut*, 302 U.S. 319, 328 (1937) (quoting *Herbert v. Louisiana*, 272 U.S. 312 (1926)).

65. See chapter 2.

66. *Wolf v. Colorado*, 338 U.S. 25 (1949).

67. *Mapp v. Ohio*, 367 U.S. 643 (1961).

68. Yale Kamisar, "Equal Justice in the Gatehouses and Mansions of American Criminal Procedure: From Powell to Gideon, from Escobedo to * * *," in *Criminal Justice in Our Time* (A. E. Dick Howard, ed., Charlottesville: University Press of Virginia, 1965), 80.

69. *Betts v. Brady*, 316 U.S. 455 (1942).

70. *Gideon v. Wainwright*, 372 U.S. 335, 344 (1963).

71. *Duncan v. Louisiana*, 391 U.S. 145 (1968).

72. Markus Dirk Dubber, "The Criminal Trial and the Legitimation of Punishment," in Duff et al., *Trial on Trial*, at 87.

73. Id. at 88.

74. Dripps, *About Guilt and Innocence*, at 125.

75. Carol S. Steiker, "Counter-revolution in Constitutional Criminal Procedure? Two Audiences, Two Answers, *Mich. L. Rev.* 94 (1996): 2466–2551.

76. See, e.g., Ofshe & Leo, "Decision to Confess Falsely."

77. Leo, *Police Interrogation*, ch. 6, at manuscript page 24.

78. Id.

79. Id. at 26.

80. *See* 384 U.S., at 473–74 ("If the individual indicates in any manner, at any time prior to or during questioning, that he wishes to remain silent, the interrogation must cease.").

81. Leo, *Police Interrogation*, ch. 6, at manuscript page 7.

82. *Argersinger v. Hamlin*, 407 U.S. 25 (1972).

83. *Douglas v. California*, 372 U.S. 353 (1963) (first appeal); *Ross v. Moffit*, 417 U.S. 600 (1974) (discretionary appeal in state supreme court); *Coleman v. Thompson*, 501 U.S. 722 (1991) (federal habeas corpus proceeding).

84. *Strickland v. Washington*, 466 U.S. 668 (1986). For criticisms, see the sources cited in George C. Thomas III, "History's Lesson for the Right to Counsel," *U. Ill. L. Rev.* 2004 (2004): 543.

85. *Strickland*, 466 U.S., at 690.

86. See *Burdine v. Johnson*, 231 F.3d 950 (5th Cir. 2000), rev'd, *Burdine v. Johnson*, 262 F.3d 336 (5th Cir. 2001) (en banc).

87. *Wade v. United States,* 388 U.S. 218, 228 (1967) (quoting Felix Frankfurter, *The Case of Sacco and Vanzetti* 30 (1927)).

88. James A. Strazzella, "Ineffective Identification Counsel: Cognizability Under the Exclusionary Rule," *Temple L.Q.* 48 (1975): 253.

89. *Gilbert v. United States,* 388 U.S. 263 (1967).

90. Brian L. Cutler & Steven D. Penrod, *Mistaken Identification: The Eyewitness, Psychology, and the Law* (New York: Cambridge University Press, 1995), at 157–58.

91. *Stovall v. Denno,* 388 U.S. 293 (1967).

92. Id. at 295.

93. *Kirby v. Illinois,* 406 U.S. 682 (1972) (plurality).

94. *Manson v. Braithwaite,* 432 U.S. 98, 109 (1977).

95. See Dripps, *About Guilt and Innocence,* at 117.

96. Frank, *Courts on Trial,* at 88.

97. Jerold H. Israel, "Free-Standing Due Process and Criminal Procedure: The Supreme Court's Search for Interpretive Guidelines," *St. Louis U. L.J.* 45 (2001): 303–432.

98. Bradley, *Failure of the Revolution,* at 62.

99. 126 S.Ct. 2064 (2006). *Herrera* is discussed in the introduction.

100. Id. at 2087.

101. The Court's refusal to grant House's claim of actual innocence did not doom him necessarily to execution. The Court sent the case back to determine whether he had received effective assistance of counsel during his original murder trial.

Chapter 8

1. Damaska, *Faces of Justice,* 222.

2. Hale, *History and Analysis,* at 258.

3. David Luban, *Lawyers and Justice: An Ethical Study* (Princeton: Princeton University Press, 1988), 103.

4. Erik Luna, "A Place for Comparative Criminal Procedure," *Brandeis L.J.* 42 (2003–4): 300.

5. Pizzi, *Trials Without Truth,* at 71 & 140–44.

6. Defendants have a federal constitutional right not to be held in custody without a judicial determination of probable cause, but this can be accomplished by having the prosecutor file an affidavit, without notice to the suspect. See *Riverside v. McLaughlin,* 500 U.S. 44 (1991). Similarly, the Eighth Amendment requires that a decision be made about bail. U.S. Const. amend. VIII.

7. Ninety-five percent of convictions in felony cases result from plea bargains. Bureau of Justice Statistics, Criminal Case Processing Statistics, "Sum-

mary Findings,"available at http://www.ojp.usdoj.gov/bjs/cases.htm#felony (last visited July 7, 2007).

8. Pizzi, *Trials Without Truth*, at 15–24; Luna, "Comparative Criminal Procedure," at 296.

9. Floyd Feeney & Joachim Herrmann, *One Case—Two Systems: A Comparative View of American and German Criminal Justice* (Ardsley, N.Y.: Transnational, 2005), 388.

10. Frank, *Courts on Trial*, at 81.

11. Id.

12. Id. at 82.

13. *United States v. Wade*, 388 U.S. 218, 258 (1967) (White, J., dissenting in part and concurring in part) (joined by Harlan, J., & Stewart, J.).

14. Frank, *Courts on Trial*, at 87 (quoting an unnamed English lawyer).

15. Pizzi, *Trials Without Truth*, 197.

16. Medwed, "The Zeal Deal," at 129.

17. Id. at 134.

18. See Jonakait, *The American Jury System*, 205.

19. Ryan, "Commutation Address."

20. Renée Lettow Lerner, email to author, April 19, 2007. I will draw on Professor Lerner's firsthand knowledge of the French justice system throughout the chapter.

21. French Code of Criminal Procedure, hereinafter FCCP, Art. 53.

22. FCCP Art. 81.

23. FCCP Art. 82–1.

24. FCCP Art. 92.

25. Damaska, *Faces of Justice*, at 137.

26. FCCP Art. 82–2.

27. Damaska, *Faces of Justice*, at 177.

28. Renee Lettow Lerner, email to author, April 29, 2007.

29. Damaska, *Faces of Justice*, at 33.

30. Annuaire Statistique de la Justice, 2002–6 editions, available at http://www.justice.gouv.fr/ (last visited July 9, 2007).

31. FCCP Arts. 196–205.

32. FCCP Art. 201.

33. Damaska, *Faces of Justice*, at 193.

34. FCCP Art. 310.

35. Lerner, "Intersection of Two Systems," at 808.

36. Id. at 811–12. In Norway, the presiding judge questions the witnesses after the lawyers have completed their questioning. Pizzi, *Trials Without Truth*, 102.

37. Lerner, "Intersection of Two Systems," at 818.

38. Jonakait, *The American Jury System*, at 182.

39. Lerner, "Intersection of Two Systems" at 831–32. In the past few years, interpretations of the European Human Rights Convention have led to a greater right for defendants to have witnesses appear and testify rather than have the court rely on hearsay from a deposition. Richard S. Frase, "France," in *Criminal Procedure: A Worldwide Study,* 170 (Craig M. Bradley, ed., Durham, N.C.: Carolina Academic Press, 1999).

40. Lerner, "Intersection of Two Systems," at 832.

41. FCCP Art. 353.

42. See FCCP Art. 296 (nine lay jurors), FCCP Art. 243 ("court proper consists of the presiding judge and two assessors"), & FCCP Art. 356 ("court and jury deliberate, then vote").

43. Lerner, "Intersection of Two Systems," at 814.

44. Damaska, *Faces of Justice,* at 36.

45. FCCP Art. 357.

46. FCCP Art. 359.

47. FCCP Art. 380–1.

48. Pizzi, *Trials Without Truth,* at 102.

49. Lerner, "Intersection of Two Systems," at 802.

50. FCCP Art. 567 (permitting applications to the Cour de Cassation claiming "violation of law"). That prosecution appeal is rarely pursued I infer from 1998 data showing only 6,700 criminal appeals filed in 1998. See www.cour decassation.fr/_Accueil/anglais/anglais.htm.

51. Lerner, "Intersection of Two Systems," at 814–15.

52. Id. at 815.

53. Id. at 809.

54. Id. at 809–10.

55. John A. Humphrey & Saundra A. Westervelt, "Introduction," in Westervelt & Humphrey, *Wrongly Convicted,* at 1 (expressing skepticism about that claim).

56. Uniform Code of Military Justice § 832.32 (a).

57. Gregory Maggs, email to author, July 7, 2007.

58. Id.

59. Uniform Code of Military Justice § 832.32 (b).

60. Id.

61. Id.

Chapter 9

The title and subtitle are, of course, suggested by the series of Douglas Adams novels, the first of which is *The Hitch-hiker's Guide to the Galaxy.*

1. Valerie P. Hans, "U.S. Jury Reform: The Active Jury and the Adversarial Ideal," *St. Louis U. Public L. Rev.* 21 (2002): 96.

2. Brown, "Decline of Defense Counsel," at 1591.

3. Jenny McEwan, "Ritual, Fairness and Truth: The Adversarial and Inquisitorial Models of Criminal Trials," in Duff et al., *Trial on Trial,* at 66 (English law); Peter Duff, "Changing Conceptions of the Scottish Criminal Trial: The Duty to Agree Uncontroversial Evidence," in id. at 48–49 (Scottish law).

4. ABA report *Achieving Justice.*

5. D. Michael Risinger, "Unsafe Verdicts: The Need for Reformed Standards for the Trial and Review of Factual Innocence Claims," *Hous. L. Rev.* 41 (2004): 1281–1336.

6. Id. at 1311–13.

7. Weinreb, *Denial of Justice,* at 125–44.

8. Id. at 3.

9. Id. at 11.

10. Weinreb's proposal is forty years old. The jury is still out on Risinger's 2004 proposal of a separate trial under factual innocence rules. I hope I am wrong and that some states will adopt his proposal.

11. ABA report *Achieving Justice,* at 11.

12. Id. at 63.

13. Id. at 47.

14. Id. at 93.

15. Id. at 23–26.

16. Id. at 80.

17. Id. at 79.

18. Id. at 99.

19. See Ronald F. Wright, "Parity of Resources for Defense Counsel and the Reach of Public Choice Theory," *Iowa L. Rev.* 90 (2004): 219–68.

20. Margaret Raymond, "The Problem With Innocence," *Cleveland State L. Rev.* 49 (2001): 463 (referring to Edwin M. Borchard, *Convicting the Innocent: Errors of Criminal Justice* (New Haven: Yale University Press, 1932)).

21. Bradley, *Failure of the Revolution,* at 62. The reasons are what Bradley calls uncertainty and incompleteness. The uncertainty principle is that each new decision creates more questions than it answers. The incompleteness principle is that the Court is not supposed to answer questions not posed by the case before it.

22. Id. at 145–46.

23. See, e.g., *Dickerson v. United States,* 530 U.S. 428 (2000); *City of Boerne v. Flores,* 521 U.S. 507 (1997). These cases suggest that once the Court "constitutionalizes" a field, as in did with police interrogation in *Miranda,* Congress can do nothing that appears to supersede the Court's interpretation.

24. Constitution Project, "Mandatory Justice: The Death Penalty Revis-

ited," "Summary (2005)," at xvii, available at www.constitutionproject.org/deathpenalty/index.cfm?categoryId=2.

25. Kay L. Levine, "The New Prosecution," *Wake Forest L. Rev.* 40 (2005): 1126.

26. *Strickland v. Washington*, 466 U.S. 668 (1984).

27. *Burdine v. Johnson*, 231 F.3d 950 (5th Cir. 2000), rev'd, *Burdine v. Johnson*, 262 F.3d 336 (5th Cir. 2001) (en banc).

28. *Mitchell v. Kemp*, 483 U.S. 1026 (1987) (Marshall, J., dissenting from denial of certiorari).

29. Id. See also *Romero v. Lynaugh*, 884 F.2d 871 (5th Cir. 1989).

30. *Smith v. Murray*, 477 U.S. 527 (1986).

31. *Barentine v. United States*, 728 F. Supp. 1241 (W.D. N.C. 1990).

32. See Ill. S. Ct. R. 714 (2007).

33. Constitution Project, "Mandatory Justice," at xvii.

34. Vivian O. Berger, "The Supreme Court and Defense Counsel: Old Roads, New Paths—a Dead End?" *Colum. L. Rev.* 86 (1986): 114.

35. Richard Klein, "The Emperor Gideon Has No Clothes: The Empty Promise of the Constitutional Right to Effective Assistance of Counsel," *Hastings Const. L.Q.* 13 (1986): 681–83.

36. Russell L. Weaver, "The Perils of Being Poor: Indigent Defense and Effective Assistance," *Brandeis L.J.* 42 (2003–4): 445–46.

37. Bruce A. Green, "Lethal Fiction: The Meaning of 'Counsel' in the Sixth Amendment," *Iowa L. Rev.* 78 (1993): 433–516.

38. Donald A. Dripps, "Ineffective Assistance of Counsel: The Case for an Ex Ante Parity Standard," *J. Crim. L. & Criminology* 88 (1997): 244.

39. Darryl K. Brown, "Rationing Criminal Defense Entitlements: An Argument from Institutional Design," *Colum. L. Rev.* 104 (2004): 801–35.

40. Stephen J. Schulhofer & David D. Friedman, "Rethinking Indigent Defense: Promoting Effective Representation Through Consumer Sovereignty and Freedom of Choice for All Criminal Defendants," *Am. Crim. L. Rev.* 31 (1992): 112–22.

41. See Legal Aid Ontario, available at http://www.legalaid.on.ca/en/default.asp (last visited July 9, 2007).

42. See Legal Services Act, Ontario Regulation 107/99, Amended to O. Reg. 286/05, available at http://www.e-laws.gov.on.ca/DBLaws/Regs/English/990107_e.htm (last visited July 9, 2007).

43. Bandes, "Repression and Denial," at 342.

44. Id. at 364.

45. Id. at 383.

46. Id. at 379–80.

47. Id. at 381 (quoting Randy Bellows, "Notes of a Public Defender," in

Phillip B. Heyman & Lance Liebman, *The Social Responsibilities of Lawyers: Case Studies* (1988), 79).

48. Jonakait, *The American Jury System,* 283.

49. David Bazelon, "The Defective Assistance of Counsel," *U. Cinn. L. Rev.* 42 (1973): 1–46.

50. Committee of Public Accounts, *Review of the Crown Prosecution Service, Session 1989–90* (London: HMSO, 1990), par. 1.1.

51. Id.

52. Report, *The Review of the Crown Prosecution Service,* presented to Parliament by the Attorney General, June 1998, at 106.

53. Richard L. Abel, *The Legal Profession in England and Wales* (New York: Blackwell, 1988), 115. See also "About Criminal Law Solicitors' Association," available at http://www.clsa.co.uk/Default.asp?page=52 (last visited July 9, 2007) (noting that the association is open to "any solicitor—prosecution or defence").

54. FCCP Art. 54.

55. FCCP Art. 63, 63-1, 63-2.

56. Federal Magistrates Judge's Association web page, available at http://www.fedjudge.org/index.asp.

57. Fed. R. Crim. P. 5.1.

58. Strictly speaking, no Sixth Amendment right to counsel exists in most initial appearances because, in most cases, the criminal prosecution has not yet begun. But the right to counsel in the current rule is an artifact of the Sixth Amendment, and my proposal merely makes the right a meaningful one.

59. Thomas P. Sullivan, "Police Experiences with Recording Custodial Interrogations," Special Report, Northwestern University School of Law Center on Wrongful Convictions, Number 1 (2004): 6.

60. Peter J. Nardulli, "The Societal Cost of the Exclusionary Rule: An Empirical Reassessment, *Am. B. Foundation Res. J.* 1983:594.

61. Sullivan, "Police Experiences with Recording," at 8.

62. *Dickerson v. United States,* 530 U.S. 428 (2000).

63. Costanzo & Leo, "Interrogations and Confessions," at 88.

64. Id. at 89.

65. Id.

66. See Davis & Leo, "Preventing False Confessions," 133–35. Cloud and his coauthors despair about the possibility of retarded suspects making a voluntary choice to confess. Cloud et al., "Words without Meaning," 591.

67. Costanzo & Leo, "Interrogations and Confessions," at 82–83, drawing from Ofshe & Leo, "Decision to Confess Falsely," and Ofshe & Leo, "Social Psychology."

68. Richard A. Leo, Steven A. Drizin, Peter J. Neufeld, Bradley R. Hall, & Amy Vatner, "Bringing Reliability Back In: False Confessions and Legal Safeguards in the Twenty-First Century," *Wis. L. Rev.* 2006 (2006): 531.

69. The literature here is voluminous. Some of the best works include the ABA's *Achieving Justice,* chapter 3; Saul M. Kassin & Lawrence S. Wrightsman, *The American Jury on Trial* (Bristol, Pa.: Taylor & Francis, 1988), 79–87; Margery Malkin Koosed, "The Proposed Innocence Protection Act Won't— Unless It Curbs Mistaken Eyewitness Identifications," *Ohio St. L.J.* 63 (2002): 263–314.

70. See "Attorney General Guidelines for Preparing and Conducting Photo and Live Lineup Procedures," April 18, 2001, John Farmer, Attorney General of New Jersey, available at www.psychology.iastate.edu/ FACULTY/gwells/ njguidelines.pdf.

71. Koosed, "Proposed Innocence Protection Act," at 311–12. Koosed's recommendation was limited to capital cases, but I would extend it to all cases.

72. Stanley Z. Fisher & Ian McKenzie, "A Miscarriage of Justice in Massachusetts: Eyewitness Identification Procedures, Unrecorded Admissions, and a Comparison with English Law," *B.U. Pub. Int. L.J.* 13 (2003): 11–12 .

73. Id. at 19.

74. Cutler & Penrod, *Mistaken Identification,* at 186. See also Hans & Vidmar, *Judging the Jury,* at 128.

75. Cutler & Penrod, *Mistaken Identification,* at 186.

76. Id. at 250.

77. Elizabeth F. Loftus, *Eyewitness Testimony* (Cambridge: Harvard University Press, 1996), ix.

78. Cutler & Penrod, *Mistaken Identification,* at 263.

79. Tracey Maclin, "Is Obtaining an Arrestee's DNA a Valid Special Needs Search Under the Fourth Amendment? What Should (and Will) the Supreme Court Do?" *J.L. Med. & Ethics* 34 (2006): 165–81.

80. Cynthia E. Jones, "Evidence Destroyed, Innocence Lost: The Preservation of Biological Evidence Under Innocence Protection Statutes," *Am. Crim. L. Rev.* 42 (2005): 1239–70.

81. Weinreb, *Denial of Justice,* at 3.

82. Pizzi, *Trials Without Truth,* 114.

83. Susan R. Klein, "Enhancing the Judicial Role in Criminal Plea and Sentencing Bargaining," *Tex. L. Rev.* 84 (2006): 2023–53.

84. Rule 16 contains 1,716 words. My favorite Hemingway short story, "A Clean, Well-Lighted Place," contains about 1,500 words.

85. Richard S. Frase, "Comparative Criminal Justice as a Guide to American Law Reform: How the French Do It, How We Can Find Out, and Why We Should Care," *Cal. L. Rev.* 78 (1990): 672.

86. See Brown, "Decline of Defense Counsel," at 1625.

87. The task of deciding which offenses would be exempt from the new discovery rules would fall to the legislature. Certain federal crimes were created to deal with organized crime and drug enterprises and would presumably be made exempt from the new rule. See, e.g., RICO (Racketeer Influenced and Corrupt Organizations Act), 18 U.S.C. §§ 1963–68 & CCE (Continuing Criminal Enterprise), 21 U.S.C. § 848.

88. Frase, "Comparative Criminal Justice," at 625 n. 461.

89. Roy B. Flemming, "Elements of the Defense Attorney's Craft: An Adaptive Expectations Model of the Preliminary Hearing Decision," *Law & Pol'y* 8 (1986): 33, 40.

90. Compendium of Federal Justice Statistics, 2003, at 34 [page 36 of the PDF], table 2.4, available at http://www.nicic.org/Library/020950 (last visited July 9, 2007).

91. Brown, "Decline of Defense Counsel," at 1638–41.

92. See Florida R. Crim. P. 3.220 (2007).

93. Ill. S. Ct. R. 416 (2007).

94. See *Williams v. Florida,* 399 U.S. 78 (1970).

95. Daniel Medwed, email to the author, September 19, 2006.

96. See McConville & Baldwin, *Courts, Prosecution, and Conviction,* at 189.

97. Id. at 53.

98. Id. at 61, table 3.

99. Id. at 61, table 3.

100. The Baldwin & McConville study found that 36 percent of the acquittals in their sample were "doubtful." Baldwin & McConville, *Jury Trials,* at 54.

101. *United States v. Williams,* 504 U.S. 36 (1992).

102. Peter J. Henning, "Prosecutorial Misconduct in Grand Jury Investigations," *S. Car. L. Rev.* 51 (1999): 7.

103. Brenner, "Voice of the Community," 124.

104. Andrew D. Leipold, "Why Grand Juries Do Not (and Cannot) Protect the Accused," *Cornell L. Rev.* 80 (1995): 260–324.

105. Mike McConville & Chester L. Mirsky, *Jury Trials and Plea Bargaining: A True History* (Oxford: Hart, 2005), 1.

106. McConville & Baldwin, *Courts, Prosecution, and Conviction,* at 195.

107. Ronald F. Wright, "Trial Distortion and the End of Innocence in Federal Criminal Justice," *U. Penn. L. Rev.* 154 (2005): 102.

108. Id. at 147–48.

109. Id. at 86 & 151.

110. Duff, "Introduction," in Duff et al., *Trial on Trial,* at 14.

111. 434 U.S. 357 (1978).

112. Id. at 358–59.

113. Pizzi agrees. See William T. Pizzi, "Do Jury Trials Encourage Harsh Punishments in the United States?" *St. Louis U. Pub. L. Rev.* 21 (2002): 62.

114. Klein, "Enhancing the Judicial Role," at 2042–52.

115. Peter Duff, "Changing Conceptions of the Scottish Criminal Trial," in Duff et al., *Trial on Trial,* at 34–35.

116. Id. at 49.

117. Saul M. Kassin & Lawrence S. Wrightsman, "On the Requirement of Proof: The Timing of Judicial Instruction and Mock Juror Verdicts," *J. Personality & Soc. Psych.* (1979): 1877–87.

118. Erik Lillquist, "Absolute Certainty and the Death Penalty," *Am. Crim. L. Rev.* 42 (2005): 89.

119. Jonakait, *The American Jury System,* 187. See also Frank, *Courts on Trial,* 80–93.

120. Jonakait, *The American Jury System,* 187.

121. See Jackson, "Managing Uncertainty and Finality," at 123.

122. *Chambers v. Mississippi,* 410 U.S. 284 (1973).

123. McEwan, "Ritual, Fairness and Truth," at 66.

124. Id. at 69.

125. *Holmes v. South Carolina,* 126 S.Ct. 1727 (2006).

126. Id. at 1731 (quoting *State v. Gregory,* 198 S.C. 98 (1941)).

127. *Taylor v. Illinois,* 484 U.S. 400 (1988).

128. Laurie L. Levenson, "Change of Venue and the Role of the Criminal Jury," *S. Cal. L. Rev.* 66 (1993): 1533.

129. Matt Matravers, "'More Than Just Illogical': Truth and Jury Nullification," in Duff et al., *Trial on Trial,* at 77.

130. Jonakait, *The American Jury System,* at 74. Indeed, perhaps juries should be encouraged to question witnesses, a practice that is currently permitted in many American states. See Mott, "Debate on Juror Questions," at 1099. Following the logic of community-based blameworthiness to its end, one could also inform juries of their power to "nullify" the evidence or the law by returning an unjustified acquittal. These ideas are outside the scope of my current project.

131. ABA report *Achieving Justice,* at 70.

132. See Cassidy, "Soft Words of Hope," at 1172; Steven M. Cohen, "Effective Screening for Truth-Telling: Is It Possible? What Is True. Perspectives of a Former Prosecutor," *Cardozo L. Rev.* 23 (2002): 827; Yaroshefsky, "Cooperation with Federal Prosecutors," at 964.

133. Steven Skurka, "Perspectives on the Role of Cooperators and Informants: A Canadian Perspective," *Cardozo L. Rev.* 23 (2002): 770.

134. Daniel S. Medwed, "Anatomy of a Wrongful Conviction: Theoretical Implications and Practical Solutions," *Villanova L. Rev.* 51 (2004): 369.

135. *Dodd v. State*, 993 P.2d 778 (Okla. Crim. App. 2000).

136. ABA report *Achieving Justice*, 76–77; Clifford S. Fishman, "Defense Witnesses as 'Accomplice': Should the Trial Judge Give a 'Care and Caution' Instruction?" *J. Crim. L. & Criminology* 96 (2005): 2.

137. *Dodd*, 993 P.2d at 784.

138. Id. (Strubhar, P.J., specially concurring).

139. Id.

140. Abramson, *We the Jury*, 204.

141. See George C. Thomas III & Barry S. Pollack, "Rethinking Guilty, Juries, and Jeopardy," *Mich. L. Rev.* 91 (1992): 24, table 3 (predicting a negligible risk of error with unanimous verdict, a 4.6 percent chance with a nine-to-three verdict, and 13.4 percent chance with an eight-to-four verdict).

142. See Weinreb, *Denial of Justice*, at 141.

143. See George C. Thomas III & Mark Greenbaum, "Justice Story Cuts the Hung Jury Gordian Knot," *Wm. & Mary Bill of Rts. L.J.* 15 (2007): 920–25.

144. Feeney & Herrmann, *One Case—Two Systems*, at 446.

145. Damaska, *Faces of Justice*, 145.

146. *Jackson v. Virginia*, 443 U.S. 307 (1979).

147. Id. at 318.

148. Id. at 324.

149. Id. at 319.

150. All information in the text about the case is drawn from a transcript of the trial in 1976, *State v. Powell*, and the unpublished 1977 opinion of the appellate court, *Powell v. State*, Tenn. Ct. Crim. App. 1977; copies available from author.

151. *Watson v. State*, 204 S.W.3d 404, 424 (Tex. Ct. Crim. App. 2006).

152. Feeney & Herrmann, *One Case—Two Systems*, at 446. See also Thomas Weigend, "Germany," in Bradley, *Criminal Procedure*, at 212.

153. Feeney & Herrmann, *One Case—Two Systems*, at 447.

154. Constitution Project, "Mandatory Justice," at xx.

155. See *United States v. Bagley*, 473 U.S. 667 (1985) (plurality); *United States v. Agurs*, 427 U.S. 97 (1976).

156. See *Burks v. United States*, 437 U.S. 1 (1978).

157. Daniel S. Medwed, "Up the River Without a Procedure: Innocent Prisoners and Newly Discovered Non-DNA Evidence in State Courts," *Ariz. L. Rev.* 47 (2005): 681.

158. Thomas et al., "Too Late for Innocence," at 264.

159. Charles I. Lugosi, "Executing the Factually Innocent: The U.S. Constitution, Habeas Corpus, and the Death Penalty: Facing the Embarrassing Question at Last," *Stan. J. Civ. Rts. and Civ. Liberties* 1 (2005): 496.

160. Belloni & Hodgson, *Criminal Injustice,* at 175, table 9.4.

161. Id. at 181.

162. Geoffrey Bennett, "Wrongful Conviction, Lawyer Incompetence, and English Law—Some Recent Themes," *Brandeis L.J.* 42 (2003–4): 203.

163. Belloni & Hodgson, *Criminal Injustice,* at 175, table 9.4.

164. Robert Carl Schehr, "The Criminal Cases Review Commission as a State Strategic Selection Mechanism," *Am. Crim. L. Rev.* 42 (2005): 1295.

165. Lissa Griffin, "The Correction of Wrongful Convictions: A Comparative Perspective," *Am. U. Int'l L. Rev.* 16 (2001): 1277.

166. National Association to Abolish the Death Penalty, "Do Not Execute Sedley Alley," at http://www.democracyinaction.org/dia/ organizations/ncadp/campaign.jsp?campaign_KEY=3439 (last visited July 9, 2007).

167. Andrew E. Taslitz, "Eyewitness Identification, Democratic Deliberation, and the Politics of Science," *Cardozo Pub. L. Pol'y & Ethics J.* 4 (2006): 271–325.

168. *State v. Michaels,* 642 A.2d 1373, 1380 (N.J. 1994).

169. Jacqueline McMurtrie, "Social Science and Wrongful Convictions," *Am. Crim. L. Rev.* 42 (2005): 1283–86.

170. *State v. Michaels,* 642 A.2d 1372 (N.J. 1994).

171. Id. at 1384.

172. *The Economist,* February 11, 2006, at 48.

173. Frank, *Courts on Trial,* at 88.

BIBLIOGRAPHY

Note: The bibliography is divided into five categories: legislative enactments; books; articles and book chapters; reports and monographs; and other sources, which includes Web sites. Cases are cited in the notes and are not listed here.

Statutes, Rules, and Resolutions

Act of January 25, 1889, sec. 6, 25 Stat. 1889.

Act of June 23, 1874, sec. 3, 18 Stat. 254.

Fifth Congress, Sess. II, ch. 58, 1 U.S. Statutes at Large 570–71 (1798).

18 U.S. Code § 115.

18 U.S. Code §§ 1963–68.

21 U.S. Code § 848.

6–7 William & Mary, ch. 2 (1696).

30 Charles II, st. 2, ch. 1 (1679).

Assize of Clarendon, 1166, ch. 1. Sources of British History. Available at http://britannia.com/history/docs/assize.html (last visited July 9, 2007).

Uniform Code of Military Justice.

French Code of Criminal Procedure.

Federal Rule of Criminal Procedure 5.1.

Federal Rule of Criminal Procedure 16, Proposed Amendment, at 1975 U.S. Code Cong. & Admin. News 716.

Legal Services Act, Ontario Regulation 107/99, Amended to O. Reg. 286/05. Available at http://www.e-laws.gov.on.ca/DBLaws/Regs/English/9901 07_e.htm (last visited July 9, 2007).

Resolutions of the Stamp Act Congress, October, 1765, introductory paragraph. Available at http://www.historyplace.com/unitedstates/revolu tion/stamp-res.html (last visited July 9, 2007).

Books

Abel, Richard L. *The Legal Profession in England and Wales.* New York: Blackwell, 1988.

Abramson, Jeffrey. *We the Jury: The Jury System and the Ideal of Democracy.* New York: Basic Books, 1994.

Adams, Douglas. *The Hitch-Hiker's Guide to the Galaxy.* New York: Crown, 1979.

Armstrong, Zella. *The History of Hamilton County and Chattanooga Tennessee.* Chattanooga: Lookout Publishing, 1931.

Ashley, Mike. *The Mammoth Book of British Kings and Queens.* New York: Carroll & Graf, 1998.

Ashworth, Andrew. *The Criminal Process: An Evaluative Study.* New York: Oxford University Press, 1998.

Baldwin, John, & Michael McConville. *Jury Trials.* New York: Oxford University Press, 1979.

Bartels, Robert. *Benefit of Law: The Murder Case of Ernest Triplett.* Ames: Iowa State University Press, 1988.

Bartlett, Robert. *England Under the Norman and Angevin Kings, 1075–1225.* Oxford: Clarendon Press, 2000.

Bartlett, Robert. *Trial by Fire and Water.* New York: Oxford University Press, 1996.

Belloni, Frank, & Jacqueline Hodgson. *Criminal Injustice: An Evaluation of the Criminal Justice Process in Britain.* New York: St. Martin's Press, 2000.

Blackstone, William. *Commentaries on the Laws of England, Book the First.* Oxford: Clarendon Press, 1765.

Blackstone, William. *Commentaries on the Laws of England, Book the Fourth.* Oxford: Clarendon Press, 1769.

Bracton. *De Legibus et Consuetudinibus Angliae.* George E. Woodbine, trans. & ed. Vol. 3. Cambridge: Belknap Press, Harvard University Press, 1977.

Bradley, Craig M., ed. *Criminal Procedure: A Worldwide Study.* Durham, N.C.: Carolina Academic Press, 1999.

Bradley, Craig M. *The Failure of the Criminal Procedure Revolution.* Philadelphia: University of Pennsylvania Press, 1993.

Cantor, Norman F. *Imagining the Law: Common Law and the Foundations of the American Legal System.* New York: HarperCollins, 1997.

Clarkson, Paul S., & R. Samuel Jett. *Luther Martin of Maryland.* Baltimore: Johns Hopkins Press, 1970.

Cogan, Neil H., ed. *The Complete Bill of Rights: The Drafts, Debates, Sources, and Origins.* New York: Oxford University Press, 1997.

Cohen, Stanley. *The Wrong Men: America's Epidemic of Wrongful Death Row Convictions.* New York: Carroll & Graf, 2003.

Coke, Edward. *The Third Part of the Institutes of the Laws of England: Concerning High Treason and Other Pleas of the Crown and Criminal Causes.* London: W. Clark and Sons, Law Booksellers, 1817.

Collins, Charles Wallace. *The Fourteenth Amendment and the States: A Study of the Operation of the Restraint Clauses of Section One of the Fourteenth Amendment to the Constitution of the United States.* New York: Da Capo Press, 1974, reprint of original Boston: Little, Brown publication.

Connery, Donald S., ed. *Convicting the Innocent: The Story of a Murder, a False Confession, and the Struggle to Free a "Wrong Man."* Cambridge, Mass.: Brookline Books, 1996.

Curriden, Mark, & Leroy Phillips, Jr. *Contempt of Court: The Turn-of-the-Century Lynching That Launched a Hundred Years of Federalism.* New York: Faber & Faber, 1999.

Cutler, Brian L., & Steven D. Penrod. *Mistaken Identification: The Eyewitness, Psychology, and the Law.* New York: Cambridge University Press, 1995.

Dershowitz, Alan M. *The Best Defense.* New York: Random House, 1982.

Dinnerstein, Leonard. *The Leo Frank Case.* New York: Columbia University Press, 1968.

Dostoevski, Fyodor. *Crime and Punishment.* Constance Garnett, trans. New York: Modern Library, 1950.

Doyle, Don H. *Nashville in the New South, 1880–1930.* Knoxville: University of Tennessee Press, 1985.

Drew, Kathleen Fischer, trans. *The Laws of the Salian Franks.* Philadelphia: University of Pennsylvania Press, 1991.

Dripps, Donald A. *About Guilt and Innocence: The Origins, Development, and Future of Constitutional Criminal Procedure.* Westport, Conn.: Praeger, 2003.

Duff, Antony, Lindsay Farmer, Sandra Marshall, & Victor Tadros, eds. *The Trial on Trial: Truth and Due Process.* Vol. 1. Oxford: Hart, 2005.

Elliot, Jonathan. *The Debates in the Several State Conventions on the Adoption of the Federal Constitution as Recommended by the General Convention at Philadelphia in 1787.* Washington, D.C., 1847.

Everitt, Anthony. *Cicero, The Life and Times of Rome's Greatest Politician.* New York: Random House, 2003.

Faigman, David L. *Laboratory of Justice.* New York: Times Books, Henry Holt, 2004.

Feeney, Floyd, & Joachim Herrmann. *One Case—Two Systems: A Comparative View of American and German Criminal Justice.* Ardsley, N.Y.: Transnational, 2005.

Fine, John V. A. *The Ancient Greeks: A Critical History.* Cambridge: Harvard University Press, 1983.

Frank, Jerome. *Courts on Trial.* Princeton: Princeton University Press, 1949.

Franklin, Benjamin. *The Writings of Benjamin Franklin.* Albert Henry Smith, ed. Vol. 9. New York: Haskell House, 1907.

Goebel, Julius, & T. Raymond Naughton. *Law Enforcement in Colonial New York: A Study in Criminal Procedure (1664–1776).* 1944; reprinted, Montclair, N.J.: Patterson Smith, 1970.

Goodman, James. *Stories of Scottsboro.* New York: Random House, Times Book, 1994.

Govan, Gilbert E., & James W. Livingood. *The Chattanooga County: From Tomahawks to TVA.* New York: Dutton, 1952.

Hale, Matthew. *The History and Analysis of the Common Law of England: Written by a Learned Hand.* 1713; reprinted, Birmingham, Ala.: Legal Classics Library, 1987.

Hall, G. D. G., ed. & trans. *The Treaty on the Laws and Customs of the Realm of England Commonly Called Glanvill.* London: Thomas Nelson & Sons, 1965.

Hans, Valerie P., & Neil Vidmar. *Judging the Jury.* New York: Plenum Press, 1986.

Harding, Alan. *A Social History of English Law.* London: Penguin Books, 1966.

Hermann, Robert, Eric Single, & John Boston. *Counsel for the Poor: Criminal Defense in Urban America.* Lexington, Mass.: Lexington Books, 1977.

Heward, Edmund. *Matthew Hale.* London: Robert Hale, 1972.

Holdsworth, Sir William. *A History of English Law.* Vol. 1. London: Sweet and Maxwell, 1903.

Huber, Peter W. *Galileo's Revenge: Junk Science in the Courtroom.* New York: Basic Books, 1993.

Jonakait, Randolph. *The American Jury System.* New Haven: Yale University Press, 2003.

Jones, A. H. M. *The Criminal Courts of the Roman Republic and Principate.* Totowa, N.J.: Rowman and Littlefield, 1972.

Kalven, Harry, Jr., & Hans Zeisel. *The American Jury.* Boston: Little, Brown, 1966.

Kassin, Saul M., & Lawrence S. Wrightsman. *The American Jury on Trial.* Bristol, Pa.: Taylor & Francis, 1988.

Kunkel, Wolfgang. *An Introduction to Roman Legal and Constitutional History.* Oxford: Clarendon Press, 1966.

Langbein, John H. *The Origins of Adversary Criminal Trial.* Oxford: Oxford University Press, 2003.

Lassers, Willard J. *Scapegoat Justice: Lloyd Miller and the Failure of the American Legal System.* Bloomington: Indiana University Press, 1973.

Leo, Richard A. *Police Interrogation and the American Process of Justice.* Cambridge: Harvard University Press, forthcoming 2008. Manuscript on file with author.

Levy, Leonard W. *Origins of the Fifth Amendment: The Right Against Self-Incrimination.* New York: Oxford University Press, 1968.

Lewis, Edward R., Jr. *Reflections of Canton in a Pharmacist's Show Globe: A Comprehensive History of Canton, Illinois and the Important Events in Fulton County.* Self-published, 1967.

Loftus, Elizabeth F. *Eyewitness Testimony.* Cambridge: Harvard University Press, 1996.

Luban, David. *Lawyers and Justice: An Ethical Study.* Princeton: Princeton University Press, 1988.

McConville, Michael, & John Baldwin. *Courts, Prosecution, and Convictions.* New York: Oxford University Press, 1981.

McConville, Mike, & Lee Bridges, eds. *Criminal Justice in Crisis.* Aldershot, England: Hants, 1994.

McConville, Mike, Jacqueline Hodgson, Lee Bridges, & Anita Pavlovic. *Standing Accused: The Organisation and Practices of Criminal Defense Lawyers in Britain.* New York: Oxford University Press, 1994.

McConville, Mike, & Chester L. Mirsky. *Jury Trials and Plea Bargaining: A True History.* Oxford: Hart, 2005.

McConville, Mike, Andrew Sanders, & Roger Leng. *The Case for the Prosecution: Police and the Construction of Criminality.* London: Routledge, 1991.

McCullough, David. *John Adams.* New York: Simon & Schuster, 2001.

Mello, Michael A. Mello. *Dead Wrong.* Madison: University of Wisconsin Press, 1997.

Miller, Merle. *Plain Speaking: An Oral Biography of Harry S. Truman.* New York: Berkley Paperback Books, 1984.

Newmyer, R. Kent. *John Marshall and the Heroic Age of the Supreme Court*. Baton Rouge: Louisiana State University Press, 2002.

Packer, Herbert L. *The Limits of the Criminal Sanction*. Palo Alto: Stanford University Press, 1968.

Penn, William. "The Peoples Liberties Asssrted [*sic*] in the Tryal of William Penn and William Mead, 1670." Available at http://tarlton.law.utexas.edu/lpop/etext/penntrial.html (last visited July 6, 2007).

Pizzi, William T. *Trials Without Truth*. New York: New York University Press, 1999.

Pollock, Sir Frederick, & Frederick William Maitland. *The History of English Law Before the Time of Edward I*. 2 vols. Cambridge: Cambridge University Press, 2d ed., 1899.

Radelet, Michael L., Hugo Adam Bedau, & Constance Putnam. *In Spite of Innocence: Erroneous Convictions in Capital Cases*. Boston: Northeastern University Press, 1992.

Rand, Ayn. *Atlas Shrugged*. New York: Dutton Adult, 2002.

Rawls, John. *A Theory of Justice*. Cambridge: Harvard University Press, 1972.

Rose, David. *In the Name of the Law: The Collapse of Criminal Justice*. London: J. Cape, 1996.

Scheck, Barry, Peter Neufeld, & Jim Dwyer. *Actual Innocence: Five Days to Execution and Other Dispatches from the Wrongly Convicted*. New York: Doubleday, 2000.

Scott, S. P., ed. *The Civil Law: Including the Twelve Tables, the Institutes of Gaius, the Rules of Ulpian, the Opinions of Paulus, the Enactments of Justinian, and the Constitutions of Leo*. S. P. Scott, trans. 1932, reprinted Union, N.J.: Lawbook Exchange, 2001.

Simon, David. *Homicide: A Year on the Killing Streets*. Boston: Houghton Mifflin, 1991.

Smith, Jean Edward. *John Marshall: Definer of a Nation*. New York: H. Holt, 1996.

Spiegel, Andrew Page. "Sir Matthew Hale and the English Law." Ph.D. diss., University of Wisconsin, 1959.

Stenton, Doris M. *English Justice Between the Norman Conquest and the Great Charter, 1066–1215*. Philadelphia: American Philosophical Society, 1964.

Strachan-Davidson, James. L. *Problems of the Roman Criminal Law*. 2 vols. Oxford: Clarendon Press, 1969.

Sundby, Scott E. *A Life and Death Decision: A Jury Weighs the Death Penalty*. New York: Palgrave Macmillan, 2005.

Thomas, George C., III. *Double Jeopardy: The History, the Law*. New York: New York University Press, 1998.

Tomkovicz, James J. *The Right to the Assistance of Counsel: A Reference Guide to the United States Constitution.* Westport, Conn.: Greenwood Press, 2002.

Tonry, Michael. *Thinking about Crime.* New York: Oxford University Press, 2004.

Trevelyan, Raleigh. *Sir Walter Raleigh.* New York: Henry Holt, 2002.

Van Caenegem, R. C., ed. *English Lawsuits from William I to Richard I.* 2 vols. London: Selden Society, 1990.

Victor, Orville J. *The History, Civil, Political, and Military, of the Southern Rebellion.* Vol. 2. New York: J. D. Torrey, 1861.

von Drehle, David. *Among the Lowest of the Dead: the Culture of Death Row.* New York: Times Books, 1995; reprinted, Ann Arbor: University of Michigan Press, 2006.

Warren, W. L. *Henry II.* Berkeley and Los Angeles: University of California Press, 1973.

Weinreb, Lloyd. *Denial of Justice: Criminal Process in the United States.* New York: Free Press, 1977.

Westervelt, Saundra D., & John A. Humphrey, eds. *Wrongly Convicted: Perspectives on Failed Justice.* New Brunswick, N.J.: Rutgers University Press, 1996.

White, Welsh S. *Miranda's Waning Protections: Police Interrogation After Dickerson v. United States.* Ann Arbor: University of Michigan Press, 2001.

Wigmore, John Henry. *A Treatise on Evidence.* Vol. 2. Boston: Little, Brown, 2d ed., 1923.

Wolfe, Tom. *Bonfire of the Vanities.* New York: Bantam Books, 1987.

Yant, Martin. *Presumed Guilty: When Innocent People Are Wrongly Convicted.* Buffalo, N.Y.: Prometheus Books, 1991.

Yarbrough, Tinsley. *John Marshall Harlan: Great Dissenter of the Warren Court.* New York: Oxford University Press, 1992.

Articles and Book Chapters

Backus, Mary Sue, & Paul Marcus. "The Right to Counsel in Criminal Cases: A National Crisis." *Hastings L.J.* 57 (2006): 1031–1130.

Bandes, Susan. "Loyalty to One's Convictions: The Prosecutor and Tunnel Vision." *Howard L.J.* 49 (2006): 475–94.

Bandes, Susan. "Patterns of Injustice: Police Brutality in the Courts." *Buff. L. Rev.* 47 (1999): 1275–1341.

Bandes, Susan. "Repression and Denial in Criminal Lawyering." *Buffalo Crim. L. Rev.* 9 (2006): 339–89.

Bandes, Susan. "Simple Murder: A Comment on the Legality of Executing the Innocent." *Buff. L. Rev.* 44 (1996): 501–25.

Bandes, Susan. "Tracing the Pattern of No Pattern: Stories of Police Brutality." *Loy. L.A. L. Rev.* 34 (2001): 665–80.

Bazelon, David. "The Defective Assistance of Counsel." *U. Cinn. L. Rev.* 42 (1973): 1–46.

Bennett, Geoffrey. "Wrongful Conviction, Lawyer Incompetence, and English Law—Some Recent Themes." *Brandeis L.J.* 42 (2003–4): 189–205.

Berger, Vivian. "*Herrera v. Collins:* The Gateway of Innocence for Death-Sentenced Prisoners Leads Nowhere." *Wm. & Mary L. Rev.* 35 (1994): 943–1023.

Berger, Vivian O. "Justice Delayed or Justice Denied?—a Comment on Recent Proposals to Reform Death Penalty Habeas Corpus." *Colum. L. Rev.* 90 (1990): 1665–1714.

Berger, Vivian O. "The Supreme Court and Defense Counsel: Old Roads, New Paths—a Dead End?" *Colum. L. Rev.* 86 (1986): 9–116.

Bernstein, David. "Junk Science in the United States and the Commonwealth." *Yale J. Int'l L.* 21 (1996): 123–82.

Bodet, Gerald P. "Sir Edward Coke's Third Institutes: A Primer for Treason Defendants." *U. Toronto L.J.* 20 (1970): 469–77.

Braun, Richard L. "The Grand Jury—Spirit of the Community?" *Ariz. L. Rev.* 15 (1973): 893–917.

Brenner, Susan W. "The Voice of the Community: The Case for Grand Jury Independence." *Va. J. Social Pol'y & L.* 3 (1995): 67–131.

Brown, Darryl K. "The Decline of Defense Counsel and the Rise of Accuracy in Criminal Adjudication." *Calif. L. Rev.* 95 (2005): 1585–1645.

Brown, Darryl K. "Rationing Criminal Defense Entitlements: An Argument from Institutional Design." *Colum. L. Rev.* 104 (2004): 801–35.

Cassidy, R. Michael. "'Soft Words of Hope': Giglio, Accomplice Witnesses, and the Problem of Implied Inducements." *Nw. U. L. Rev.* 98 (2004): 1129–77.

Cloud, Morgan. "The Dirty Little Secret." *Emory L.J.* 43 (1994): 1311–49.

Cloud, Morgan, George B. Shepherd, Alison Nodvin Barkoff, & Justin V. Shur. "Words Without Meaning: The Constitution, Confessions, and Mentally Retarded Suspects." *U. Chi. L. Rev.* 69 (2002): 495–624.

Cohen, Ronald L., & Mary Anne Harnick. "The Susceptibility of Child Witnesses to Suggestion." *Law and Human Behavior* 4 (1980): 201–10.

Cohen, Steven M. "Effective Screening for Truth-Telling: Is it Possible? What Is True. Perspectives of a Former Prosecutor." *Cardozo L. Rev.* 23 (2002): 817–28.

Colb, Sherry F. "Profiling with Apologies." *Ohio St. J. Crim. L.* 1 (2004): 611–25.

Colb, Sherry F. "What Is a Search? Two Conceptual Flaws in Fourth Amendment Doctrine and Some Hints of a Remedy." *Stan. L. Rev.* 55 (2002): 119–89.

Costanzo, Mark, & Richard A. Leo. "Research and Expert Testimony on Interrogations and Confessions." In *Expert Psychological Testimony for the Courts,* Mark Costanzo, Daniel Krauss, & Kathy Pezdek, eds. Mahwah, N.J.: Lawrence Erlbaum Associates, 2007.

Davis, Deborah, & Richard Leo. "Strategies for Preventing False Confessions and Their Consequences." In *Practical Psychology for Forensic Investigations and Prosecutions,* Mark R. Kebbell & Graham M. Davies, eds., 121–49. West Sussex, England: 2006.

Dripps, Donald A. "Ineffective Assistance of Counsel: The Case for an Ex Ante Parity Standard." *J. Crim. L. & Criminology* 88 (1997): 242–307.

Dubber, Markus Dirk. "The Criminal Trial and the Legitimation of Punishment." In *The Trial on Trial: Truth and Due Process,* Antony Duff, Lindsay Farmer, Sandra Marshall, & Victor Tadros, eds., vol. 1, 85–100. Oxford: Hart, 2005.

Duff, Antony. "Introduction: Toward a Normative Theory of the Criminal Trial." In *The Trial on Trial: Truth and Due Process,* Antony Duff, Lindsay Farmer, Sandra Marshall, & Victor Tadros, eds., vol. 1, 1–28. Oxford: Hart, 2005.

Duff, Peter. "Changing Conceptions of the Scottish Criminal Trial." In *The Trial on Trial: Truth and Due Process,* Antony Duff, Lindsay Farmer, Sandra Marshall, & Victor Tadros, eds., vol. 1, 29–50. Oxford: Hart, 2005.

Ekman, Paul, & Maureen O'Sullivan. "Who Can Catch a Liar?" *Am. Psychologist* 46 (1991): 913–20.

Fehlings, Gregory. "Storm on the Constitution: The First Deportation Law." *Tulsa J. Comp. & Int'l. L.* 10 (2002): 63–114.

Fisher, George. "The Jury's Rise as Lie Detector." *Yale L.J.* 107 (1997): 575–708.

Fisher, Stanley Z. "The Prosecutor's Ethical Duty to Seek Exculpatory Evidence in Police Hands: Lessons from England." *Fordham L. Rev.* 68 (2000): 1379–1452.

Fisher, Stanley Z. "In Search of the Virtuous Prosecutor: A Conceptual Framework." *Am. Crim. L. Rev.* 15 (1988): 197–261.

Fisher, Stanley Z., & Ian McKenzie. "A Miscarriage of Justice in Massachusetts: Eyewitness Identification Procedures, Unrecorded Admissions, and a Comparison with English Law." *B.U. Pub. Int. L.J.* 13 (2003): 1–19.

Fishman, Clifford S. "Defense Witnesses as 'Accomplice': Should the Trial Judge Give a 'Care and Caution' Instruction?" *J. Crim. L. & Criminology* 96 (2005): 1–23.

Flemming, Roy B. "Elements of the Defense Attorney's Craft: An Adaptive

Expectations Model of the Preliminary Hearing Decision." *Law & Pol'y* 8 (1986): 33–57.

Frase, Richard S. "Comparative Criminal Justice as a Guide to American Law Reform: How the French Do It, How We Can Find Out, and Why We Should Care." *Cal. L. Rev.* 78 (1990): 539–683.

Frase, Richard S. "France." In *Criminal Procedure: A Worldwide Study,* Craig M. Bradley ed., 143–85. Durham, N.C.: Carolina Academic Press, 1999.

Gelfand, Alan E., & Herbert Solomon. "Considerations in Building Jury Behavior Models and in Comparing Jury Schemes: An Argument in Favor of 12-Member Juries." *Jurimetrics J.* 17 (1977): 292–313.

Gershman, Bennett L. "Effective Screening for Truth Telling: Is It Possible? Witness Coaching by Prosecutors." *Cardozo L. Rev.* 23 (2002): 829–63.

Givelber, Daniel. "The Adversary System and Historical Accuracy: Can We Do Better?" In *Wrongly Convicted: Perspectives on Failed Justice,* Saundra D. Westervelt & John A. Humphrey, eds., 253–68. New Brunswick, N.J.: Rutgers University Press, 1996.

Givelber, Daniel. "Lost Innocence: Speculation and Data About the Acquitted." *Am. Crim. L. Rev.* 42 (2005): 1167–99.

Givelber, Daniel. "Meaningless Acquittals, Meaningful Convictions: Do We Reliably Acquit the Innocent?" *Rutgers L. Rev.* 49 (1997): 1317–96.

Green, Bruce A. "Lethal Fiction: The Meaning of 'Counsel' in the Sixth Amendment." *Iowa L. Rev.* 78 (1993): 433–516.

Griffin, Lissa. "The Correction of Wrongful Convictions: A Comparative Perspective." *Am. U. Int'l L. Rev.* 16 (2001): 1241–1308.

Groot, Roger D. "The Jury of Presentment Before 1215." *Am. J. Legal Hist.* 26 (1982): 1–24.

Gross, Samuel, et al. "Exonerations in the United States, 1989–2003." *J. of Crim. L. & Criminology* 95 (2004): 523–60.

Hans, Valerie P. "U.S. Jury Reform: The Active Jury and the Adversarial Ideal." *St. Louis U. Public L. Rev.* 21 (2002): 85–97.

Henning, Peter J. "Prosecutorial Misconduct in Grand Jury Investigations." *S. Car. L. Rev.* 51 (1999): 1–61.

Holly, Wayne D. "Rethinking the Sixth Amendment for the Indigent Criminal Defendant: Do Reimbursement Statutes Support Recognition of a Right to Counsel of Choice for the Indigent." *Brooklyn L. Rev.* 64 (1998): 181–230.

Israel, Jerold H. "Free-Standing Due Process and Criminal Procedure: The Supreme Court's Search for Interpretive Guidelines." *St. Louis U. L.J.* 45 (2001): 303–432.

Jackson, John D. "Managing Uncertainty and Finality: The Function of the Criminal Trial in Legal Inquiry." In *The Trial on Trial: Truth and Due*

Process, Antony Duff, Lindsay Farmer, Sandra Marshall, & Victor Tadros, eds., vol. 1, 121–45. Oxford: Hart, 2005.

Jones, Cynthia E. "Evidence Destroyed, Innocence Lost: The Preservation of Biological Evidence Under Innocence Protection Statutes." *Am. Crim. L. Rev.* 42 (2005): 1239–70.

Jung, Heike. "Nothing but the Truth? Some Facts, Impressions and Confessions About Truth in Criminal Procedure." In *The Trial on Trial: Truth and Due Process,* Antony Duff, Lindsay Farmer, Sandra Marshall, & Victor Tadros, eds., vol. 1, 147–56. Oxford: Hart, 2005.

Kahan, Dan M. "Is Chevron Relevant to Federal Criminal Law?" *Harv. L. Rev.* 110 (1996): 469–521.

Kamisar, Yale. "Equal Justice in the Gatehouses and Mansions of American Criminal Procedure: From Powell to Gideon, from Escobedo to * * *." In *Criminal Justice in Our Time,* A. E. Dick Howard, ed., 3–95. Charlottesville: University Press of Virginia, 1965.

Kassin, Saul M., & Lawrence S. Wrightsman. "On the Requirement of Proof: The Timing of Judicial Instruction and Mock Juror Verdicts." *J. Personality & Soc. Psych.* (1979): 1877–87.

Katz, Stanley N. "Introduction." *William Blackstone's Commentaries on the Laws of England.* Chicago: University of Chicago Press, 1979.

King, Victoria. "The Domesday Book." *History Magazine,* October–November 2001. Available at http://www.history-magazine.com/domesday.html.

Klarman, Michael J. "The Racial Origins of Modern Criminal Procedure." 99 *Mich. L. Rev.* 99 (2000): 48–97.

Klein, Richard. "The Emperor Gideon Has No Clothes: The Empty Promise of the Constitutional Right to Effective Assistance of Counsel." *Hastings Const. L.Q.* 13 (1986): 625–93.

Klein, Susan R. "Enhancing the Judicial Role in Criminal Plea and Sentencing Bargaining." *Tex. L. Rev.* 84 (2006): 2023–53.

Koosed, Margery Malkin. "The Proposed Innocence Protection Act Won't— Unless It Curbs Mistaken Eyewitness Identifications." *Ohio St. L.J.* 63 (2002): 263–314.

Lain, Corinna Barrett. "Countermajoritarian Hero or Zero: Rethinking the Warren Court's Role in the Criminal Procedure Revolution." *U. Pa. L. Rev.* 152 (2004): 1361–1452.

Langbein, John H. "Shaping the Eighteenth-Century Criminal Trial: A View from the Ryder Sources." *U. Chi. L. Rev.* 50 (1983): 1–136.

Lefcourt, Gerald B. "Responsibilities of a Criminal Defense Attorney." *Loy. L.A. L. Rev.* 30 (1996): 59–68.

Leipold, Andrew D. "How the Pretrial Process Contributes to Wrongful Convictions." *Am. Crim. L. Rev.* 42 (2005): 1123–65.

Leipold, Andrew D. "Why Grand Juries Do Not (and Cannot) Protect the Accused." *Cornell L. Rev.* 80 (1995): 260–324.

Leo, Richard A. "From Coercion to Deception: The Changing Nature of Police Interrogation in America." *Crime, Law, and Soc. Change* 18 (1992): 35–59.

Leo, Richard A. "Inside the Interrogation Room." *J. Crim. L. & Criminology* 86 (1996): 266–303.

Leo, Richard A. "Rethinking the Study of Miscarriages of Justice: Developing a Criminology of Wrongful Convictions." *J. Contemp. Crim. Just.* 21 (2005): 201–23.

Leo, Richard A. "The Third Degree and the Origins of Psychological Interrogation in the United States." In *Interrogations, Confessions, and Entrapment,* Daniel Lassiter, ed., 37–84. New York: Kluwer Academic, Plenum Publishers, 2004.

Leo, Richard A., Steven A. Drizin, Peter J. Neufeld, Bradley R. Hall, & Amy Vatner. "Bringing Reliability Back In: False Confessions and Legal Safeguards in the Twenty-First Century." *Wis. L. Rev.* 2006 (2006): 479–539.

Leo, Richard A., & Richard J. Ofshe. "The Consequences of False Confessions: Deprivations of Liberty and Miscarriages of Justice in the Age of Psychological Interrogation." *J. Crim. L. & Criminology* 88 (1998): 429–96.

Lerner, Renée Lettow. "The Intersection of Two Systems: An American on Trial for an American Murder in the French Cour D'Assises." *U. Ill. L. Rev.* 2001:791–856.

Levenson, Laurie L. "Change of Venue and the Role of the Criminal Jury." *S. Cal. L. Rev.* 66 (1993): 1533–70.

Levine, Kay L. "The New Prosecution." *Wake Forest L. Rev.* 40 (2005): 1125–1214.

Lillquist, Erik. "Absolute Certainty and the Death Penalty." *Am. Crim. L. Rev.* 42 (2005): 45–91.

Lillquist, Erik. "The Capital Jury: False Positives and False Negatives in Capital Cases." *Indiana L.J.* 80 (2005): 47–52.

Lugosi, Charles I. "Executing the Factually Innocent: The U.S. Constitution, Habeas Corpus, and the Death Penalty: Facing the Embarrassing Question at Last." *Stan. J. Civ. Rts. & Civ. Liberties* 1 (2005): 473–503.

Luna, Erik. "A Place for Comparative Criminal Procedure." *Brandeis L.J.* 42 (2003–4): 277–327.

Luna, Erik. "System Failure." *Am. Crim. L. Rev.* 42 (2005): 1201–18.

Lynch, Gerard E. "Our Administrative System of Criminal Justice." *Fordham L. Rev.* 66 (1998): 2117–51.

Maclin, Tracey. "A Criminal Procedure Regime Based on Instrumental Values." Review of Donald A. Dripps, *About Guilt and Innocence: The Origins,*

Development, and Future of Constitutional Criminal Procedure. *Constitutional Commentary* 22 (2005) 197–239.

Maclin, Tracey. "Is Obtaining an Arrestee's DNA a Valid Special Needs Search Under the Fourth Amendment? What Should (and Will) the Supreme Court Do?" *J.L. Med. & Ethics* 34 (2006): 165–81.

Matravers, Matt. "'More Than Just Illogical': Truth and Jury Nullification." In *The Trial on Trial: Truth and Due Process*, Antony Duff, Lindsay Farmer, Sandra Marshall, & Victor Tadros, eds., vol. 1, 71–83. Oxford: Hart, 2005.

McEwan, Jenny. "Ritual, Fairness and Truth: The Adversarial and Inquisitorial Models of Criminal Trials." In *The Trial on Trial: Truth and Due Process*, Antony Duff, Lindsay Farmer, Sandra Marshall, & Victor Tadros, eds., vol. 1, 51–69. Oxford: Hart, 2005.

McMurtrie, Jacqueline. "The Role of Social Science in Preventing Wrongful Convictions." *Am. Crim. L. Rev.* 42 (2005): 1283–86.

Mcnair, Mike. "Vicinage and the Antecedents of the Jury." *Law & Hist. Rev.* 17 (1999): 537–90.

Medwed, Daniel S. "Anatomy of a Wrongful Conviction: Theoretical Implications and Practical Solutions." *Villanova L. Rev.* 51 (2004): 337–77.

Medwed, Daniel S. "Up the River Without a Procedure: Innocent Prisoners and Newly Discovered Non-DNA Evidence in State Courts." *Ariz. L. Rev.* 47 (2005): 655–718.

Medwed, Daniel S. "The Zeal Deal: Prosecutorial Resistance to Post-conviction Claims of Innocence." *B.U. L. Rev.* 84 (2004): 125–83.

Mott, Nicole L. "The Current Debate on Juror Questions: 'To Ask, or Not to Ask, That Is the Question.'" *Chi.-Kent L. Rev.* 78 (2003): 1099–1125.

Musson, Anthony. "Twelve Good Men and True? The Character of Early Fourteenth-Century Juries." *Law & Hist. Rev.* 15 (1997): 115–44.

Nardulli, Peter J. "The Societal Cost of the Exclusionary Rule: An Empirical Reassessment." *Am. B. Foundation Res. J.* (1983): 585–609.

Ofshe, Richard J. "I'm Guilty If You Say So." In *Convicting the Innocent: The Story of a Murder, a False Confession, and the Struggle to Free a "Wrong Man,"* Donald S. Connery, ed., 95–108. Cambridge, Mass.: Brookline Books, 1996.

Ofshe, Richard J., & Richard A. Leo. "The Decision to Confess Falsely: Rational Choice and Irrational Action." *Denver U. L. Rev.* 74 (1997): 979–1122.

Ofshe, Richard J., & Richard A. Leo. "The Social Psychology of Police Interrogation: The Theory and Classification of True and False Confessions." *Stud. in Law, Pol., and Soc'y* 16 (1997): 189–251.

Olson, Trisha. "Of Enchantment: The Passing of the Ordeals and the Rise of the Jury Trial." *Syracuse L. Rev.* 50 (2000): 109–96.

Pillsbury, Samuel H. "On Corruption and Possibility in LA." *Loy. L.A. L. Rev.* 34 (2001): 657–64.

Pizzi, William T. "Do Jury Trials Encourage Harsh Punishments in the United States?" *St. Louis U. Public L. Rev.* 21 (2002): 51–63.

Richman, Daniel. "Prosecutors and Their Agents, Agents and Their Prosecutors." *Colum. L. Rev.* 103 (2003): 749–832.

Risinger, D. Michael. "Unsafe Verdicts: The Need for Reformed Standards for the Trial and Review of Factual Innocence Claims." *Hous. L. Rev.* 41 (2004): 1281–1336.

Roach, Kent. "Four Models of the Criminal Process." *J. Crim. L. & Criminology* 89 (1999). 671–716.

Roach, Kent. "Wrongful Convictions and Criminal Procedure." *Brandeis L.J.* 42 (2003–4): 349–68.

Schehr, Robert Carl. "The Criminal Cases Review Commission as a State Strategic Selection Mechanism." *Am. Crim. L. Rev.* 42 (2005): 1289–1302.

Schulhofer, Stephen J., & David D. Friedman. "Rethinking Indigent Defense: Promoting Effective Representation Through Consumer Sovereignty and Freedom of Choice for All Criminal Defendants." *Am. Crim. L. Rev.* 31 (1992): 73–122.

Shapiro, Alexander H. "Political Theory and the Growth of Defensive Safeguards in Criminal Procedure: The Origins of the Treason Trials Act of 1696." *L. & Hist. Rev.* 11 (1993): 215–33.

Siegel, Andrew M. "Moving down the Wedge of Injustice: A Proposal for a Third Generation of Wrongful Conviction Scholarship and Advocacy." *Am. Crim. L. Rev.* 42 (2005): 1219–37.

Skurka, Steven. "Perspectives on the Role of Cooperators and Informants: A Canadian Perspective." *Cardozo L. Rev.* 23 (2002): 759–70.

Steiker, Carol S. "Counter-revolution in Constitutional Criminal Procedure? Two Audiences, Two Answers." *Mich. L. Rev.* 94 (1996): 2466–2551.

Strazzella, James A. "Ineffective Assistance of Counsel Claims: New Uses, New Problems." *Ariz. L. Rev.* 19 (1977): 443–84.

Strazzella, James A. "Ineffective Identification Counsel: Cognizability Under the Exclusionary Rule." *Temple L.Q.* 48 (1975): 241–80.

Stuntz, William J. "The Uneasy Relationship Between Criminal Procedure and Criminal Justice." *Yale L.J.* 107 (1997): 1–76.

Tague, Peter. "An Indigent's Right to the Attorney of His Choice." *Stan. L. Rev.* 27 (1974): 73–99.

Taslitz, Andrew E. "Eyewitness Identification, Democratic Deliberation, and the Politics of Science." *Cardozo Pub. L. Pol'y & Ethics J.* 4 (2006): 271–325.

Thomas, George C., III. "Colonial Criminal Law and Procedure: The Royal Colony of New Jersey 1749–57." *NYU J. L. & Liberty* 1 (2005): 671–711.

Thomas, George C., III. "History's Lesson for the Right to Counsel." *U. Ill. L. Rev.* 2004:543–97.

Thomas, George C., III. "*Miranda*'s Illusion: Telling Stories in the Police Interrogation Room." Review of Welsh S. White, *Miranda's Waning Protections: Police Interrogation After Dickerson v. United States. Tex. L. Rev.* 81 (2003): 1091–1120.

Thomas, George C., III. "Stories About Miranda." *Mich. L. Rev.* 102 (2004): 1959–2000.

Thomas, George C., III. "When Constitutional Worlds Collide: Resurrecting the Framers' Criminal Procedure." *Mich. L. Rev.* 100 (2001): 145–231.

Thomas, George C., III, & Mark Greenbaum. "Justice Story Cuts the Hung Jury Gordian Knot." *Wm. & Mary Bill of Rts. L.J.* 15 (2007): 893–925.

Thomas, George C., III, & Barry S. Pollack. "Rethinking Guilty, Juries, and Jeopardy." *Mich. L. Rev.* 91 (1992): 1–33.

Thomas, George C., III, Gordon G. Young, Keith Sharfman, & Kate Briscoe. "Is It Ever Too Late for Innocence? Due Process, Finality, Efficiency, and Claims of Innocence." *U. Pitt. L. Rev.* 64 (2003): 263–302.

Trott, Stephen S. "Word of Warning for Prosecutors Using Criminals as Witnesses." *Hastings L.J.* 47 (1996): 1381–1432.

"The Vindication of a Prosecutor." *J. Crim. L. & Criminology* 59 (1968): 335–37.

Weaver, Russell L. "The Perils of Being Poor: Indigent Defense and Effective Assistance." *Brandeis L.J.* 42 (2003–4): 435–46.

Weigend, Thomas. "Germany." In *Criminal Procedure: A Worldwide Study,* Craig M. Bradley ed., 187–216. Durham, N.C.: Carolina Academic Press, 1999.

Wolson, Richard J., & Aaron M. London. "The Structure, Operation, and Impact of Wrongful Conviction Inquiries: The Sophonow Inquiry as an Example of the Canadian Experience." *Drake L. Rev.* 52 (2004): 677–93.

Wood, Alex. "Lying Accepted Investigative Tool." In *Convicting the Innocent: The Story of a Murder, a False Confession, and the Struggle to Free a "Wrong Man,"* Donald S. Connery, ed., 39–45. Cambridge, Mass.: Brookline Books, 1996.

Wright, Ronald F. "Parity of Resources for Defense Counsel and the Reach of Public Choice Theory." *Iowa L. Rev.* 90 (2004): 219–68.

Wright, Ronald F. "Trial Distortion and the End of Innocence in Federal Criminal Justice." *U. Penn. L. Rev.* 154 (2005): 79–156.

Yaroshefsky, Ellen. "Cooperation with Federal Prosecutors: Experiences of Truth Telling and Embellishment." *Fordham L. Rev.* 68 (1999): 917–64.

Zacharias, Fred C. "Structuring the Ethics of Prosecutorial Trial Practice: Can Prosecutors Do Justice?" *Vand. L. Rev.* 44 (1991): 45–114.

Zacharias, Fred C., & Bruce A. Green. "Reconceptualizing Advocacy Ethics." *Geo. Wash. L. Rev.* 74 (2005): 1–67.

Reports and Monographs

Achieving Justice: Freeing the Innocent, Convicting the Guilty; Report of the ABA Criminal Justice Section's Ad Hoc Innocence Committee to Ensure the Integrity of the Criminal Process. American Bar Association Criminal Justice Section, 2006.

Annuaire Statistique de la Justice, 2002–6 editions. Available at http://www.justice.gouv.fr/ (last visited July 9, 2007).

Bureau of Justice Statistics. "Felony Convictions in State Court." 2002, http://www.ojp.usdoj.gov/bjs/glance/tables/felcovtab.htm (last visited July 9, 2007).

Committee of Public Accounts. *Review of the Crown Prosecution Service, Session 1989–90* (London: HMSO, 1990).

Connors, Edward, Thomas Lundregan, Neil Miller, & Tom McEwan. *Convicted by Juries, Exonerated by Science: Case Studies in the Use of DNA Evidence to Establish Innocence After Trial.* Washington, D.C.: U.S. Dept. of Justice, Office of Justice Programs, National Institute of Justice, 1996.

Constitution Project. "Mandatory Justice: The Death Penalty Revisited." Summary (2005). Available at www.constitutionproject.org/death penalty/index.cfm?categoryId=2.

Department of Justice. Federal Bureau of Investigation. *Crime in the United States 2004,* "Persons Arrested." tbl. 29. Available at http://www.fbi.gov/ucr/cius_01/01crime4.pdf, tbl. 29 (last visited July 9, 2007).

"Guidelines for Preparing and Conducting Photo and Live Lineup Procedures." April 18, 2001. John Farmer, Attorney General of New Jersey. Available at www.psychology.iastate.edu/FACULTY/gwells/njguide lines.pdf (last visited July 9, 2007).

Province of Manitoba. Manitoba Justice Publications. Thomas Sophonow Inquiry. Available at http://www.gov.mb.ca/justice/publications/ sophonow/ (last visited July 9, 2007.

Report of the Florida Supreme Court's Commission on Criminal Discovery. February 1, 1989.

The Review of the Crown Prosecution Service. Presented to Parliament by the Attorney General, June 1998.

Royal Commission on Criminal Justice. *Report to Parliament, July, 2003.* 1993.

Sullivan, Thomas P. "Police Experiences with Recording Custodial Interrogations." Special Report, Northwestern University School of Law Center on Wrongful Convictions, Number 1. 2004.

Wickersham Commission. *Report on Lawlessness in Law Enforcement,* June 25, 1931. Available at www.heinonline.org, under Legal Classics, Library, U.S. Wickersham Commission Reports.

Newspapers

D'Amour, Mike. "Last Words Deny Killing." *Calgary Sun,* March 30, 2005. Available at http://www.injusticebusters.com/05/Arnold_Terry.shtml (last visited July 9, 2007).

Graczyk, Michael. "Man Executed for Killing Police Officer." *Dallas Morning News,* May 13, 1993.

Liptak, Adam. "County Says It's Too Poor to Defend the Poor." *New York Times,* April 15, 2003.

Thompson, Jennifer. "I Was Certain, but I Was Wrong." *New York Times,* June 18, 2000.

Yellin, Emily. "Lynching Victim Is Cleared of Rape, 100 Years Later." *New York Times,* February 27, 2000.

Other Sources

Aeschylus. *Eumenides.* Ian Johnston, trans., 2003. Available at http://www .mala.bc.ca/~johnstoi/aeschylus/aeschylus_eumenides.htm (last visited July 9, 2007).

Akesson, Per. "The Cog." Available at http://www.abc.se/~m10354/mar/ cog.htm (last visited July 9, 2007).

Air Force, Judge Advocate Recruiting FAQs. "Areas of Practice for Judge Advocates." Available at http://www.jagusaf.hq.af.mil/FAQs/lawtypes.htm (last visited October 15, 2007).

"Almanac, Historical Information, Chattanooga, Tennessee." Available at http://www.myforecast.com/bin/climate.m?city=29744&metric=false (last visited July 9, 2007).

"Arms and Armor in Medieval Europe." Available at http://www.metmu seum.org/toah/hd/arms/hd_arms.htm (last visited July 9, 2007).

Army JAG Corps, Areas of Practice, Criminal Law. Available at http://www.goarmy.com/jag/areas_of_practice.jsp (last visited October 15, 2007).

Associated Press. "FBI Apologizes to Lawyer Held in Madrid Bombings." May 25, 2004. Available at http://www.msnbc.msn.com/id/5053007/ (last visited July 9, 2007).

"Atomic Nucleus." Wikipedia. Available at http://en.wikipedia.org/wiki/ Atomic_nucleus (last visited July 9, 2007).

Berry, Sheila Martin. "When Experts Lie." Available at http://www.truthin
justice.org/expertslie.htm (last visited July 9, 2007).

Bureau of Justice Statistics. Criminal Case Processing Statistics. "Summary
Findings." Available at http://www.ojp.usdoj.gov/bjs/cases.htm#felony
(last visited July 7, 2007).

The Canons of the Fourth Lateran Council. Medieval Sourcebook. "Twelfth
Ecumenical Council." Available at http://www.fordham.edu/halsall/ba
sis/lateran4.html (last visited July 9, 2007).

"The Chattanooga Confederate Cemeteries, The Silverdale Cemetery." Available at http://www.utc.edu/Academic/Communication/ConfCem/Con
federateCem.html (last visited July 9, 2007).

Cicero. *ad Quintum Fratrem*, II, 4. 1. Available at http://www.thelatin
library.com/cicero/fratrem2.shtml#4 (last visited July 9, 2007).

"Compendium of Federal Justice Statistics, 2003." Available at http://www
.nicic.org/Library/020950 (last visited July 9, 2007).

Dixon, Richard. "John Marshall, Birth to 1785, Early Education." Available at
http://www.let.rug.nl/usa/B/jmarshall/marsh (last visited July 9, 2007).

Domesday Book Online. "How Was It Compiled?" Available at http://www
.domesdaybook.co.uk/compiling.html#how (last visited July 9, 2007).

"East Tennessee Anti-secession Resolutions." Available at http://alpha.fur
man.edu/~benson/tennres1.htm (last visited July 9, 2007).

Federal Magistrates Judge's Association web page. Available at http://www
.fedjudge.org/index.asp (last visited July 10, 2007).

Galloway, Tammy H. "John M. Slaton (1866–1955)." Available at New Georgia Encyclopedia, http://www.georgiaencyclopedia.org/nge/Article.jsp?
id=h-2137 (last visited July 9, 2007).

Grace, Roger M. "Great Norwegians, Earl Warren." Available at http://www
.mnc.net/norway/ (last visited July 9, 2007).

Innocence Project. Case of Jimmy Ray Bromgard. Available at http://www.in
nocenceproject.org (last visited July 8, 2007).

Innocence Project. Case of Ray Krone. Available at http://www.innocence
project.org (last visited July 8, 2007).

Innocence Project. Case of Clark McMillan. Available at http://www.inno
cenceproject.org (last visited July 8, 2007).

Innocence Project. Causes and Remedies of Wrongful Convictions. Available
at http://www.innocenceproject.org/understand/ (last visited July 9,
2007).

"John Marshall Harlan." Constitutional Law, Supreme Court Justices. Available at http://www.michaelariens.com/ConLaw/justices/harlan.htm
(last visited July 9, 2007).

Legal Aid Ontario. Available at http://www.legalaid.on.ca/en/default.asp (last visited July 9, 2007).

Legal Services Act. Ontario Regulation 107/99, Amended to O. Reg. 286/05. Available at http://www.e-laws.gov.on.ca/DBLaws/Regs/English/990 107_e.htm (last visited July 9, 2007).

Leitch, Alexander. "Aaron Burr, Jr." A Princeton Companion. Available at http://etcweb.princeton.edu/CampusWWW/Companion/burr_aaron_jr (last visited July 9, 2007).

Linder, Douglas. "The Treason Trial of Aaron Burr." 2001. Available at http://www.law.umkc.edu/faculty/projects/ftrials/burr/burraccount.htm l (last visited July 9, 2007).

Linder, Douglas. "The Trial of Sheriff Joseph F. Shipp et al., 1907." Available at http://www.law.umkc.edu/faculty/projects/ftrials/shipp/shipp.html (last visited July 9, 2007).

Livingood, James W. "A History of Hamilton County, Tennessee." Partly available at http://www.hamiltontn.gov/courthouse/Default.aspx (last visited July 13, 2007).

Medieval Sourcebook. *Charter of Liberties of Henry I, 1100,* ch. 1. Available at http://www.fordham.edu/halsall/source/hcoronation.html.(last visited July 9, 2007).

Merritt, Jeralyn. "Death of Lying Chemist Fred Zain." Available at http://www.talkleft.com/new_archives/001077.html (last visited July 9, 2007).

Mortality Statistics, 1905. Sixth Annual Report (G.P.O., 1907). Available at http://www.cdc.gov/nchs/data/vsushistorical/mortstatsh_1905.pdf (last visited July 9, 2007).

"Nathan Bedford Forrest." Available at http://www.civilwarhome.com/nat bio.htm (last visited July 7,2007).

National Association to Abolish the Death Penalty. "Do Not Execute Sedley Alley." Available at http://www.democracyinaction.org/dia/organiza tions/ncadp/campaign.jsp?campaign_KEY=3439 (last visited July 9, 2007).

Navy Manual of the Judge Advocate General. Sec. 0130 (b). Available at http://www.jag.navy.mil/documents/JAGMAN.pdf (page 60) (last visited October 15, 2007).

Ryan, George H., Governor of Ill. "Commutation Address." Northwestern Center for Wrongful Convictions, January 11, 2003. Available at http://www.law.northwestern.edu/depts/clinic/wrongful/RyanSpeech.htm (last visited July 9, 2007).

"The Selection and Confirmation of Justices: Criteria and Process, Policy Preferences." Congressional Quarterly. Available at http://www.cq

press.com/incontext/SupremeCourt/the_selection.htm (last visited July 9, 2007).

Sourcebook of Criminal Justice Statistics. 2002. Available at http://www. albany.edu/sourcebook/pdf/t5442002.pdf.

Twain, Mark. "Fourth of July Speech, 1873." Available at http://www.twain quotes.com/Jury.html (last visited July 9, 2007).

INDEX

Sophronow conviction and inquiry
(Manitoba), 3, 227 (*see also*
Sophronow, Thomas)
Cantor, Norman F., 65, 66, 76
"capital litigation trial bar," created
by Illinois Supreme Court, 186
Central Park Jogger case, 16–19
Centurion Ministries, 11
Chambers v. Mississippi, 208–9
Cheng, Thomas, 34
children
as suspects, 195
threat to remove, 152
as witnesses, 14, 225
Cicero, Marcus Tullius, 59, 60, 61,
242n. 43
citizenship, and the Fourteenth
Amendment, 149
civil litigation
"preponderance of evidence" standard, 199
pretrial discovery in, 202
right to jury trial, 98
Clarendon
Assize of (*see* Assize of Clarendon)
Constitutions of, 78
Clark, Tom, 155
"A Clean, Well-Lighted Place" (Hemingway), 266n. 84
clergy as magistrates, 75–77
and Lateran Council prohibition
on ordeals, 82
Cloud, Morgan, 33, 237n. 117, 265n.
66
Cobb, Sherry, 52
Cobham, Lord (Henry Brooke),
88
coercion, in confessions, 49, 186
cog (boat), 73, 244n. 25
Cohen, Ronald A., 14
Coke, Sir Edward, 87, 88–89
The Collapse of Criminal Justice (Rose),
3
colonial law, in British America,
94–95
Colorado v. Connelly, 115–16
combat, trial by. *See* battle, trial by
Commentaries on the Laws of England
(Blackstone), 64, 102–3
committal papers, English, study of,
201–2

Communists, American, and the
Supreme Court, 156–57
compurgation, 65–66, 83
confessions
to clergy, and legal innocence,
75–76
coerced, 49, 186
consistency with existing evidence,
196
defense challenges to, under "factual innocence" rules,
182
false (*see* false confessions)
involuntary, 151–52
proposed reforms to evaluation of,
195–96
true, 49
confrontation of state's witnesses, 52,
162. *See also* cross-examination:
of state's witnesses
Connelly v. Colorado, 49–50
conspiracies, vast, 192, 198
Constitution, U.S.
Bill of Rights (*see* Bill of Rights)
drafting of, 96, 248n. 8
prohibits ex post facto laws, 96,
101
ratification of, 147–48
"constitutionalizing" a field, by
Supreme Court, 263n. 23
Constitution Project
calls for "professional competence"
standard, 186
urges "reasonable doubt" standard
in capital case appeals, 217
Constitutions of Clarendon (Henry
II), 78
constructive treason, 109, 110
contest, trial as, 171. *See also* adversarial system
convictions
dubious (*see* questionable convictions)
of innocent persons (*see* wrongful
convictions)
review of, 2 (*see also* appeals)
corroboration of informants' stories,
34
Costanzo, Mark, 16
Cotton, Ronald, 14
country, putting oneself on the, 83

exemptions from proposed expansion of, 267n. 87
liberalizing and simplification of, proposed, 197–98, 200
and the screening magistrate, 222
dismissal, from pretrial judicial review, 199. *See also* acquittals
divine right of kings, 85–86, 89
DNA evidence, 31, 41, 222
  denied to condemned man, 222
  and the Duke rape case, 26
  exculpatory, 24, 171
  flaws in collection and storage of, 37
  prisoners exonerated by, 2, 7, 8, 14, 18, 160
  screening judge's supervision of, 197, 201
Dodd v. State, 212
Domesday Book, 69–70
Douglas, William O., 153
Dripps, Donald, 2, 46, 55, 166, 186–87
drug enterprises, 267n. 87
Dubber, Markus, 159
due process
  comprises protection of innocence, 45, 185, 209
  as constitutional right (*see* Due Process Clause)
  evolution of, 46–47
  failed by "third degree" interrogations, 50
  and Herrera execution, 5
  procedural requirements, 52
  reliability of, 47
  suits based on, before Supreme Court, 149–50
Due Process Clause, 2, 149, 158–59, 161, 165, 166
  and false confession, 115
Duff, Antony, 46, 53–54
Duff, Peter, 207
Duke rape case, 26, 29, 189
"duty counsel," Canadian, 187

Eadmer (English chronicler), 75
Eaton, William, 101, 104
Eisenhower, Dwight D., 154
Ekman, Paul, 33
Eleanor of Aquitaine, queen of England, 78, 80

elusive truth, 1–2
Ely Inquest, 70
Emma, queen mother, 64
emperor, Roman, as magistrate, 60–61
English Bill of Rights (1689), 89, 92
English Court of Appeal, 221
epistemology
  of innocence, 41, 92
  and justice systems, 1
  of trials by ordeal, 67–68
"equal before the law" standard, and the right to counsel, 158
equal protection clause, 149, 157
Europe
  medieval, guilt and innocence in, 62–68
  modern, inquisitorial model of justice in, 62
European Human Rights Convention, and witness testimony, 262n. 39
evidence
  in ABA's *Achieving Justice,* 183
  collection and preservation of, 183, 197
  confession leading to new, 196
  DNA (*see* DNA evidence)
  exculpatory, prosecutors' obligation to disclose, 53, 217
  false, 12, 32–39, 50, 160, 201–2
  of innocence, excluded by procedural rules, 208–9
  insufficient, and appeals, 113, 172
  juries' right to nullify, 268n. 130
  misleading, 12
  mitigating, defense counsel failure to present at sentencing, 186
  newly discovered, 218, 219–22
  police fabrication of, 50
  reliable, exclusion of, 33
  rules of, 170, 177–78, 208
  scientific (*see* scientific evidence)
  truth of, 52
  weight of, and corrupt verdicts, 85
evidentiary hearings, federal, 193
examination, proposed reforms for, 208

examining magistrate (France),
172–73, 174, 178, 184, 198,
203
as model for United States, 182
excessive bail, prohibited by English
Bill of Rights, 92
expert witnesses
equal access to, 190
hearings for, 212
juries at mercy of, 37
screening testimony of, under "factual innocence" rules, 182
ex post facto laws, prohibition of, 96,
101
eyewitness identifications, 162–66,
219
in ABA's *Achieving Justice*, 183
by children, 14, 225
defense challenges to, under "factual innocence" rules, 182
failures of, 13–14
in Johnson case, 122–23, 125–26
mistaken, 11
and probable cause to indict, 172
proposed reforms in, 196–97
screening judge's supervision of,
201, 222

fabrication of evidence, by police, 50
facts
knowable only by perpetrator, 195
uncertainties in finding, 11
See also truth
factual innocence, 182
Faigman, David, 41
failed science, 36–37, 39
fairness, 55
in interrogation, 48–49
protected by right to counsel, 51
in Scottsboro Nine case, 145, 157
and Supreme Court interventions,
157–58
false confessions, 11, 16–19, 48–50,
49–50, 52, 114–16, 159–60, 161,
194, 195, 205, 265n. 66
in ABA's *Achieving Justice*, 183
Miller's, 27
Triplett's, 42
false evidence. *See* evidence: false
Federalists, 147, 148, 149
and habeas corpus, 100

Feeney, Floyd, 170, 217
Fine, John, 58
fingerprint matches, 36–37
fire ordeal, 63–64, 75, 79, 82
Fisher, Stanley, 196
"flat earth" policing theory
and failure to pursue other suspects, 15–16
and false confessions, 16–19
See also "tunnel vision"
Florida, expanding use of depositions
in, 200
"foils," in lineups, 196
Forbes, William C., 38
Forrest, Nathan Bedford, 252–53n. 17
Fortas, Abe, 155
"foul blows"
vs. "hard blows," 25–26
and the Miller case, 28–29
Fourteenth Amendment, 149–50, 158
and state regulation of slaughterhouses, 149, 257n. 35
Fourth Amendment, 158, 159
Frank, Jerome, 3, 6, 10–11, 50, 54–55,
166, 170, 227
Frank, Leo, 129–32, 143, 146, 150
Frankfurter, Felix, 13, 48, 163
Frankish justice
compurgation, 65–66
inquests, 62
trials by ordeal, 63
Franklin, Benjamin, 3
freedom of speech, in Parliament, 92
Freemasonry, 50
French Code of Criminal Procedure,
168
instruction to juries, 175–76
French criminal justice, 198,
199
prosecutors' training, 25
role of magistrates, 203 (*see also* examining magistrate; presiding
judges)
Friedman, David D., 187

Galileo Galilei, 15
gender, and equal protection, 157
Germany, appeals in, 216–17
Germond, Gate, 11
Gideon v. Wainwright, 21, 51, 158
GIGO phenomenon

instructions to juries, 171
  "beyond reasonable doubt" standard, 207
  cautionary, about eyewitness ID, 196–97
  in France, 175–76
  to ignore unadmissable testimony, 208
  modified French, proposed, 212–13
internment of Japanese-Americans, 154
interrogations
  of extraordinary length, 17, 151–52
  fairness of, 50
  improper, 226
  proposed reforms for, 195
  "third degree," 50–51
  videotaping of, 183, 194–95
  of young children, 225
  See also confessions; false confessions
intimidation
  of juries, 90
  of suspects, 194
  of witnesses, 200
  See also coercion
investigating judges. See examining magistrate (France)
investigations
  American, conducted by police, 182
  failures of, 12–13
  flawed procedures, addressed by ABA's Achieving Justice, 183
  inadequate, 34
  private, by defense, 20
  proposed reforms in, 193–98
  in U.S. military courts, 179–80
Iredell, James, 97
irrelevant testimony, 170
irreparable mistaken identification, 196
Israel, Jerry, 166

Jackson, Andrew, 104
Jackson, John, 45
Jackson v. Virginia, 113–14, 215
jailhouse informants, 11, 34–36, 211–12, 223
  in ABA's Achieving Justice, 183
  defense challenges to, under "fac-

tual innocence" rules, 182
James I, king of England, 87, 89
James II, king of England, 89
Jay, John, 103
Jefferson, Thomas, 106, 107, 110, 149
  and the 1800 election, 103–4
jeopardy bar, 199
Johnson, Ed, 118–28, 133–38, 139, 146, 150, 157, 253n. 33
  Supreme Court contempt trial after lynching of, 140–43
Johnson grass case, Texas, 149
Jonakait, Randolph, 32, 39, 189, 208, 211–12
Jones, Cynthia, 197
Jones, Howard E., 137–38
judges
  administrative, for new evidence review, 220–21, 224
  appellate, 184, 218
  to determine adequacy of defense counsel (Dripps proposal), 186–87
  examining magistrate (France), 172–73, 174, 178, 182, 198, 203
  federal magistrates, 193
  of French indicting chamber, 203
  increased screening role proposed, 184
  jury instructions (see instructions to juries)
  presiding (France), 174–75, 178, 182, 224
  screening magistrate, proposed, 193–94, 197, 201, 206–7, 222, 226
  wickedness among, 97
judicial review, pretrial, proposed, 198–202, 222–23, 226
judicial screening, failure of, 30–31
Judiciary Act of 1789, 46, 106
Jung, Heike, 55
junk science. See failed science
juries
  allowed to question witnesses, 268n. 130
  Athenian, 57–58
  attainted, 85, 90
  in civil actions, 98
  as "conscience of the community," 211
  criminal, in medieval England, 84
  deadlocked, 176, 213–14, 223

Weinreb, Lloyd, 45, 182, 197, 213, 263n. 10
Whigs
and presumption of innocence, 92
and the self-preservation principle, 89
and the Stamp Act Resolution, 94
White, Byron, 155
wickedness, among judges, 97
Wickersham Commission, 50
Wigmore, John Henry, 151
Wilkinson, James, 104–5, 109
William and Mary, king and queen of England, 89
William II (Rufus), king of England, 71, 75
Williamson, F. Lane, 26
William the Conqueror, justice under, 69–72
Wilson, James, 98
Wilson, Woodrow, 103
witnesses
depositions of, 200, 262n. 39
insulated from prosecution and defense before trial (France), 173
intimidation of, 200
narrative testimony of (France), 175
questioning of, by jury, 268n. 130
testimony of, 170
Wolf v. Colorado, 158
Wood, Alex, 17
Wright, Ron, 204
Wrightsman, Lawrence S., 207
wrongful convictions, 2
"Birmingham Six" (England), 37–38
Colorado v. Connelly, 115–16
compensation for, 182–83

Ronald Cotton, 14
Michael Crowe, 15–16, 17–18, 160
death-row, in Illinois, 24
through defense counsel failures, 19–23
through eyewitness ID errors, 14–15
through false confessions, 16–19
through failure of judicial screens, 30–31
from fallible juries, 31–32
from false evidence, 32–39
federal, 8–9
Leo Frank, 131–32
frequency of, 39–41
through investigative failures, 12–13
judicial review after, 172
Ray Krone, 6–8, 37, 189, 227
Clark McMillan, 13–14
Kelly Michaels, 225–27
Eldon Miller, 189
for misdemeanors, estimated number of, 40, 238n. 151
and police "tunnel vision," 14–15
through prosecution and adjudicative failures, 19
from prosecutor failures, 23–30
Scottsboro Nine rape case, 143–46
Thomas Sophronow, 15, 34–35, 226–27

Yaroshevsky, Ellen, 33–34

Zacharias, Fred, 25
Zain, Fred S., 38–39, 238n. 141
Zeisel, Hans, 32